Writing Across The Curriculum In Secondary Classrooms

Teaching From A Diverse Perspective

Harriet Arzu Scarborough

Merrill
Prentice Hall

Upper Saddle River, New Jersey
Columbus, Ohio

Library of Congress Cataloging-in-Publication Data

Writing across the curriculum in secondary classrooms: teaching from a diverse perspective
Harriet Arzu Scarborough, editor.

    p. cm.

Includes bibliographical references and index.

ISBN 0-13-022489-8

1. English language—Composition and exercises—Study and teaching
(Secondary)—United States. 2. Interdisciplinary approach in education
United States. 3. Multicultural education—United States. I. Scarborough, Harriet Arzu.

LB1631 .W693 2001
373.19—dc21   00-056101

Vice President and Publisher: Jeffery W. Johnston
Editor: Linda Ashe Montgomery
Editorial Assistant: Jennifer Day
Production Editor: Mary M. Irvin
Design Coordinator: Diane C. Lorenzo
Project Coordination and Text Design: Carlisle Publishers Services
Cover Design: Rod Harris
Production Manager: Pamela D. Bennett
Director of Marketing: Kevin Flanagan
Marketing Manager: Amy June
Marketing Services Manager: Krista Groshong

This book was set in Garamond by Carlisle Communications, Ltd., and was printed and bound by
R. R. Donnelley & Sons Company. The cover was printed by Phoenix Color Corp.

10 9 8 7 6 5 4 3 2 1
ISBN 0-13-022489-8

PREFACE

Every summer for the past five years I have taught a seminar on writing and thinking across the curriculum. The class usually consists of mostly middle and high school teachers. In the course of our class discussions, we gradually arrived at the realization that although the textbook we used for the class had much to offer, it had become a little out of step with the needs of an increasingly diverse student population. We were surprised that texts were being written without considering the implications of the growing diversity of students in the United States. Over the years we had become accustomed to the diversity of our classrooms and recognized that meeting student needs meant employing diverse materials and methodologies. We had the same expectations of the textbooks we used. When our expectations were not met, we toyed with the notion of writing our own text. It seemed a daunting task when the idea first surfaced: How would classroom teachers teaching five classes a day find time to write a book? Would we be able to commit time and energy to a project that might take a couple of years? Forming a study group helped make the idea become a reality.

For almost a year, we met regularly, discussing what the book might look like, what we might want to focus on in the book, and what each person's role might be. The discussions during our study group meetings surprised us because they were so positive. At the end of a busy day, we looked forward to these meetings because we were focusing on what worked in the classroom.

For the textbook we envisioned, we wanted the resonant voice of many practicing teachers. So, to complement the teachers' voices, I invited a few colleagues from the university level to contribute to this book. These were colleagues who had had experience teaching in secondary schools but were now teaching at the college level. In some cases, the positions they held at the college level called for them to maintain ties with and gather wisdom from secondary schools and secondary school teachers.

From all, we have a unique intertwining of theory and practice. From the practicing high school teachers comes practical knowledge with a sound theoretical base. From the college teachers comes theory situated in practice. No other volume provides this kind of continuity, bringing the special wisdom of those who have worked in both settings to bear on the issue of writing and learning in the secondary classroom.

I wish to thank the authors of the chapters for agreeing to participate in this venture and for their patience and indulgence at each request I have made of them. My friend and colleague Anne-Marie Hall, especially, has been extremely helpful and supportive.

I also owe a debt of gratitude to my husband, Tom, and my niece Reneé for their patience and their willingness to pick up the slack every time I had to work on the book. Tom, especially, has been a willing reader, a sounding board, and all-around cheerleader for this project.

To the many teachers across the secondary school curriculum who continue to search out ways to expand their students' literacy, my writing colleagues and I hope that this text becomes a valuable resource for you, now and in years to come.

I am grateful to the reviewers of my manuscript for their comments and insights: Angela M. Ferree, Western Illinois University; David N. Petkosh, Cabrini College; Donna J. Merkley, Iowa State University; Harold Nelson, Minot State University; Ann Lockledge, University of North Carolina–Wilmington; Cynthia G. Kruger, University of Massachusetts–Dartmouth; and Karen Kusiak, Colby College.

Finally, I am indebted to Linda Sharp McElhiney for her unwavering faith in this project. I have been most appreciative of our editorial relationship because without her support, this book would not have come to fruition.

Harriet Arzu Scarborough

ABOUT THE EDITOR:

Harriet Arzu Scarborough has taught middle school and high school language arts. She is now the high school language arts coordinator for Tucson Unified School District in Tucson, Arizona, and teaches methodology courses for preservice secondary teachers at the University of Arizona. Scarborough is the author of many journal articles and has made numerous presentations locally and nationally on teaching and learning in secondary schools as well as on diversity issues.

CONTRIBUTORS' PAGE

Carl Anderson teaches English to gifted and talented students at Palo Verde High Magnet School in Tucson, Arizona.

David Bachman-Williams is currently teaching American government at Tucson High Magnet School in Tucson, Arizona and is the bilingual coordinator for the school.

Paula Bachman-Williams has been teaching in the Tucson Unified School District, Tucson, Arizona for the past thirteen years. Her current assignment is teaching biology to freshmen at Cholla High Magnet School.

Edith Baker is a lecturer at Bradley University, Peoria, Illinois. She also directs the Writing Across the Curriculum Program there.

Loraine Chapman is an instructional technology trainer for Tucson Unified School District in Tucson, Arizona.

MaryCarmen Cruz is Cholla High Magnet School's curriculum coordinator.

Sal Gabaldón, a former high school English teacher, is a curriculum specialist in the Bilingual Education Department of Tucson Unified School District.

A former middle and high school teacher, Anne-Marie Hall is an associate writing specialist in the Department of English at the University of Arizona. She also directs the Southern Arizona Writing Project.

Carl Johannesson is an English teacher at Cholla High Magnet School in Tucson, Arizona.

A former high school English teacher, Yvonne Merrill is an associate writing specialist in the English Department at the University of Arizona in Tucson.

Michael Robinson teaches composition in the English Department at the University of Arizona in Tucson.

Amy Rusk Foushee has been a librarian at Tucson High Magnet, Tucson, Arizona, since 1994.

Alyson Whyte is a former high school English teacher. She is currently an assistant professor of education at Florida State University, Tallahassee, Florida.

CONTENTS

INTRODUCTION

HARRIET ARZU SCARBOROUGH

The impetus for writing this book came from a study group in which many of the contributors participated. Members of this study group, high school teachers from various disciplines, had previously been introduced to the notion of writing to learn at literacy workshops over the years. Often we had flirted with the idea of producing our own text, a text in which we could give voice to the many ideas we had about the use of writing to mediate learning. We also wanted an opportunity to use writing to explore our own ideas of teaching. Because of the extensive experiences of the study group participants, we were able to bring a variety of perspectives to the discussions.

A CONTEXT FOR WRITING TO LEARN

For about a year, we met twice a month after school. During our meetings we found that our discussions became broader than the idea of writing to learn. Actually, we found ourselves contextualizing writing to learn. We discussed classroom processes—how we created environments conducive to risk taking and learning, how we structured activities to make learning relevant and authentic for students, and what we did to meet the needs of all our students, especially those developing proficiency in English. And we found ourselves going back to the notion of literacy. It did not matter if we taught social studies, science, law-related education, Latino literature, or junior English. We were engaged in helping students develop and sharpen literacy skills—reading, writing, speaking, listening, and thinking—across the curriculum.

TAPPING INTO THE UNDERGROUND SPRINGS

Two discoveries became clear to us through our discussions: First, even as we taught magical realism in Latino literature, the interdependence of organisms within the environment in science, the tenets of the Constitution, or the intricacies of a civil trial, we each used writing as a tool to help students make sense of what we wanted them to learn. Second, writing had the power to activate schemata—to tap into knowledge that students brought to a new learning situation. Cummins (1996) points out the tendency of less-informed educators to equate knowledge of English with the ability to think logically. This tendency leads to viewing students who are developing proficiency in English from a deficit situation. In our study group discussions it became clear to us that the use of writing to activate the students' schemata showed the tremendous power that writing has to tap into the learners' underground springs— that is, to bring out knowledge that we did not think was there. Being able to tap into these underground springs helped us work successfully with our linguistically diverse students.

WRITING TO LEARN AND WRITING ACROSS THE CURRICULUM

In writing the book we did not lose sight of the fact that writing to learn is a component of the larger concept of writing across the curriculum. Many educators have touted writing as an important part of any successful school program for the following reasons:

1. Developing students' writing abilities is the responsibility of all teachers, not just English teachers (Lester & Onore, 1990).
2. Writing supports more complex thinking and learning about the subjects that students are expected to learn (Langer & Applebee, 1987).
3. Writing improves the learning of content (Maxwell, 1996).

The inclusion of writing in the curriculum, however, has tended to focus inordinately on the use of *writing to demonstrate learning,* putting more emphasis on the final product than on the process. Forgotten in this preoccupation with the final product are the many valuable uses of writing: to activate the schemata, to connect prior knowledge with new knowledge, to foster metacognition, to reflect, to analyze, to explore, to evaluate, to draw conclusions, to confirm or change predictions, to apply concepts, and so on.

In her book *Roots in the Sawdust,* in which she introduced the concept of writing to learn to many secondary teachers, Anne Ruggles Gere (1985) distinguished between writing to learn and writing across the curriculum. According to Gere, the goal of writing across the curriculum is to improve the quality of writing, whereas the goal of writing to learn is to improve thinking and learning. Writing to learn, in essence, is the use of writing as a tool for thinking and as a tool to mediate learning across the curriculum. When students writing in their journals make associations they may have about a particular concept or when they are asked to freewrite to explore connections they can make to a certain concept, they acquire a better understanding of that concept. The very act of writing slows down the writer enough so that there is opportunity to interact with the subject matter in an explorative manner. This informal exploratory writing, by the writer for the writer, is done both in preparation for, and quite independently of, formal writing assignments in a course. It is writing that helps students think in a probative, speculative, and generative manner to develop the language of learning. This type of writing fosters abstract thought, leading to a deeper understanding of subject matter. Teachers have identified a number of writing strategies that can be used to activate schemata, confirm or refute predictions, and apply and extend new knowledge, among others. Although these are not a set list of activities to be checked off, they can be incorporated into a well-orchestrated curriculum of reading, writing, thinking, and listening.

ATTRIBUTES OF WRITING TO LEARN

Because writing to learn is subsumed under the larger umbrella of writing across the curriculum, it is applicable in any subject area. Writing done to mediate learning continues to be of particular interest to the study group members and secondary teachers with whom I have worked because of the following attributes:

1. It does not have to be graded.
2. It does not have to be a finished product.

3. It can become a stepping-stone to more formal writing.

4. It provides a way to interact with a literary work or content material to gain understanding.

A CONCEPT, NOT A BODY OF ACTIVITIES

In the chapters that follow the various authors discuss strategies for using writing as a tool for learning across the curriculum. In his chapter, "La Voz Liberada: Writing to Learn in a Sheltered English Class," however, Salvador Gabaldón cautions us that writing to learn is a concept, or an approach to teaching, *not* a body of activities. The notion of writing to learn is not embodied in particular strategies. Rather, how the strategies are used determines whether they are mediating learning or demonstrating learning—the two major dichotomies of writing across the curriculum. Narrative is usually connected with the notion of demonstrating learning, but in chapter 6, Mary Carmen Cruz shows that narrative can also be used to work with subject matter to hone understanding. Thus narrative in that instance becomes a writing-to-learn activity.

COACH OR JUDGE?

A common dilemma for many educators surfaced in our study group discussions: "How can I serve in the roles of both coach and judge of my students' writing at the same time?" These roles are seemingly paradoxical, yet such is the nature of teaching. In a writing-to-learn classroom, these roles are seen not as contradictory but as extensions of each other. Writing to learn as informal, expressive writing is coached not judged. It can remain informal writing or can serve as a jumping-off point for more formal, transactional writing. The coach intervenes at various points (formative evaluation) of the writing process, and final (summative) evaluation becomes a natural extension. Many of the authors in this book show how this approach is used. In her chapter, Edith Baker illustrates how beginning with nonthreatening journal activities, students work through an American literature curriculum. The journal activities become seeds for more formal essays. The teacher intervenes at appropriate times, guiding the process along.

FOUR PERSPECTIVES

In this book which offers four perspectives, we delineate the many dimensions that the concept of writing as a tool for learning across the curriculum can embody. Part 1,

"Writing Across the Curriculum: Mathematics and Science," contains four chapters that focus on writing in math, science, law-related education, and social studies contexts. In Chapter 1, Paula Bachman-Williams describes how she incorporates writing-to-learn strategies into her curriculum to help students learn not only basic scientific skills but also things about themselves as members of a multicultural community. In 1987 Langer and Applebee wrote in their text *How Writing Shapes Thinking: A Study of Teaching and Learning,* "if writing is to play a meaningful role in subjects other than English, then the teachers of those subjects need to have a conception of writing specific to their disciplines" (p. 151). They further assert that the approach to writing in science and mathematics classes should be one that emphasizes what is unique about writing and (thinking) in those subjects, instead of emphasizing ways in which such activities will advance the work of English teachers. In Chapter 2, Anne-Marie Hall echoes that argument and challenges English teachers to employ in their classrooms writing activities that enhance mathematical and scientific thinking.

Carl Johannesson discusses in Chapter 3 how writing plays a vital role in helping his students understand trial concepts and develop courtroom literacy. In Chapter 4 David Bachman-Williams uses writing to encourage students to think critically about the connection between their own lives and the societal issues that affect economics and government.

In Part 2, "Writing to Learn," the focus is on the use of writing as a tool for learning. Salvador Gabaldón shows in Chapter 5 how writing can "liberate" the voice of students developing English proficiency. Likewise, in Chapter 6, MaryCarmen Cruz walks us through her classroom as she presents a number of writing strategies designed to ease students from informal, expressive writing to more formal and transactional writing. Loraine Chapman presents several strategies to make technology a tool for writing and learning (Chapter 7), and Michael Robinson details his own learning even as he uses writing-to-learn strategies to help students grapple with issues of identity (Chapter 8).

Illustrating the close relationship between writing to learn and writing across the curriculum, Part 3, "Writing Across the Curriculum: Promoting Genre Study," moves us into the use of writing to explore particular genres. In Chapter 9, Edith Baker shows how the journal can be used as a place to explore ideas—ideas that will eventually become an essay. Amy Rusk-Fousheé discusses the use of writing in a collaborative poetry unit in Chapter 10. In Chapter 11, Carl Anderson introduces the idea of using writing as a way to understand N. Scott Momaday's approach to storytelling and actually has students write their own narratives from three different perspectives.

Part 4, "Writing Across the Curriculum: Professional Perspectives," focuses on professional issues that surround writing across the curriculum. In Chapter 12, I describe another way to use writing-to-learn activities: to build community in the classroom, thereby bridging the gaps among learners and teachers. Yvonne Merrill discusses changes students encounter in the attributes of writing in the disciplines as they make the transition from high school to college and offers rhetorical analysis as a way for students to write more effective assignments across the curriculum (Chapter 13). Finally, in Chapter 14, Alyson Whyte details her own use of writing to mediate her learning during her first year as a college professor. She describes her struggles with the dilemma of "embracing contraries"—being nurturing and soft or being demanding and challenging.

In this book we present a broad notion of writing to learn by situating the strategies in a variety of multicultural classrooms across the curriculum and by showing the place of the concept of writing to learn within the broader spectrum of writing across the curriculum. We also provide insight into the possibilities that writing can bring to our own learning and to our relationships with our students. For the most part, the classrooms we speak of are in the Southwest, but as the population of the United States continues to become increasingly multicultural, the situations we speak of in this book become more applicable to schools across the nation.

REFERENCES

Cummins, J. (1996). *Negotiating identities: Education for empowerment in a diverse society.* Ontario, CA: California Association for Bilingual Education.

Gere, A. (1985). *Roots in the sawdust.* Urbana, IL: National Council of Teachers of English.

Langer, J., & Applebee, A. (1987). *How writing shapes thinking: A study of teaching and learning.* Urbana, IL: National Council of Teachers of English.

Lester, N., & Onore, C. (1990). *Learning change.* Portsmouth, NH: Boynton/Cook.

Maxwell, R. (1996). *Writing across the curriculum in the middle and high schools.* Needham Heights, MA: Allyn & Bacon.

1

PROMOTING LITERACY IN SCIENCE CLASS

PAULA BACHMAN-WILLIAMS
CHOLLA HIGH MAGNET SCHOOL

ABSTRACT

The development of student literacy cannot be left solely to English teachers. Science and other content area teachers need to make literacy development an integral part of their curriculum if they are to access the higher-level thinking necessary for meaningful learning. Included here are writing activities to help students organize their thinking and sharpen their understanding of the science they are learning.

WHY WRITE IN SCIENCE CLASS?

"We have to write again today!" I hear such comments often when I ask students to write in their science classes. Traditionally high school science teachers have left the teaching of reading and writing to English teachers. However, science teachers need to teach literacy in the content areas because literacy opens up avenues to teach the higher-level thinking necessary in our classes. Students need to read, write, and think to comprehend and learn in the content areas. If we have literate students, then we can teach our content.

LITERACY IN THE SCIENCE CLASSROOM

I teach ninth-grade biology at a high school in which about 60 percent of the students are Mexican American, 10 percent are Native American, 4 percent are African American, 1 percent are Asian American, and 24 percent are European American. Our students come to us generally not as well prepared academically as we would like them to be. They typically use the casual register (Joos, 1967) when speaking and writing, regardless of audience and situation. According to Joos the five registers of language include frozen, formal, consultative, casual, and intimate. The register appropriate for academic instruction is consultative, but my students tend to use the casual register when speaking and writing. Maria Montaño-Harmon, a professor at California State University at Fullerton, says that these are characteristics of people who do not read habitually. Indeed, the majority of my students do very little reading for pleasure. Consequently academic reading is difficult. Reading the textbook, which is written above their reading ability, frustrates them. They communicate orally in the casual language used with their friends. The challenge, then, is to make the subject relevant to their lives and teach them the literacy skills of academic reading, writing, speaking, and science.

My own journey to literacy was supported from my early years. I was read to, talked to, and encouraged to ask questions. I remember many evenings when my father would read classical poetry to us. We had magazines and books all over the house. I remember reading a series of biographies about famous people. I eagerly read any animal story I could find. However, my experience is not the experience of the majority of my students.

To meet the needs of our students my school has made literacy across the curriculum a priority. Professional development classes taught at our school site have specifically addressed teaching strategies for developing literacy skills and academic competence across the curriculum. The school district has also offered classes in English for academic purposes. In addition because of the increasing number of students in our district who are developing English proficiency, our school district has offered training for teachers to teach students English for academic purposes.

Over the years I have worked to incorporate strategies to promote writing to learn in my classes. I realized that I needed to teach my students reading and writing so that they could learn strategies that would make them more successful in school. One strategy I found especially successful is the journal. Consequently, I have incorporated journal writing into my science classes. I ask students to write in their journals daily because writing promotes thinking. I generally have the journal prompt on the board or overhead when students arrive in class. I expect them to pick up their journals and begin to write when they sit down. The journal prompt can be a variety of types, such as content oriented, personal knowledge, personal reflection, or pattern poetry. Possible journal prompts may include the following:

1. Write a paragraph describing the path of blood in the heart.
2. Tell about your favorite day last year.

MULTICULTURAL CONSIDERATIONS

An important concept in biology is genetics, a topic that generates much student interest. I have developed a "Know Your Ancestors" project to introduce the concept of genetics, and this project also provides me an opportunity to connect with students' lives. I ask students to research a country from which one of their ancestors emigrated. The Native American students generally research their tribal nation, and the African American students often choose a country in Africa to research. I suggest to students who are adopted or who have no information on a country to look at their physical features and pick a country in the area of the world that they think might be a logical choice. The project includes a four-generation chart of their ancestors, a geo poem (a modification of the bio poem) of the country, country and continent maps, a current event of the country, demographic data, and a flag with an explanation about the colors and symbols. Writing-to-learn activities in the form of journal entries help to move students through this project. Following are some of the journal prompts I have provided for students:

1. Read the short passage "What Is Culture?" and then write about your culture. What values has your family taught you?
2. Write a paragraph about what you find most interesting about the country you are researching.
3. Write a story that you have heard about one of your ancestors.
4. Write the story of why your family immigrated to the United States or a possible scenario of why family members came.

5. Of all the things you have learned about your family, what do you find most interesting?

6. Write a paragraph about your feelings about this experience of learning about your family.

7. Write a paragraph about the "Know Your Ancestors" project. What was easiest for you? What was hardest for you?

I found the geo poem in a lesson that was published with the World Geograph software program. I have modified its format for my students for this project. Students replace the words in parentheses and finish the sentence starters with entries appropriate for their situation.

Geo Poem

(Name of country)
(Four adjectives—words or statements that describe the country)
Home of . . . (something that distinguishes it from other countries)
Neighbor of . . . (name at least three neighboring countries)
Who exports . . . (three items)
Who imports . . . (three items)
Who is proud of. . . (people, places, or characteristics)
Who celebrates . . . (name three holidays)
Whose flag is . . . (name the colors in the flag)
Member of . . . (continent on which it is found)
(Local name of country and a phrase to describe the origin of the name)

The "Know Your Ancestors" project allows students to identify the origin of their genetic traits. Students then ask questions about genetics, and their questions lead to an increased interest in the topic that we are studying.

Students often come to science classrooms with misconceptions about science. The opportunity to address some of these misconceptions and the need to establish connections in my classroom prompt me to introduce a "What Is Science?" writing activity at the beginning of the school year. Science explains the world around us. Throughout time people have told stories to explain why things are the way they are in nature. Myths and legends of various cultures around the world that explain certain natural phenomena have been published as children's books. *Raven,* by Gerald McDermott, is a tale from the Pacific Northwest that explains how we got the sun. *How Mr. Dog Got Tame,* an African American legend, explains how dogs and humans became such good friends. *Why Mosquitoes Buzz in People's Ears,* by Verna Aardema, is an African tale that explains just that—why mosquitoes buzz in your ear. *Soft Child,* by Joe Hayes, is a Native American tale to explain how rattlesnakes got their fangs. In *Opossum and the Great Firemaker,* a Mexican legend, opossum learns to play possum to steal fire from the great firemaker, iguana. *The Seventh Sister* is a Chinese legend that explains why two bright stars meet in the night sky once a year.

I first ask students, with a partner, to read a myth from one of the books mentioned. They write a summary of the story, focusing on the natural phenomenon that the story explains. After a person from each group reads his or her summary to the class, our ensuing discussion on myths stimulates students' thinking about the possibilities for writing their own myths. I ask students to write down three possible ideas for a myth, and then I record an idea from each student on the overhead. Now the students have many ideas to help them choose their own story topics. Again with a partner students write their own myths to explain some natural phenomenon or happening. For example, they could explain why there is snow, thunder, earthquakes, change of season, rain, spines on cacti, and so forth. Favorite topics for students have been to explain why we have stars or rain or to provide a reason for particular animal features, such as why zebras have stripes. Collaborative writing is difficult, but it becomes an opportunity for students to get to know their classmates. In addition, I want to establish quite early on that collaboration is something to be valued in this classroom. After writing their myths, students make colored illustrations to go with them. The myths are typed, and the students' work is displayed. Monica wrote this myth to explain why we see rainbows:

The Magical Birds

Once upon a time there lived two brothers Roman and Raman. Raman was jealous of Roman, and would do anything to hurt him. So Raman thought hard. "What can I take away from him that will make him sad. I know! I will let loose his precious birds that he loves so much. So that they will fly away and he will never see them again." For Raman knew that the birds were magical; with their unique colors such a blue, green, yellow, orange, red and purple. In their special way and unlike any other birds, they had great speed to fly once let out in the open. No one could see them with their naked eye.

That night the two brothers went to sleep. Raman woke up and opened the cage to the magical birds. He watched with pleasure as each bird rose to the midnight sky and vanished in a flash before his eyes.

In the morning the two brothers woke up. Raman secretly laughed at Roman that was very depressed when he found out that his magical birds were gone from their cage. He guessed that from the terrible weather that they have been having, the wind must have opened the cage doors and that is how they had gotten loose.

The evil brother, Raman, was pretending to comfort his brother by saying that maybe it was better for the birds to be finally free. Roman was still very sad and just sat looking into the sky hoping that maybe he would see his birds. As it started to rain, he still continued to stare at the sky. Then he saw these streaks of bright colors that stretched from one side of the earth to the other. Roman knew that these were the colors of his birds as they searched for a place to nest. He ran back home with joy so he could tell his brother that he had seen his magical birds. Raman did not believe him because you cannot see the birds if they are flying with just the naked eye because they are too fast. Soon the brother found out that they could see the birds fly for the rain slowed them down just enough. You could then see their colors as they flew in perfect form from one another. And today the birds are called a rainbow and the evil brother is still trying to make his brother unhappy. For Roman has been filled with joy by the fact that his birds are set free and he can still see them when it rains.

The following myth is a final result of Mike and Philip's collaboration. Their first story was about two paragraphs long; in it they explained that deer had antlers because when the deer scratched its head on a tree, the branches stuck to its head. My probing question "Does your story explain why the deer would need antlers?" prompted a revision, and the result was a much-improved myth.

Why Do Deer Have Antlers

There was a deer that was always getting jumped by all the bigger animals in the forest. They would bite him and slash him with their claws. Every time they did this to him he would be severely injured. This deer wanted to find a way to scare off the bigger animals or to protect himself from them.

One day he was walking through the forest trying to find something that will scare off the other animals. His head started to itch, so he rubbed his head on a tree. At that moment two branches with sharp ends fell onto his head. He tried to pull them off but they were stuck to his head. Then he realized that he could scare away something or protect himself from predators.

All of a sudden a fox came out of his den so the deer stood over him to show off his new items. The fox was so scared of him that he ran back into his den and never came out. The deer was so proud of himself that he jumped for joy.

Later that afternoon all the bigger animals went after the deer to jump him, but when they found him they were in for a big surprise. When they attacked him he fought back with several mighty blows. The animals cowered back from him and from that day forth nothing bothered that deer again.

Another strategy used to help students think about what they are learning is a structured writing prompt for an "I Understand" poem. This prompt is used to help students clarify what they know about a subject. The part that they do not understand can be the basis for teacher explanation, review, or further class work. I have written this one in English and Spanish because my classes include some beginning-level English-as-a-second-language (ESL) students. I encourage them to write in the language with which they are most comfortable because the thinking about what to write is where the learning takes place.

The Brain Poem/El Poema del Cerebro

I understand . . . /Yo entiendo . . .
I understand . . . /Yo entiendo . . .
I understand . . . /Yo entiendo . . .
But I really do not understand . . . Pero realmente no entiendo . . .

Another activity that my students do early in the school year is to write a science autobiography. They write a paragraph that describes their feelings about science, what science courses they have taken in the past, why they are taking biology, and what career they are interested in pursuing. Sylvia's autobiography is an example of this assignment.

Sylvia's Autobiography

Science to me is my favorite subject because it's fun. I'm taking biology because it's a start to having all my science classes for a university and because it sounds fun. And because I'm interested in being a veterinarian or a marine biologist, something fun with animals, or even a marine animal trainer like at Sea World and places like that. In past years we have studied astronomy, ocean, animals in the ocean, erosion, purifying water, etc.

This autobiography gives me information I can use in planning my curriculum. If there are areas of biology that most of the students have studied in the past, I know these are areas that I can either build on or extend. Sylvia's career choices gave me an opportunity to talk with her about the importance of her science and math classes in high school to help her reach her goal.

I also give students the opportunity to practice some science skills such as observation. One year we raised silkworms in my classroom. Students showed great interest in how the silkworm grew and developed. One way students recorded their findings was by using the following poem outline. This poem is another variation of Gere's (1985) bio poem. Students finish the sentence starters and replace the words in the parentheses.

The Mulberry Silkworm

Line 1   The mulberry silkworm
Line 2   (Four adjectives that describe the silkworm)
Line 3   (Four stages of metamorphosis)
Line 4   As a caterpillar it likes to eat . . .
Line 5   To survive it needs . . . (three things)
Line 6   Who changes . . . (describe at least one)
Line 7   To grow it needs to . . .
Line 8   Whose cocoon . . . (describe the cocoon)
Line 9   (Your silkworm's name)

Brandi's poem follows:

The mulberry silkworm
    soft, fuzzy, messy, silky
egg, larva, pupa, and adult
    as a caterpillar it likes to eat mulberry leaves
to survive it needs fresh leaves, air, and light
who changes three times throughout life
to grow it needs to eat and stay alive
whose cocoon is white sometimes yellow and made of silk
Spot

Brandi has included her observations about what she has learned about silkworms in her poem. I was looking for more detailed descriptions of the silkworms in the poem, but this attempt is a beginning. In the future I would have the class brainstorm observations; then students would have more details to use in the poems.

Rather than asking students to memorize definitions and spelling words, I find **acrostics** help them integrate knowledge. I find that writing acrostics helps to ease the tedium of learning the vocabulary of science. In writing acrostics students use the word written vertically as the first letter of each phrase. Here is Steve's acrostic on the brain:

> Blood brings oxygen
> Records memories
> Always working
> Imagines plans
> Neurons tell the body what to do

The various writing assignments that I have described are some of the ways that my students practice the skills of a literate person in a science class. These assignments not only allow students to speak from their own experiences but also give them a variety of creative ways to express their thoughts. Finally, as these writing-to-learn activities help students organize their thinking and sharpen their understanding of the science they are learning, they also allow students to employ diverse academic skills to complete the assignments.

EXTENSION ACTIVITIES

1. Describe some activities that you have used to deal with possible student misconceptions about your content area.

2. Have your students write subject autobiographies. List about five other questions (besides the ones used in this chapter) that you might want students to address regarding their history with your subject area.

3. Describe your experience using journals in your classes. How successful has it been in enhancing students' literacy skills?

REFERENCES

Aardema, V. (1975). *Why mosquitos buzz in people's ears*. New York City: Putnam.

Chang, C. (1994). *The seventh sister*. Mahawah, NJ: Troll Association.

Gere, A. (1985). *Roots in the sawdust*. Urbana, IL: National Council of Teachers of English.

Hayes, J. (1993). *Softchild-how rattlesnake got its fangs*. Niwot, CO: Robert Rinehart Pub.

Johnson, J. (1997). *How my dog got tame*. Mahawah, NJ: Troll Association.

Joos, M. (1967). *The five clocks*. New York: Harcourt Brace Jovanovich.

Mike, J. M. (1993). *Opposum and the great firemaker*. Mahawah, NJ: Troll Association.

2

MATH AND SCIENCE IN MY ENGLISH CLASS? WHY NOT?

ANNE-MARIE HALL

UNIVERSITY OF ARIZONA

ABSTRACT

This chapter takes a broad-lens view of math and science as more than just computation. It argues that mathematical and scientific ways of thinking can be enhanced and reinforced in other content areas, particularly language arts. Making a sharp distinction between writing to learn and writing to display learning, the chapter offers eleven activities for English teachers to use to support math and science literacies.

A BROAD-LENS VIEW OF LITERACIES

Teachers are well aware of the advantages of using writing and literacy events in math and science. We have all read countless articles and attended workshops in which writing activities and the theory of writing to learn are richly integrated into a math or science course (Tchudi, 1991, 1993; Walvoord, 1982). But what about using math and science literacies in English? Why not? Before you panic, let me explain that I am not asking English teachers to teach the Pythagorean theorem, decimals, fractions, ratios, or even statistics. I am talking about reinforcing the *thinking* of the disciplines of mathematicians and scientists in our language arts curricula.

In my experiences as director of a writing project, I have had the opportunity to visit dozens of classrooms and see teachers teaching other teachers. As I observe math and science teachers participate in the writing project, it becomes obvious to me that the idea of writing as a tool to enhance learning has caught on in the content areas. Teachers (in math and science as well as in other content areas) are aware that writing is an important part of helping students learn content. My intent here is not to ignore other content areas, but to fulfill the purpose of this chapter I need to concentrate on math and science.

At a recent writing project workshop, math, science, social studies, modern language, general education, and English teachers from a local high school were working on a semester-long professional development program called "Literacies across the Curriculum." Initially, the workshop leaders (writing project teacher-consultants) met the participants' expectations by offering lots of ways to integrate reading and writing into their curricula. The English teachers were wonderful resources to their colleagues in brainstorming ways to use writing without being overburdened by paper grading. But soon discussion moved beyond ways these practices might improve learning and writing in content areas to issues of reciprocity; in other words, how can teachers reinforce math and science literacies in the English classroom? Reflecting on my own preoccupation with English as *literacy* and as one-dimensional, I realized that it need not be such a one-way street. It need not be just writing and reading in the content areas but literacies across the curriculum. Indeed, there is more than one kind of literacy.

Viewing literacy as diverse and involving multiple disciplines (math literacy, science literacy, computer literacy, and so forth) also seems to meet the needs of today's students in more pragmatic ways than in the past. For example, many of my undergraduate students at the university are not going to be English majors. In fact, my courses are frequently the only and last English courses they will take beyond high school. Other students who do not go to college end their formal education in English in high school. Yet all of these students will be citizens of the world, reading widely in newspapers, the Internet, magazines, journals, and so forth. What we read in our lives beyond schooling (particularly formal schooling in English) requires the ability to recognize patterns, to make valid inferences and decisions and arguments to solve a variety of real-world problems, and to have a sense of numbers in relationship to basic facts. Students must be able to determine the reasonableness of results. All of these are basic mathematical principles. Aren't they also basic language arts principles?

Besides reading, English teachers teach writing. And in a writing curriculum, we know that students with a developed number sense are more easily able to engage in style analysis. They can look at their own writing and count the number of words in a sentence, complicating their syntactic maturity by recognizing ways to combine sentences or vary them in diction and length. This kind of metacognition (being able to understand how you write and why you write the way you do) is basic to helping students take responsibility for their own writing. Without a basic number sense, it is futile to teach students to analyze their own writing style.

I want to argue for an expanded notion of literacy across the curriculum, one that includes a basic grasp of mathematical principles to aid in reading and in critical thinking within the language arts classroom. In this chapter I will first explore the theory behind writing to learn and writing across the curriculum in the hope of building a rationale for using writing, thinking, speaking, and reading in the English classroom while integrating basic principles of mathematical and scientific reasoning. I will then talk about specific mathematical and scientific principles and suggest activities for integrating them into the English curriculum.

WRITING TO LEARN

Since the 1960s, several theorists have researched and written about language and learning. Jerome Bruner (1966) told us that when people articulate connections between new information and what they already know, they learn and understand that new information better. Lev Vygotsky (1962) helped us see that when people think and figure things out, they do so in symbol systems commonly called languages, most often verbal, but also mathematical, musical, visual, and so on. Janet Emig (1977) brought linguistics and cognitive psychology together, arguing that when people learn things, they use all of the language modes—reading, writing, speaking, and listening—to do so, with each mode helping people learn in a unique way. James Britton, Tony Burgess, Nancy Martin, Alex McLeod, and Harold Rosen (1975) gave overwhelming evidence of how important speaking can be in developing writing. Additionally, they launched the earliest rationale for writing across the curriculum in arguing that when people write about new information and ideas—in addition to reading, talking, and listening—they learn and understand them better. Finally, James Moffett (1968) reminded us (like Plato did) that when people really care about what they read and write, when they see relevance to their own lives, they both learn and write better.

WRITING ACROSS THE CURRICULUM

There are distinctions in the literature between writing to learn and writing across the curriculum (Elbow, 1973; Fulwiler, 1987; Gere, 1985). Ann Ruggles Gere explains it this way:

> Writing to learn has different goals from writing across the curriculum. Although writing to learn, like writing across the curriculum, emphasizes writing in all disciplines, its goal is different. Writing across the curriculum aims to improve the quality of writing, while writing to learn focuses on better thinking and learning. To be sure, students who use writing as a way of learning often produce better written products, but this is a side benefit, not the chief purpose. (1985, p. 5)
>
> (Reprinted with permission from Gere, A. R. [1985]. *Roots in the sawdust: Writing to learn in the disciplines.* Urbana, IL: National Council of Teachers of English.)

Certainly the idea of creating a classroom environment in which students talk about their ideas to teachers and peers and write about what they are learning is nothing new. But the idea that writing should occur in all disciplines got lost for a while. The whole-language movement, which has strongly influenced elementary school environments, has long recognized the importance of integrating all the language arts with content area learning (Freeman & Freeman, 1992; Goodman, 1986; Strickland & Strickland, 1993). Nonetheless, there is a transition that begins in middle school and hardens by secondary school into a belief that there are content area disciplines in which "covering the curriculum" is the most important goal (Tchudi, 1991, 1993). The isolation of the disciplines in secondary school, then, has made a fertile ground for a movement to integrate reading, writing, speaking, and listening into content area courses such as math, social studies, science, art, and so on.

Beginning with the British Schools Council Project in Writing across the Curriculum in the 1960s, it became obvious that in science and math classrooms, students who were able to write about the new information they were learning engaged in more lively ways with the topic and they learned more. Classrooms filled with rich and varied literacy experiences produced students who were more interested in learning (Britton, 1970; Martin, D'Arcy, Newton, & Parker, 1976).

The basic concepts of writing across the curriculum are obvious; writing in the content area is an opportunity to improve writing, and writing can be used to learn content. In writing-to-learn classrooms students pose questions, generate ideas for class discussions or other projects, provide feedback to the teacher, and just write to help themselves think about what they are learning. The writing makes their thinking process more visible. A key difference here between writing a literary analysis in an English classroom and a writing-to-learn activity in *any* classroom is this: one is *writing to display learning,* whereas the other is *writing to learn.* Table 2.1 explains the types of writing assignments that distinguish between writing to learn and writing to display learning.

Many of the types of writing in the *Writing to Learn* column are used as prewriting or invention (helping students generate ideas for longer and more formal writing)

TABLE 2.1   Writing across the Curriculum: Two Concepts

WRITING TO LEARN	WRITING TO DISPLAY LEARNING
Types of Writing	
Journals	Essays
Lab notebooks	Book reports
Notes on readings	Research papers
Quick one-minute essays	Essay exams
Freewriting	Lab reports
Rough drafts of more formal assignments	Final reports
	Formal letters
Characteristics	
Informal	Formal
Exploratory	Conclusive
Self-expressive	Authoritative
Messy	Clear, concise, focused
Ways to Respond	
In brief notes, comments	In marginal or end comments
In a one-to-one conference	In a one-to-one conference
In a reader-response sort of first impression	In a balanced evaluation explaining both strengths and weaknesses
By praising good ideas	by pointing out ways to improve future writing tasks of the same nature
By ignoring grammar	By correcting mistakes in the first paragraph
By pointing out connections and suggesting ways to explore them more fully	and using check marks for repeated errors
By having students respond to each other's writing	

for the types of writing in the column *Writing to Display Learning,* although a distinguishing feature of writing-to-learn activities is that they do not have to lead to polished writing. Again, it is helpful to refer to Ann Ruggles Gere's distinction between writing to learn and writing across the curriculum: writing to learn can be made into a performance product, a display of knowledge, but this is not its chief purpose. Writing across the curriculum, like writing to display knowledge, is an umbrella concept under which writing-to-learn activities reside. This theory (writing to learn) informs practice (writing across the curriculum) and the search for pedagogy. Christopher Thaiss (1984) tells us that faculty training programs stressing writing across the curriculum proliferated in the 1970s. Teachers and researchers such as Pamela Farrell-Childers, Anne Ruggles Gere, & Art Young (1985, 1994), Toby Fulwiler (1982, 1987), and Stephen Tchudi (1991, 1993) wrote books encouraging content area teachers not to be experts in teaching writing but rather to use dozens of easy-to-use techniques (which they explain) for applying language to content areas.

In sum, there are two things to remember about writing to learn and writing across the curriculum. First, there is substantial evidence (from cognitive psychologists, linguists, etc.) that writing enhances learning because it is multirepresentational, is integrative, provides immediate feedback, provides a record of the thought processes of the writer, provides connections between abstract and concrete ideas, is active, and is self-rhymed (Britton, 1970; Britton et al., 1975; Bruner, 1966; Emig, 1977; Martin et al., 1976; Moffett, 1968; Vygotsky, 1962). Second, implied in the writing across the curriculum movement is the notion that one does not have to be a specialist or an expert in the teaching of writing to use literacy events to enhance learning in the content areas.

MATHEMATICS AND SCIENCE LITERACIES ACROSS THE CURRICULUM

Let's start with what we can agree on. If the implication that underlies writing across the curriculum is true—that one does not have to be a writing specialist or an expert to use writing in a non-English discipline—then surely there are ways in which English teachers can teach, reinforce, and stress mathematical and scientific principles in their classrooms without being experts in math or science. It is the other side of the same coin.

The argument for the transfer of writing-to-learn theory to using math and science concepts in the English classroom is also straightforward. If writing enhances learning (in all subjects), then we would still be using writing in English classes to enhance learning. We would just be more explicitly aware of how math and science thinking can be taught within our existing curriculum, particularly when helping students read and write material (such as nonfiction, newspaper, and textbook prose) that requires the ability to use mathematical structure and logic to make conjectures, to test the validity of arguments, or simply to describe patterns and relationships involving data, graphs, numbers, and the like. We would more consciously intrude in order to use math and science principles of reasoning and problem solving in our English classrooms. It is still writing to learn, just casting a wider net to draw in the thinking that is intrinsic to math and science when reading, when helping students analyze their own writing, or when teaching research papers or persuasive writing (analyzing evidence, collecting data, making valid inferences from statistics, etc.).

Relying on the standards for mathematics and science, Steven Zemelman (1998) lists the best practice in teaching mathematics and the best practice in teaching science. When you look at the concepts that need to be increased in mathematics, for example, it is easy to see many ways to reinforce these practices in an English classroom. The same is true with science.

In mathematics, teaching practices that are encouraged include questioning and making conjectures, justifying ways of thinking, and problem solving. If you look at the large concepts in mathematics—those that help students think like a mathematician— you see mathematics as problem solving, as communication, as reasoning, and you see the use of statistics and probability to describe, analyze, evaluate, and make decisions. You look for patterns and describe them, you identify relationships, and you use variables to express relationships (Zemelman, 1998). Aren't those the guiding principles of critical thinking when students write an argument about an issue they care about, compare and contrast characters in a novel, or justify a critical stance on a poem?

So, too, in science, students are encouraged to focus on underlying concepts about how natural phenomena are explained. They question, think, and problem solve. Skepticism, the willingness to question common beliefs, the acceptance of ambiguity when data are not decisive, the ability to stay open to others' views and to change one's opinion, and the ability to use logic in hypothesizing and inferring (Zemelman, 1998) all sound like the basic premises of my composition class. Yet being aware of how these concepts help our students think like scientists in the English classroom is an important step in making the connections among math, science, and English more explicit.

THEORY INTO PRACTICE

In the following sections I describe some ways that math and science thinking can be reinforced in the English classroom.

Mysteries

Teach mysteries in English to help students make predictions, inquire, and look at variables and constants. Students can be detectives as they go in search of evidence to rule in or out a theory about "whodunit." This type of scientific analysis could also produce an excellent literary analysis.

Inferences

Teach students to make inferences by walking through the classroom or across campus and writing down observations. After students make inferences from what they see, they should test the inferences to see if they are justifiable, reasonable, and believable.

Nonfiction Genres

Teach genres other than fiction, poetry, and drama. Bring nonfiction into the classroom and learn to distinguish between the literature of fact and the literature of imagination.

For example, bring in articles from science magazines, popular magazines, and essays printed in anthologies. Have students analyze them rhetorically (Who is the audience? What is the purpose?). Learn to recognize the differences between scientific and literary writing. Practice writing in all genres. In other words, write for different purposes and audiences but include nonfiction and science writing in your curriculum.

Investigations

Have students investigate how inventions (or something else) change over time. Look at car engines, eggbeaters, furniture, skis, running shoes, and so on. Besides reinforcing cause-effect reasoning, it is a great topic for a research paper. Also, if you teach science fiction in your classroom, this type of investigation (e.g., looking at some aspect of technology) works especially well. Seeing the incremental steps between inventions and looking at the historical context surrounding the invention provide a wonderful way to understand consequential reasoning and patterns over time.

Vocabulary

Stress key words from science in your weekly vocabulary lessons such as observation, prediction, sequences, inferences, facts versus opinions, interpretations, investigations, relevancy, classification, cause and effect, and clarification. Ask students to relate these terms to some aspect of the language arts curriculum that you are presently covering (*Romeo and Juliet,* Gary Soto's poems, etc.).

Lists

Assign groups of students different discussion topics related to what you are reading. Each group puts a list on the board arranged according to a theory (most important to least important, steps in a process, causes, effects, reasons, examples, items, suggestions, ideas, conclusions, etc.). It cannot be random; there must be a logic and coherence to the list. Students can state their rationale at the beginning or end of the list. This type of listing is a great way to study for an exam on a large unit, for example.

Problem a Week, Month, or Unit

Have students work on open-ended problems related thematically to a literature unit you are teaching (on envy, love, friendship, communities, neighborhoods, etc.). Groups of students can extend this assignment into a problem-solving project using inductive and deductive reasoning, drawing logical conclusions, justifying their solutions, and analyzing their processes. With inductive reasoning, the students collect details, facts, opinions, and so forth about a particular theme (racism in their school while reading Maya Angelou's *I Know Why a Caged Bird Sings,* for example) and try to organize the data and arrive at a generalization or truism about racism. With deductive reasoning, the students start with a theory or generalization and go in search of the particulars to support the theory. After this process, they may revise their theory.

Patterns

Look for patterns within genres, between genres, with a particular author, with a particular literary period, and so on. Help students generalize from the particulars they notice (inductive reasoning). Try the opposite. Begin with a generalization and go in search for particulars that support or contradict the generalization (deductive reasoning). For example, when reading poetry by Luci Tapahanso, have students look for common themes in her early work, later work, and so forth. Does she write in the same literary genre throughout? Are there significant differences in her poetic form from her early work to her later work? Does the form depend on what theme she writes on?

Linguistic Analysis

Have students analyze the style of a Morrison or a Faulkner work. Count the number of sentences and the number of words in each sentence in the prologue to *A Farewell to Arms,* for example. Then figure out the average sentence length. Then count the number of nouns, verbs, adverbs, conjunctions (there will be many), and the like. What does that tell you about Hemingway's style? Students can figure out the math and come up with ratios (number of conjunctions per 100 words or per sentence, number of verbs per 100 words, etc.). They can compare Hemingway's style and Morrison's style, choosing 250 words from each, for example. Then they can try imitating the two styles. And they can conduct linguistic analyses on their own writing and each other's. Syntactic maturity is a goal in teaching students writing; that means students can create long and varied sentences yet do not lose control of their ideas. I have had mathematically inclined students who loved doing this kind of linguistic analysis on the writing of authors and on their own writing. And it is very revealing about the craft of writing, throwing light on the artistic act of "making" a text (to quote W. H. Auden).

Random Data

Bring in a list of random data—perhaps from a novel, a current event, or a newspaper clipping. Have groups of students arrange the data in an order that shows consequential relationships (because this, then that). If all the groups are working with the same data, they can compare their results, arguing for their reasons for arranging the data in a particular order. This activity helps them in writing sustained arguments that are logical and reasonable, and it particularly helps students use sources (outside research) in ways that are apparent to a reader (i.e., logical).

Thematic Literature Units

Teach a unit on nature. Explore the evolution of the contemporary environmental movement by looking at its roots through literature: religion (origin myths—Genesis, Navajo, etc.), romanticism and nature (Henry David Thoreau), transcendentalism and nature (Ralph Waldo Emerson), conservation (Aldo Leopold), environmentalism (John Muir), ecology (Rachel Carson), and ecodefense (Ed Abbey). Encourage students to be curious about nature and to develop deeper understandings of the evolution of the current environmental movement.

A CAVEAT OR TWO

While I have been arguing that teachers do not need to be experts in math or science to support math or science literacies, I have also been implying that math and science teachers need not be experts in the teaching of writing to use writing in their classrooms. However, there is a tension between teaching content and teaching writing. Many content area teachers (math, science, history, fine arts, etc.) are uncomfortable using writing in their classes. Furthermore, they may be uncertain about the place of writing in their curriculum and their goals when they ask students to write in their classes. And when they evaluate their students' writing products, they may pay attention only to content at the exclusion of syntax, mechanics, organization, and other writing concerns. If the main objective of the writing activity is understanding of the concept being taught (writing to learn), then focusing exclusively on content (what the student said) is usually enough. However, sometimes writing-to-learn activities in the content areas develop into writing to display knowledge—and thus need to be brought to the level of a "public" performance.

During a recent portfolio-grading session in which high school and university teachers were assessing high school writing portfolios for placement into university composition courses, several high school teachers had one of those collective "aha" moments. They represented different urban and rural high schools, most of which had some kind of writing across the curriculum program. Some writing across the curriculum programs were elaborate—lots of professional development workshops, opportunities for interdisciplinary teams, requirements for writing from each content area and each level—and others were more informal. But there was almost a smugness on the part of all the teachers because the program was in place. The "aha" moment came in reading the portfolios, each of which included expository writing from a discipline other than English. The writing was noticeably weaker in this selection.

In other words, the reflective letter, literary analysis, and expressive writing (the other three selections, which came out of English classrooms) were substantially stronger. One teacher expressed her disappointment that writing across the curriculum was, well, not having the results she expected:

> Mary: I feel discouraged when we read the other content area papers. For as long as we've been at Tucson High, writing across the curriculum, working in partnership with our social studies peers and science peers, I felt discouraged. There still seems to be a gap between what I felt were pieces coming from English and the other content areas . . . So I'm so thoroughly, philosophically committed to that idea that all teachers should be teachers of writing and yet I felt discouraged by the products I was reading today because it's not happening.

The point here is that we may have become complacent about writing across the curriculum. We think it is happening, and the evidence in this portfolio-grading session is that it is not working all that well. Other researchers have recognized that as we try to institutionalize writing across the curriculum, there are numerous pitfalls (Farrell-Childers, Gere, & Young, 1994). Teachers cannot assume that because their schools' administrators, curriculum coordinators, and department chairs have made some overture to writing across the curriculum the program is being practiced soundly in the classrooms. For example, writing to learn in math and science classrooms may include (expressive) writing-to-learn activities, but it should also include writing assignments typical of the writing scientists and mathematicians really do. These teachers talk about that problem:

> Sharon: I was really surprised by the science papers I was getting . . . . I was wondering why those particular assignments had seemed so creative and why that's considered writing in science class[.] My first thoughts for curriculum were let's do the sort of writing scientists do; let's work on doing multiple revisions of lab reports, or on scientific research papers. Not doing advertisements and . . . stuff like that which I am seeing.

> Paulette: I don't think these students are exposed to much real writing. That's where curriculum comes in. Maybe these students are not seeing a variety of papers, even trade papers out of *Scientific American* or scholarly history journals.

Sharon pointed out that the kinds of writing from science that she was seeing included poems on amoebas, biopoems of the word *virus,* television scenes using the words *proteins, lipids,* and *carbohydrates,* and fictional stories incorporating a habitat studied in science—all of which are fine and good if students are learning science in the process. On the other hand, making science understandable to the general public is a special skill. Articles in *Discover* magazine and nonfiction books by Carl Sagan, Isaac Asimov, or Annie Dillard are especially good examples. But Sharon's argument is that this is simply an infusion of English genres into science, not true science writing. More importantly, she does not believe that it enhances science *thinking.*

But the types of writing that Sharon listed are those that teachers generally use as writing-to-learn strategies. Perhaps what needs to happen is for science teachers to see that there are different types of writing to be done in the science classrooms and that they need to equip their students with enough skills to make good decisions about the appropriate types of writing for particular tasks. Perhaps the problem has been letting content area teachers believe that writing to learn equals writing across the curriculum.

It may be time to go back to the drawing board. We need to reopen the dialogue with our colleagues from all disciplines. And this time English teachers need to be open to bringing math and science concepts into a more explicit role in their own classrooms. They need to teach English, but they can reinforce scientific and mathematical thinking in their writing, speaking, thinking, and reading assignments. It is nothing new. As you can see from the practical ideas cited earlier, many of these learning strategies are already in use in English classrooms. Now is the time to make them a calculated intrusion, to start the conversation again with our math and science colleagues, to ask for ways to affirm the thinking of mathematicians and scientists in science, math, and English classrooms. One teacher suggested a way to begin this reciprocal arrangement:

> Mary: One thing we can do is try block scheduling. English teachers with social studies, science, math teachers, etc. And the students are writing papers together. . . . I think the blocking . . . those kinds of collaborations that occur in the high schools where you have a natural collegiality that begins to build and then suddenly someone doesn't say to you, "well, you're the English teacher, I'll give you the papers to edit. My kids will do the ideas." You begin this framework that everyone is going to work on the writing together.

And the math. And the science.

A NEW MODEL OF PROFESSIONAL DEVELOPMENT

We have grown numb by now to editorials (designed to make us feel guilty) about how Johnny can't read or write. But what is disturbing is how ignorance of mathematics has become socially acceptable (Doran, 1998). We know the consequences to citizens of not being able to read or write. But what are the consequences of not being able to do math? In a recent newspaper column, Robert S. Doran, the math department chair at Texas Christian University, writes that "people openly admit they aren't good at math. Only in America do adults openly proclaim their ignorance of mathematics as if it were some sort of merit badge." Aside from the evidence that students who take math are far more likely to be successful in college and the workplace, he also reports on a white paper from October 1997 in which Education Secretary Richard Riley "showed that students with a basic grasp of higher level math are more likely to succeed regardless of family income or public or private schooling."

My argument, then, is that English teachers can help lay the groundwork for students to move inside the world of mathematics, to become comfortable with the thinking of the discipline. Whether we are thinking about our weight, shoe size, the speed we drive, computers, electronics, gadgets in the home, percentages, cost of living indexes, coefficients of friction, or the Dow-Jones average, we live in a society saturated with math (Doran, 1998). And science thinking helps us keep an inquiring mind, an intellectual curiosity that is careful and reasoned. Curriculum is interdisciplinary today. We are educating the whole student. And in the language arts classroom, our students use mathematical skills almost every day. They will need to use them even more when they engage in real-world problem solving beyond our classroom walls.

Perhaps what we need is a new model of professional development. We might configure it vertically, like the National Writing Project Institutes. We could look at three strands—math, science, and English—from the standards and gaze at them from the multiple levels of college through the primary grades. Bringing different disciplines and levels together to develop instructional strategies might help all of us think vertically and horizontally across the curriculum, like scientists, mathematicians, and English educators. Why not?

EXTENSION ACTIVITIES

1. Can you think of other ways of connecting mathematics to English? To the real world? Perhaps have your students list all the ways they use mathematics each day—not just computation but the concepts (statistics and probability, patterns and functions, measurement, etc.). Then have them make a parallel list of situations in which they need to communicate those concepts to someone else. Ask students who their ideal readers might be for their lists. What would these readers have to know to understand their lists?

2. Science thinking involves questioning, thinking, and problem solving. Have students make a list of things that puzzle them (rules they do not understand, people they have never talked to, things that frighten them, a club on campus they are curious about, something they have never tried before but want to try, or something that makes them mad). Then ask them to use their science thinking and their writing skills to problem solve: be skeptical, question common beliefs, accept ambiguities when data are not decisive, modify explanations, be willing to change their opinions, use logic, plan their inquiry, hypothesize, and infer.

3. What strategies that you are already using in your classroom to teach scientific and mathematical thinking can you add to the list? What about writing strategies to enhance types of thinking done in other subject areas such as physical education, home economics, and so forth?

RESOURCES ON THE INTERNET (MATH AND SCIENCE)

National Council of Teachers of Mathematics (http://www.nctm.org)

Links to good mathematics Web sites (http://members.aol.com/mathwise2)

American Association for Advancement of Science (http://aaas.org)

National Committee on Science Education Standards (http://ncrl.org/sdrs)

National Science Teachers Association (http://www.nsta.org)

REFERENCES

Britton, J. (1970). *Language and learning*. Harmondsworth, U.K.: Penguin.

Britton, J., Burgess, T., Martin, N., McLeod, A., & Rosen, H. (1975). *The development of writing abilities*. London: Macmillan Education.

Bruner, J. S. (1966). *Toward a theory of instruction*. Cambridge, MA: Harvard University Press.

Doran, R. S. (1998). (1998, March 10). We may not like it, but math really does matter. *Arizona Daily Star,* p. A13.

Elbow, P. (1973). *Writing without teachers*. London: Oxford University Press.

Emig, J. (1977). Writing as mode of learning. *College Composition and Communication, 28*(2). pp. 122–128.

Farrell-Childers, P., Gere, A. R., & Young, A. (1994). *Programs and practices: Writing across the secondary school curriculum*. Portsmouth, NH: Heinemann.

Freeman, Y., & Freeman, D. (1992). *Whole language for second language learners*. Portsmouth, NH: Heinemann.

Fulwiler, T. (Ed.). (1987). *The journal book*. Portsmouth, NH: Heinemann.

Gere, A. R. (1985). *Roots in the sawdust: Writing to learn across the disciplines*. Urbana, IL: National Council of Teachers of English.

Goodman, K. S. (1986). *What's whole about whole language?* Portsmouth, NH: Heinemann.

Martin, N., D'Arcy, P., Newton, B., & Parker, R. (1976). *Writing and learning across the curriculum*. London: Ward Lock.

Moffett, J. (1968). *Teaching the universe of discourse*. Boston: Houghton-Mifflin.

Strickland, K., & Strickland, J. (1993). *Uncovering the curriculum*. Portsmouth, NH: Boynton/Cook.

Tchudi, S. (1991). *Travels across the curriculum: Models for interdisciplinary learning*. Richmond Hill, Ontario: Scholastic.

Tchudi, S. (Ed.). (1993). *The astonishing curriculum: Integrating science and humanities through language.* Urbana, IL: National Council of Teachers of English.

Thaiss, C. (1984). *Language across the curriculum.* ERIC/RCS. EJ371798.

Vygotsky, L. (1962). *Thought and language.* Cambridge, MA: Harvard University Press.

Walvoord, B. E. F. (1982). *Helping students write well: A guide for teachers in all disciplines.* New York: Modern Language Association.

Zemelman, S. (1998). *Best practice: New standards for teaching and learning in America's schools* (2nd ed.). Portsmouth, NH: Heinemann.

3

Writing in a Law-Related English Class

Carl Johannesson

Cholla High Magnet School

ABSTRACT

In an effort to provide authentic experiences for students in a law-related English class, the author uses writing as a tool for students to acquire basic legal literacy. Students are asked to put the antagonist in a fairy tale on trial, and in the process they create a play of the trial that incorporates legal concepts. Student samples showing the incorporation of the different legal concepts are provided.

THE GENESIS OF A MAGNET PROGRAM

In the mid-1980s the Office of Civil Rights of the U.S. Department of Education ordered Tucson Unified School District to implement a desegregation plan that would achieve a more balanced ethnic distribution across the district. Cholla High School was included in the order because the percentage of minority students was significantly higher in the school than in the Tucson community at large. The district proposed a remedy that has been used in other cities and that was acceptable to the Office of Civil Rights: magnet schools that would attract students from schools with an Anglo overabundance. At Cholla High School we began to explore possible magnet themes and finally settled on an international-intercultural studies theme and law-related education theme.

Coincidentally, I had developed a few law-related activities not long before this new program was thrust on us. I had created mock trial activities for Shakespeare's *Julius Caesar* and Steinbeck's *Of Mice and Men*. I saw from students engaged in the process an enthusiasm and a care for close reading that in previous years had been missing. I liked this approach because my students liked it and because they took charge of their learning. When I was asked if I was interested in teaching English with a law-related focus, I knew I was.

Those on the faculty who had decided to get involved took part in in-service training and curriculum development. Meanwhile, authentic, state-of-the-art facilities were constructed, including a courtroom modeled after the University of Arizona College of Law's "courtroom of the future," a computerized law library, and a computerized conference center for electronic meetings and learning activities modeled after a similar facility at the University of Arizona's College of Management Information Systems.

Tucson Unified School District's high school magnet programs are schools within comprehensive high schools. The idea is to offer magnet courses in every discipline alongside the preexisting course offerings in those content areas. Students who take enough course work in either the law-related or the international-intercultural program receive a special endorsement on their diplomas.

The magnet program has been officially in place since 1996, and in 1998 the National Council of Teachers of Social Studies awarded Cholla High Magnet School's social studies curriculum its Program of Excellence Award in recognition of our innovative program.

LEARNING THEORY

Creating the magnet program gave us the opportunity to establish a pedagogy that incorporated the principles and practices of current theory. In doing so, we had to ask ourselves a question: What do we know should go on in school that traditional learning does not recognize? The answers came from the works of Piaget, Vygotsky, Maslow, Bloom, Bruner, Gardner, MacLean, Lave, and other cognitive researchers and educators whose work references and builds on their findings. We looked at the ideas of constructivist theory, social development theory, situated learning, anchored instruction, and other emerging views of learning and school.

We found that what should go on in school is the same thing that goes on outside of school. School should not be an artificial environment, alienated from the real world. The world is authentic. Education should be authentic, too. We have known for a long time that knowledge is not as Plato saw it: an immutable form in another sphere, hovering beyond the grasp of lowly subjectivity. Instead, it is a creation of the learner.

We know that the measure of learning is not the regurgitation of a vast repertoire of facts, the model traditional education presented. We know that intelligence is expressed in a multitude of ways (Gardner, 1983). Yet most people accept this now eclipsed view, and too many educators pander to that outcome, an outcome that requires that students spend an inordinate amount of time exercising only one of the many realms of intelligence, and at the lower end of Bloom's taxonomy at that. Furthermore, an acceptance of the traditional education approach diminishes the amount of time that could be allotted to a broader vision of learning and to higher-order activity.

We know that learning should engage students in the thought processes people in the real world use, but teachers rarely provide students with learning experiences in which knowledge emerges from authentic processes. We know that a piecemeal approach to literacy in any domain is cognitively ineffective. Breaking the whole into its parts and then asking students to experience the parts in isolation for later integration into the whole is more than a waste of time. It is ineffectual, condescending, and boring. How old is the adage that the whole is greater than the sum of its parts?

We know about collaboration, but how many actually know how to design collaborative activities, and how many actually practice or even accept the notion of student-teacher collaboration? In traditional classrooms student-teacher collaboration very likely would have entailed giving the student the answers to the upcoming test because the dominant strategy involved the dissemination of information through the process of lecture with the student as passive receiver of knowledge. We have found ourselves in that position. We know now that such a situation occurs because we have designed the learning experience improperly.

Outcomes should be achieved through student-teacher participation in a process in which the student is the apprentice and the teacher is the expert practitioner (Brown, 1989). If this relationship seems wrong, we should rethink the process we have designed. As teachers, we should never feel we are doing the students' thinking for them by contributing to the task at hand. Instead, if the task is cognitively appropriate, our contributions will provide vital pieces of scaffolding (Bruner, 1960) that facilitate learning in the zone of proximal development (Vygotsky, 1978). (See also Chapter 12.)

LAW-RELATED ENGLISH AND THE LANGUAGE OF THE LEGAL DOMAIN

My ninth-grade law-related English class has as one of its primary objectives the preparation of students to operate in the activity-rich learning environment of the courtroom. In the courtroom learners are authentically engaged in processes of the legal domain. This active engagement requires students to acquire basic legal literacy of concepts, not simply of terms:

1. Roles, functions, and duties: Judge, counsel, bailiff, clerk, and jurors
2. Opening statements: Purpose, structure, style, and content
3. Examinations: Direct and cross
4. Rules of evidence: Avoiding and guarding against fallacious reasoning
5. Closing arguments: Purpose, structure, style, and content

Law-related activities such as pleadings, motions, and mock trials require a foundation in the vocabulary of the law. Dozens of concepts underpin the thinking and reasoning that these processes demand. Therefore, a dominant feature of the first-semester curriculum is the acquisition of legal vocabulary because students must acquire that specialized language before they can engage in these and other activities. However, the students choose this course because they are interested in participating in courtroom proceedings. Ideally, I would like them to learn the language and speak it at the same time.

THEORY INFORMS PRACTICE

They want to dive right in. They want to enter the fray. As a teacher it is fruitless to lament the impetuousness and impatience of students. As teachers we must devise strategies that work. There was a time when the concerns of students would have been dismissed as foolish impudence, and they would have been told that the work is necessarily tedious and that they simply must do it. But cognitive psychology, writing theory, and brain-based learning have revealed that the impatience of youth can be appreciated not in acquiescence but because it has authenticity.

The paradigm of deductive, teacher-centered learning has been overturned not by adolescent protest or cultural decline but by adults—scientists and intellectual pioneers—whose work in often unrelated pursuits has converged and has resulted in a new paradigm that in all respects, whether social, political, or intellectual, simply makes more sense. Learners' minds can no longer be thought of as clean slates on which the teacher writes.

As it turns out, the students' impatience with the traditional practice of separating the contents from the process in order to build understanding one step at a time is justifiable. Isolating the parts from the whole is inimical to what cognitive psychology tells us leads to knowledge. Learning must proceed holistically. Seeing vocabulary within the wholeness of the situation in which it exists promotes acquisition because those situations structure cognition (Brown, 1989).

The terms and concepts that comprise a basic language of the law are the cognitive tools the students need to operate in that domain. The students need to know and comprehend these ideas, be able to apply them, know how to analyze circumstances with regard to them, and be able to synthesize and evaluate with them (Bloom, 1977). If it is a mistake to separate content from process and look at the parts one at a time, the alternative was to keep everything in context and look at everything all at once. English teachers who know James Moffett's *Teaching the Universe of Discourse* (1968) will feel the resonance in his belief that students should learn to write by writing, not by learning about writing. I decided that they would learn the legal language by "speaking" it, not by learning about speaking it. What may seem too big a leap is nonetheless the way to go.

WRITING TO LEARN THROUGH LEGITIMATE PERIPHERAL PARTICIPATION

I felt that I needed an intermediate step that did not bore students on the one hand (what constructivists term "readiness") or frustrate them on the other. It had to actively involve them in a task they really wanted to do even though they did not yet have all the skills. What I really wanted to do was immerse them in an authentic activity, a real-world activity in which they could learn the language and use it at the same time. What I decided to do was an adaptation of what Lave and Wenger (1991) call "legitimate peripheral participation." The idea is that learners start at the periphery of the domain they are entering and, through authentic practice, move toward full competence; only in this case the students would learn about one domain (the law) through performance in another domain (playwriting).

I liked this strategy because, as all good English teachers know well, the imagination is a safe place where time and the unforgiving consequences of its inexorable march forward do not rule, where time can stand still or move ahead at any pace we wish to impose, and where hindsight has the power to reverse that which has already happened. Things can be built up, torn down, and reconfigured as learning leads to increased knowledge and meaning. This is not a "school" activity, either; it is what people do for a living. We call them playwrights.

MULTICULTURAL CONSIDERATIONS

I decided that students could apply legal concepts to an imaginary reality and through this process optimize their understanding of those concepts while at the same time not feel bored or shortchanged. The more familiar the imaginative reality, the greater the likelihood of successful application. What imaginative realities do all fourteen- and fifteen-year-old American students know regardless of their cultural heritage? Fairy tales and folktales.

These stories are found in all cultures around the world. Children who have grown up in the United States know the stories that have become Disney movies, and through the phenomenal success of foreign sales Hollywood has brought these stories to children around the world. But other possibilities abound. All cultures have such stories, stories with moral and ethical conflict in which children or their animal equivalents struggle to find justice.

Teenagers also know about courts of law. Although constitutions and legal rights differ from country to country, law exists even at a tribal level. They all know that allegations have led to a legal arena in which questions are asked and answers are given, resulting in a decision that resolves the matter. Their awareness often comes from personal experience, literature, film, or television. However rudimentary and linguistically uninformed their familiarity may be, they possess an inner sense from which the semantics of law can emerge as tools of reasoning, making possible the capacity to understand and use this awareness with ever-increasing degrees of complexity (Vygotsky, 1978).

COLLABORATION

This learning activity cannot succeed without collaboration between students and teachers. Teachers must act as coauthors and practitioners. Teachers need to establish a cognitive apprenticeship of sorts, "first by making explicit their tacit knowledge or by modeling their strategies for students in authentic activity. Then teachers and colleagues support students' attempts at doing the task" (Brown, 1989). Finally students can continue the task on their own. At the start of this project students easily grasp a great deal of the knowledge required to move forward. But as cognitive demands spiral upward, the experts must add scaffolding for the apprentices' knowledge to expand.

The plays the students write are extended, attenuated writing-to-learn activities that evolve and "morph" through the regular infusion of new concepts. What begins with a structure that includes a sense of character, action, and outcome—what Caine and Caine would call "the familiar" (1994, p. 23)—is wide open to revision. Essentially, students flesh out a story they know very well with details about which they may initially have little or no understanding: "novel stimuli" (Caine & Caine, 1994, p. 23). In a sense, they are writing something they do not know enough about to write. The nexus between the flow of concepts and the stories they are writing creates a looping effect that causes their plays to expand, often in unanticipated directions.

For example, a previously "completed" direct examination of a witness may be revisited and revised to include a concept that the writer has just learned. This in turn could lead to an infusion of objections, arguments, rulings, and subsequent cross-examination that would add dimension to the plot and deepen the student's understanding. If plot is the recognition of a problem, and the postponement of its solution, then the concepts become plot heuristics and sources of creative possibilities.

Brain-Compatible Characteristics

Brain-based learning theory uses the terms *upshift* and *downshift* to describe how anxiety affects thinking (Caine & Caine, 1994). Teachers want their students to be upshifted, to operate within the neocortex, where language and speech reside, and the prefrontal cortex, where creativity, intuition, and critical thinking take place. When students feel threatened or anxious, the limbic system, where emotions are centered, shifts cognitive focus into the brain stem (fight or flight). Here the mode of thought is defensive. The attendant behaviors observable here are all those off-task behaviors that torment teachers, running the gamut from disruptiveness to boredom and listlessness. Ironically, teachers can bring this torment on themselves by prescribing coercive behavioral modification (heavy doses of consequences), high in the active ingredients threat and anxiety. The classic line is:"If it's late I won't accept it." If, however, tasks are characterized by affect-positive qualities, the limbic system will upshift brain function into the neocortex, where access to the prefrontal cortex (and learning) is possible.

Good writing is good thinking, and it does not emanate from the brain stem or the limbic system. It comes from the cerebral cortex (MacLean, 1978). Students who see themselves as academic losers, who have developed elaborate brain stem–centered "I-don't-care" behaviors to protect themselves from the pain of failure, are given a chance to experience the realms of the brain where they can feel intellectually empowered and begin to build positive mental programs.

How do we optimize the chances that our students' writing will flow from this part of the brain? An important nontraditional quality of this whole process is the orientation it has to time. I have found that my own writing performance is adversely affected when temporal parameters become a conscious element in the cognitive-productive process. We all know that time runs out and that as it runs out it looms ever larger, occupying more and more of our available consciousness just when we need that capacity most. There is something a little perverse about a quality that increases the more it diminishes.

Writing practices should accommodate and account for unanticipated meanderings that do not follow the itinerary. Sometimes these unscheduled excursions lead to ideas or understanding we could not have found had we followed the guide. Ultimately the ideas or understanding may be discarded. But they may transform the task they had wandered away from or become the core of a new product altogether. Sometimes these tangents are prompted by intuitions that are instrumental in our innate search for meaning. Teachers need to encourage this kind of activity. Brain-compatible learning, according to Caine and Caine (1994, p. 92), "always involves conscious and unconscious processes."

Ideally, I wanted time to go away, and, so, when the inevitable question students have been sadly conditioned to ask—"When is this due?"—was asked, my somewhat ingenuous albeit thunderously well received reply was "Never." Although my answer was not true, and they knew it just could not be, it was an opportunity to frame the project within the neocortex and minimize interference from the limbic system (MacLean, 1978).

I announced that I would be intruding from time to time to congratulate them on their latest accomplishment: their latest objection on grounds of relevance, their latest impeachment of perjured testimony, their latest argument that an out-of-court statement is an exception to the hearsay rule.

"But, how long?" some persisted.

I told them that we would go to the writing lab maybe once a week, all semester, trying to minimize their time anxiety. In my planning of this project I had pictured a writing-to-learn activity developing into a finished product, but I did not want them to think of it in that way. I did not want them to think that everything rested on some final product. Instead, they would be given credit along the way.

THE PROJECT AND METACOGNITION

I was interested in how students revisited previously written parts of their plays and revised with the new concepts they would receive at intervals and with my collaborative input. I would have them print early drafts of the work in progress, against which we could compare subsequent revisions and together observe our progress.

The idea is to have the students put the antagonist in the fairy tale on trial. They create a play of the trial, incorporating legal concepts (terms and processes), the tools they need to learn how to use. Even though the students do not know the concepts going in, by being asked to use them, they have to wrestle with them and imagine situations in which they would be utilized. By doing so, understanding is enhanced through metacognition (Flavell, 1979) because the creative process requires strategic planning, problem solving, and self-evaluation.

If, for example, a student using the tale of "Goldilocks and the Three Bears" wants to find a way to include an objection on the grounds of relevance, she first has to deal with the concept's definition and the examples provided. Second, she has to imagine what might come up in the course of the trial that would be objected to on the basis of relevance. At this point, the student simultaneously visualizes the facts of the story, the motivations and needs of the characters, and the meaning of relevance and explores possible pieces of action (plot) in which this issue is played out. Following are the guidelines I provide for students:

The Project Guidelines

1. Choose a story you know very well.
2. Decide who is the defendant.

3. Decide on the charges.

4. Pick witnesses for both sides.

5. Begin the play with the judge calling for opening statements.

6. Create opening statements for both sides.

7. Create the prosecution's or plaintiff's case.

8. Create the defense case.

9. Incorporate at least thirty terms from the vocabulary.

10. Incorporate the rules of evidence through at least ten objections.

11. Create closing arguments for both sides.

STUDENT EXAMPLES

The following excerpts from students' work are examples of how this activity turned out. I gave students the following guidelines for writing **opening statements:**

1. Use opening statements as previews of the case intended to give the jury a road map to follow.

2. Tell a story using the following structure:

   a. Start with the theme. "This case is about . . . "

   b. Introduce the witnesses and say what evidence they will provide.

   c. Provide the theory of the case, each side's version of the facts.

   d. Do not argue. Say "We expect the evidence to show that . . . "

3. Say what you expect the jury to conclude.

Francisco Terrazas chose not to go with a ready-made story. Instead, he took a simple nursery rhyme and created an original story. The following opening statements for the prosecution and the defense follow the previously mentioned essential ingredients.

Prosecution Opening

Ladies, and gentlemen of the jury, this is a case of robbery. Plain, and simple. We're in this court, because on the night of November 30, 1997, the defendant, one Peter Piper trespassed on my client's farm. The farm into which he pours his heart and soul. Mr. Piper then proceeded to rob him of $5,000 worth of pickled peppers.

We expect the evidence in this case to show that on the night of November 30, which is in the middle of pickled pepper season, the defendant drove out to Mr. Pepper's farm just outside of Goosetown. He stopped the car and checked to see if anyone was around. After making sure that there would be no witnesses to i.d. him, he got out, and sent his dog to one end of the farm in order to distract Mr. Pepper, so the defendant could sneak out to the pickled pepper patch. While poor Mr. Pepper was out chasing the dog out by the cabbages, Mr. Piper, without consent of the Peppers went out into the pickled pepper patch on the other side of the farm, and placed an entire peck of pickled peppers into a brown potato sack and ran back to his car.

Once he reached his car, he whistled for his dog, and sped off down the dark highway. However, while he was in the garden, Mrs. Pepper saw him, and called the sheriff. The first patrol car got there just as Mr. Piper was speeding away; but the officer was still able to get a license plate number.

The next day, the police obtained a search warrant for Mr. Piper's house. Inside, they found a brown burlap bag, along with $5,000, which is what a peck of pickled peppers is worth. Inside the bag, they also found some leaves, which were determined to have come from a pickled pepper plant. Inside a desk drawer they found a pair of pruning shears. Mr. Piper was then arrested, and is now on trial for trespassing, and theft of pickled peppers.

In this trial, you will hear from several witnesses, who will give testimony which proves far beyond a reasonable doubt, that Mr. Piper is indeed the thief.

You will hear from Mr. Pepper, who will testify that on the night of November 30, he had just sat down for a nice dinner, after a long, hard day of work on the farm. When all of a sudden, he heard a dog barking out in his cabbage patches. He then got up, and ran out to bring the dog in, and call the owner. After about twenty minutes of running in circles, he was able to grab a hold of the dog's collar, however, the dog managed to slip out of the collar, and evade capture. While poor Mr. Pepper was left standing there with an empty dog collar. Mr. Pepper proceeded to run back to the house, to call the number on the dog tag. When he reached the porch, he saw someone running from his prized pickled pepper patch. He also noticed that the figure had some kind of bundle slung over his shoulder. He then ran inside to tell his wife what he saw.

You will also hear from Mr. Pepper's delightful wife, Mrs. Pepper. She will testify that she also saw the figure in the pepper patch. She saw the person stuff several pickled peppers into some kind of sack. She then saw the thief run out to a car, which appeared to be a 1996 Jallopiemobile. She heard the thief whistle, wait about half a minute, then jump in he car, and speed away. She also saw a small animal jump into the car. She would have stopped the thief, but you never know what type of weapons a pickled pepper thief might be carrying these days. She ran to the phone, and called the sheriff.

The next witness you will hear from will be Officer Rogers, who was the first officer on the scene. He arrived at Mr. Pepper's house just in time to see the prowler speeding away. He then began to give chase. He was close enough to get a license plate number, and make of the car. However, Mr. Piper was just too fast for the police car to catch.

You will also hear from Detective Dave Rogers, who was one of the detectives who searched the defendant's apartment. He will testify to what was found in Mr. Piper's apartment.

You will hear from Mrs. Smith who is a cashier at Cocoa Foods. She was working the register on November 29, when Mr. Piper purchased a bag of potatoes. The kind that come in a burlap sack. The same type of sack found in his apartment!

And so ladies, and gentlemen of the jury, it is because of these witnesses, their testimonies, and the other pieces of evidence that will be shown in this case that I ask you this. When it comes time to deliberate, you come back with the only verdict that is impartial, and just, a verdict of GUILTY.

Defense Opening

Ladies, and gentlemen, good morning. First of all, these allegations against my client are completely ludicrous. My client is a kind man who would never steal from anyone, and is in no way liable for the missing pickled peppers. And besides, why would he? He's got a steady job, and a steady flow of income. Here's what really happened on the night of November 30, 1998.

My client had just gotten home from a bad day at work, when his mother called him on the phone. For some reason or another, they got into an argument, and Mr. Piper's mother hung up on him. Well, after the argument, and the bad day at work, my client thought it would be a good idea to go for a drive.

He went outside, and jumped into his car. Mr. Piper's dog, Peppy likes going for rides, so he took the dog with him. Once Peppy got in, Mr. Piper drove off down the road. After about an hour of driving along the highway, Mr. Piper started to feel bad about arguing with his mom. About five minutes later, he passed Mr. Pepper's house. He decided that he would stop, and ask to use the phone to call his mom, and apologize, because he was feeling so guilty about the argument.

He stopped in front of the farmhouse, and as soon as he opened the door, the dog jumped out of the car, and ran off into the farm. Mr. Piper took off in the direction he thought the dog had run, which was into the pickled pepper patch. Mr. Piper spent several minutes looking for his dog, and then decided to go back to his car, hoping that Peppy had found his way back. He got back to his car, and whistled for Peppy, who came running, and jumped in the car.

He then saw Mrs. Pepper open the door, and he jumped into the car, and drove off, fearing that she might think he was a robber.

Ladies, and gentlemen of the jury, there is no crime in this case, simply a misunderstanding. There is no way that the prosecution can prove that my client stole pickled peppers, when the mere thought wasn't even in his mind. Trust me, the prosecution's evidence will in no way prove to you beyond a reasonable doubt that my client is anything but innocent. And so, when it comes time to deliberate, ask yourself. Is my client guilty of these ridiculous charges, or is he simply the victim of the Peppers' misunderstanding? And believe me ladies, and gentlemen, I'm sure that you'll come to this conclusion: Not guilty. Thank you.

The students were given the following guidelines for writing **closing arguments:**

1. Review the evidence that came out during the trial, showing how it proves your theory of the case.

2. Refute the other side's evidence if it hurts your case.

3. Tell the jury what verdict you are asking for.

The following closing arguments are by Francisco Terrazas.

Prosecution Closing Argument

Yes, thank you, Your Honor. Ladies, and gentlemen of the jury, throughout the course of this trial you have heard testimony, and seen evidence that proves two things: one, that Mr. Piper did indeed set foot on the Peppers' farm without any type of consent, and two that Mr. Piper did in fact steal an entire peck of pickled peppers, and sell it for $5,000.

You have heard testimony from both Mr. and Mrs. Pepper which proves that there was a sign warning people NOT to enter their property without permission, and Mr. Piper admitted that he could, and did see the sign. By admitting that he saw the sign, and still proceeded to set foot on their property, he is also admitting that he DID trespass.

Now, on the theft charge, you heard from Mr. Pepper, who said that indeed, after Mr. Piper had entered his pickled pepper patch, a peck of pickled pepper had been cut right off the plant! You also heard his wife, Mrs. Pepper say that she saw Mr. Piper with a sack slung over his shoulder. Mr. Pepper also saw the sack, and saw a bundle inside, which was the same size as a pickled pepper. Coincidence? I find that hard to believe. Mr. Piper said himself, that he did have a potato sack, the same kind that the Peppers saw slung over his shoulder. When police searched his apartment, they found the sack, and took it, so it could be analyzed. When it was, they found traces of a pickled pepper.

Now, Mr. Piper wants you to believe that they got there because he bought one at the store, and put it in the bag, for storage during the drive home. Ladies, and gentlemen, that's just a little unbelievable for me. After carefully reviewing the facts I have just gone over, I am sure that you will reach a verdict of guilty, on both counts.

Defense Closing Argument

Ladies and gentlemen, I am not even going to talk about the trespassing charge because my client has already admitted that he did trespass. He's not glad he did it. He's not proud he did it. Now as for the theft charge, well, that's a completely different story.

Mr. Piper in no way stole anything from the Peppers' farm, let alone a pickled pepper. He did have one in his possession, but he got it at the store. The bag the Peppers saw on Mr. Piper's shoulder never existed. The only reason my client was in the pepper patch was to look for his poor dog.

After you have deliberated on the facts at hand, I'm sure you will find that there is reason to doubt the evidence that suggests Mr. Piper committed this crime. I'm sure that you will find that there is no possible choice other than not guilty.

Ladies and gentlemen, thank you for your time and patience.

I gave students the following criteria for the rule regarding **opinions:**

1. Only experts recognized by the court may offer opinions, and then only if the opinion is with regard to the witness's expertise.

2. An exception is when the opinion is with regard to a common experience (e.g., "He was driving slowly").

Mary Zeller adapted the story "Sleeping Beauty." Here is how she incorporated different rules of evidence into her play:

Prosecution Prince, could you describe how the defendant treated you on the night of December 12?

Prince Yes. That night I was heading to the home of the Princess to tell her that I was in love with her, and wanted to marry her. I knocked on the door, and it swung open!

Prosecution What happened next?

Prince A dozen weird little creatures jumped on me. They were fast, and tied me up before I could even react! Then they took me to a small room. Miss Ficent was there, waiting for me.

Prosecution   What did she say to you?

Prince   She told me that I was her prisoner and would never escape. Then she told the creatures to take me away. Then she vanished, just like that.

Prosecution   Where did the creatures take you?

Prince   To a dungeon.

Prosecution   Did anyone talk to you while you were there?

Prince   Yes. Miss Ficent told me a story about how she set a curse on the Princess on the day of her birth, and that the Princess was the same peasant girl that I was in love with.

Prosecution   Sadly, yes. I think she's crazy, really. She needs to be locked up!

Defense   Objection, Your Honor! The Prince may be a prince, but he's not an expert in psychology.

Judge   Sustained. Mr. Prosecutor, ask another question.

The criterion for the rule regarding **relevance** of evidence is as follows:

> **1.** Questions must directly relate to the issues in the case. For example (in a medical malpractice case), "Have you ever been arrested for speeding?" is not relevant.

Prosecution   Did you leave?

Prince   Yes, I did. And I went straight to the palace. But some thorns got in my way, and I couldn't get to the door.

Prosecution   What did you do then?

Prince   I used my sword to cut down the thorns.

Prosecution   Then what?

Prince   All of a sudden I saw a gigantic dragon looming before me! It was the biggest dragon I had ever seen!

Defense   Objection, Your Honor! Dragons are irrelevant to this case.

Prosecution   As you will soon find out, Your Honor, dragons have plenty to do with this case.

Judge   Overruled. Mr. Prosecutor, you may continue.

Criteria for the rule regarding **argumentative questions** (also called "badgering") are as follows:

> **1.** Attorneys cannot pose an argument and then ask the witness to agree with it.
>
> **2.** Attorneys may not argue with witnesses.

Judge   Does the defense wish to question the witness?

Defense   Yes, Your Honor. Prince, you say that Miss Ficent was already in the house when you went in, correct?

Prince   Yes, that is correct.

Defense   How do you propose she got into the house?

Prince   I really can't answer that question, sir. I never saw her go in.

Defense   And you say she took you to a dungeon?

Prince   Correct.

Defense	And three fairies rescued you?
Prince	Correct.
Defense	Do you expect this court to believe a story like that?
Prosecution	Objection, Your Honor! Counsel is badgering the witness.
Judge	Sustained! Let's move on.

Following are the criteria for the rule regarding **leading questions:**

1. Leading questions include the desired answer.
2. Leading questions may not be asked in direct examination.
3. Leading questions may be (and usually should be) used in cross-examination.

Prosecution	Miss Fairy, you have identified yourself as one of Princess Aurora's godmothers, is that right?
Flora	Yes, sir. It is.
Prosecution	Why were you living with her in a secluded area of a forest?
Flora	Well, on the day of her birth, Miss Ficent set a curse on her, and told her that she would die before she reached the age of sixteen. This startled her parents, and they were willing to do anything to ensure her safety. So we volunteered to keep her with us in the forest, and we would pretend she was our niece.
Prosecution	Isn't it true that you never told her that she was really the princess so she wouldn't find out about the curse?
Defense	Objection, Your Honor. The counsel is leading the witness.
Flora	No, sir. We didn't want to scare her.
Judge	Sustained. Would the jury please disregard that statement. Mr. Prosecutor, you may continue.
Prosecution	So there's no way she could have known that Miss Ficent had set this curse on her, right?
Defense	Objection, Your Honor. The prosecutor is continuing to lead the witness!
Judge	Sustained. Mr. Prosecutor, please be more careful in your questioning of the witness.

Criteria for the rule on **hearsay** are as follows:

1. Hearsay is an out-of-court statement.
2. An exception is if the statement was made by the defendant.

Prosecution	Miss Fairy, could you describe what happened to you on the night of the Princess's birth?
Fauna	We were celebrating her birth. It was a rather exciting celebration. We were giving the young princess her blessings when Miss Ficent appeared. The Queen told me that she was trouble, and . . .
Defense	Objection, Your Honor! This is hearsay. It should not be allowed.
Prosecution	If I'm not mistaken, Your Honor, Queen Sarah is present in this courtroom. In fact she is one of the defense's own witnesses.
Judge	Overruled. Miss Fairy, you may continue to answer the question.

The criterion for the rule regarding **personal knowledge** is that witnesses may not testify regarding matters they have not directly seen, heard, or experienced.

Judge   Does the prosecution wish to cross-examine the witness?

Prosecution   Yes, Your Honor. Queen Sarah, you say the fairies took your daughter to live in the forest, is that right?

Sarah   That is correct.

Prosecution   Did they ever bring back any reports of unusual behavior?

Sarah   No, sir. I had no reason to think she wasn't acting like a princess should act.

Prosecution   So, there really wouldn't be any reason to assume that the Princess committed suicide, right?

Defense   Objection, Your Honor! Queen Sarah has no idea what the Princess was going through in the forest. She never even saw her. How could she know?

Judge   Sustained. Please ask another question, Mr. Prosecutor.

REFLECTION ON THE PROJECT: BRAIN COMPATIBILITY, METACOGNITION, AND LEARNING

The playwriting project is always brain compatible. While students are challenged to incorporate new concepts that by themselves could be intimidating, they are able to explore them within the safe, known context of the story they already know so well. This relationship between learner and task sets up a motivation to learn that is intrinsic, based on the brain's need to make meaning. The students want to learn (to succeed at understanding and incorporating the new trial concepts and terms) because they want the whole (the known story into which they are being incorporated) to continue to make sense (Caine & Caine, 1994). This desire to learn the new concepts inevitably sets up the primary thought process—metacognition, or thinking about thinking—with the brain's need to make meaning supplying the persistence.

By the end of the first semester, the students are preparing mock trials and applying the trial concepts they have learned (and are still learning) in writing their plays. As the fourth quarter approaches, students begin to select pieces of writing for inclusion in their freshman portfolios. Virtually every student chooses the play as one of her or his five samples. More than twenty weeks have passed since they began the project, and close to ten have gone by since they last looked at their products. In the interim they continued to develop their courtroom literacy. Looking anew at the plays with an eye to polishing them, they are able to see inadequacies that they very quickly amend. They discover that what had always been a writing-to-learn activity is also something else: a piece of writing that is complete enough to polish and publish in one or two periods in the writing lab.

EXTENSION ACTIVITIES

1. What do you do to make your content area relevant to your students? In other words, how do you provide some real-life experiences in your content area for your students?

2. What are some writing activities that you could use to provide real-life experiences for your students?

REFERENCES

Bloom, B. S. (Ed.). (1977). *A taxonomy of educational objectives. Handbook 1: Cognitive domain*. New York: Longman.

Brown, J. S. (1989). Situated cognition and the culture of learning. *Educational Researcher, 18*(1), 32–42.

Bruner, J. (1960). *The process of education*. Cambridge, MA: Harvard University Press.

Caine, R., & Caine, G. (1994). *Making connections: Teaching and the human brain*. New York: Addison-Wesley.

Flavell, J. (1979). Metacognition and cognitive monitoring: A new area of cognitive-developmental inquiry. *American Psychologist, 34*(10), pp. 906–911.

Gardner, H. (1983). *Frames of mind*. New York: Basic Books.

Lave, J., & Wenger, E. (1991). *Situated learning: Legitimate peripheral participation*. Cambridge, U.K.: Cambridge University Press.

MacLean, P. (1978). A mind of three minds: Educating the triune brain. In J. Chall & A. Mirsky (Eds.), *Education and the brain: The seventy-seventh yearbook of the National Society for the Study of Education, part II*. Chicago: University of Chicago Press.

Maslow, A. (1968). *Toward a psychology of being* (2nd ed.). New York: Van Nostrand Reinhold.

Moffett, J. (1968). *Teaching the universe of discourse*. Boston: Houghton-Mifflin.

Vygotsky, L. S. (1978). *Mind in society*. Cambridge, MA: Harvard University Press.

4

USING WRITING FOR POLITICAL AWARENESS

DAVID BACHMAN-WILLIAMS

TUCSON HIGH MAGNET SCHOOL

ABSTRACT

Politically alienated students are challenged to reexamine their views of government. Through writing assignments that help them discover their interactions with government, students open doors to positive critical thinking about politics. The author describes two assignments in detail and provides sample student writings.

THE CHALLENGE OF TEACHING GOVERNMENT IN AN URBAN HIGH SCHOOL

Every year they walk into my classroom. Among this year's group is Gexabel, whose boyfriend skipped a court date; Alejandra, who received a jury summons and did not go; and Cory, who was subpoenaed as a witness and only wanted to know how to avoid testifying. Many of my students have had only negative interactions with the government, much of that with the police and courts in one form or another. Others have helped their parents talk with welfare or Immigration and Naturalization Service officials. They distrust government as an unknown or as a source of pain and frustration. My classes are listed as sheltered and/or bilingual. Most of my students are Chicanos (Mexican Americans) or recent emigrants from Mexico. The rest are European American, with a few African American, Native American, and other recent emigrants from non-Spanish-speaking countries.

My challenge is to find ways of teaching them about government not only to let them know that there are some positive and useful interactions they can have with government but also to help them cope better in the less desirable encounters. Their personal writing is perhaps the most powerful tool available to me as a teacher in this task. Through writing exercises they learn to use the higher-level thinking skills that are necessary for satisfactory relationships with government entities. They can begin to see ways other than the gut-level primal reactions they are accustomed to prior to my class.

WRITING TO FOSTER POLITICAL AWARENESS

In workshops I have learned about several forms of writing that are useful. The standard essay questions are useful on tests. In class work other forms of writing are challenging but also interesting to the students. We have written letters to judges and prosecutors asking for explanations of judicial proceedings. We have drawn up political action plans and critiqued them. We have written letters to friends explaining a governmental process. Frequently I ask students for a paragraph giving an opinion on some controversial topic and explaining why they take that particular position. In all this writing I find that my students learn not only to express themselves better but also to see the benefits of constructive approaches to dealing with government.

TWO SUCCESSFUL ASSIGNMENTS

Two favorite assignments have evolved that help students become more knowledgeable and hopeful about government. The end result is that they gain confidence for future encounters. The first major assignment of the year is for students to write their own declaration of independence. As growing and changing individuals they begin to feel connections with the live and evolving organism that government is. The exercise brings out the parallels between individual and group struggles for freedom and equality. It naturally crosses cultural lines and even encourages positive comparisons. The other writing experience I favor is the concluding major assignment of the year, titled "My Life Is a Political Statement." This assignment is intended as a summary of what students have learned concerning their inescapable and interactive connection with the economic, political, and legal structures of society.

Both of these assignments require extensive scaffolding through prewriting activities. The first time I asked my classes to write a declaration of independence I had gone over what I expected in the finished product and had quickly given some pointers on the structure of the content. This approach yielded unsatisfactory and shallow results. I found that students needed to learn the difference between persuasive and declarative writing. Typical of many young people of this age, their natural tendency was to argue for independence rather than sensing and using the declarative form. They also needed to learn the necessity of stating the principles on which the declaration rests. These were new forms of expression for many of the students. Lastly, they needed to appreciate the logical connection among principles, complaints, and the concluding declaration and view of the future.

The "Declaration of Independence" assignment now begins with a guided analysis of the original document. The students read our historical treasure in silence. In small groups they start analyzing it. I give them exploratory questions such as the following: Who is the audience? What principles of government are illustrated? (This question asks for a connection to John Locke's idea of the government existing at the consent of the people to serve their needs, which we have just finished studying.) What complaints are there? What promises do you find in the concluding paragraph? The groups then determine the outline of the Declaration of Independence, specifying the beginning and end of each of the four sections. I ask if they find any opening for dialogue in the document or whether it is a definitive statement that leaves no room for negotiation. Without this analysis, which serves as a prewriting exercise, most of the students would not know enough to write a similar declaration.

After the often agonizing analysis students are ready to write their own declaration of independence. They first pick the situation they want to focus on. I ask them to think of the same questions that we have used to analyze the original Declaration of Independence. I suggest strongly that they begin with the complaints and principles and then write the introduction and conclusion. Writing their own declaration gives them practice and reinforcement of the critical analysis they have done in the first part of the assignment. Truthfully, it is also where the fun begins. Despite the frustrations concerning discernment of the structure, most students have enjoyed the idea of writing a declaration of independence.

As can be guessed, most choose to declare themselves independent from their parents or a brother or sister with whom they share a room. There have been some very creative themes, too. One student took on the persona of her mother's car and declared her independence from the "neglectful" owner and the desire to belong, predictably, to the daughter instead. Another claimed the role of her goldfish yearning to swim freely in a stream. A married student chose to declare the independence of the remote control from her husband's grasp. The science fiction enthusiasts wanted the Martian colonies to be independent from the dictatorial Earth. What is key in this assignment is that the students are making strong connections between events and situations in their own lives or the lives of other groups or nations and the life of our nation. Having grasped the similarities, their interest grows about how governments evolve and operate.

A Mexican American student with bilingual abilities wrote the declaration of a new ownership for her mother's car. Minnette is a fair student who is typical of many of my students in several ways. Her writing is a classic example of the casual style (note how she begins with "Hi!") documented by Dr. Maria Montaño-Harmon from California State University at Fullerton. Her critical thinking skills are underdeveloped for a senior and her spelling and grammar are representative of informal rather than academic language, according to Montaño-Harmon's categories. She blithely hops from first to third person and makes mistakes of agreement in number. But she enjoyed this writing assignment. What follows is the last draft she turned in to me.

> Hi! My name is Grouchy. I am declaring independens from my current owner. Decent respect for the laws of ownership force me to show my reasons.
>
> Grouchy should have more than one owner. The gods of Nissan created this car such that it should have more than one owner.
>
> My complaints towards my current owner is that I can get washed only once in a long time. I don't get my oil changed as often as I need to. I get unleaded gas instead of supreme. She doesn't vacum my rug except about once a month, & she doesn't check my poor old tires. She wears off my Goodyear shoes. Then when I start breaking so hard I start squeaking & all she does is ignore me. Instead she highers up the radio, & here I am falling apart anxiously whating for her to replace my broken shoes. So that my joints can feel strong again. As it is now I feel like I have authoritis. I also have to include that she drives me all around town each day and it gets me so very tired. I also get extream severe headaches, because I am always running into the sidewalk when she turns.
>
> There for I declare for now on & for ever more independence from my current owner Margarita Felix that she may not have the privilege to drive me. She will not even have the advantage to place a foot in my exceleration pettle not in (even) my brake. If she tries to open the door from the drivers side or any other door I will just slam it.
>
> There for I declare for always and for eternity Minnette Felix as my new owner. Minnette will give me the proper care that I need. she will make sure I get proper cleaning when I need it. Get my oil changed every 3 months. She will give me supreme gas instead of unleaded. she will check my Goodyear shoes and take proper care of them. She will have my brakes checked so they won't squeak so loud. She won't take me all around town each day. She shall make sure I get proper rest. I believe, and know that she will be a careful driver & have caution when she turns, so I wont have anymore of thos severe headaches.

Obviously, more revision is needed, along with editing, to improve the spelling, grammar, and punctuation. One would have hoped for a more logical connection between the principle and the rest of the piece. Yes, there is room for improvement, but for me the fact remains that Minnette enjoyed the task and had a very positive attitude toward the class for the rest of the year. In the process she did some very good analysis and engaged in critical thinking. And she learned to appreciate the Declaration of Independence as a living document.

Some students in the bilingual class have been in the United States for only a short time. They are learning English but are not yet able to do this type of assignment in English. I allow those students, all of whom speak Spanish, to do the assignment in their primary language. Krashen's (1998) research shows that literacy transfers from primary to secondary languages very well. The issue of writing in English is important; however, more important is the cognitive connections they are making. Lydia Arballo is an excellent example. She reads the English text we use and understands the English-only oral discussions in class. Her theme is independence from her parents. Her Spanish version is followed by my translation.

Cuando en el curso de la vida de un ser humano llega el momento en que uno tiene el derecho de independencia y de tomar sus propias decisiones, es bueno dar nuestras razones al aire libre para que el mundo entero se da cuento de que tan bien son nuestras razones de independizarnos.

Diós nos ha dado derechos que nadie nos puede quitar y que todos deben de respetar. Ese derecho es libertad de vivir nuestra vida como nos paresca mejor. Todos fuimos creados igual y por eso todos debemos de tratarnos con respeto. Pero cuando muchos son los abusos que los padres had dado a sus hijos, es nuestro derecho de pedir justicia y libertad de tomar nuestras propias decisiones sin que nuestros padres nos obliguen a hacer algo que no queremos.

Para comprobar esto, aqui estan algunos datos;

Mis padres me han prhibido que gaste el dinero que gano en mi trabajo.

Mis padres me han prohibido que salga con mis amigas.

No me permiten que compre la ropa que yo quiero.

No me permiten escuchar la música que yo quiero.

No me permiten que mis amigas vengan a visitarme.

No me permiten salir a otra parte que no sea la escuela.

No me permiten hablar por teléfono.

No me permiten manejar su carro, teniendo ya 16 años y mi licencia de manejar.

No me permiten mirar televisión.

Me obligan a hacer todas las cosas yo sola.

Me obligan a lavar toda la ropa sucia.

No me dan dinero para gastar en cosas que yo quiero. Ellos escojen lo que quieren a su gusto.

He tratado de hablar con mis padres pero no me escuchan. He tratado de pedirles que me dejen tomar mis propias decisiones, pero en lugar de escucharme y darme la razón, me castigan. Por lo cuanto mis padres han violado mis derechos de vivir mi vida como yo quiera.

Me declaro independiente de mis padres y un joven libre a tomar mis propias decisiones y hacer con mi vida lo que mejor me paresca. Con el apoyo de Diós y la ayuda del gobierno podré al fín ser una persona independiente.

Translation:

> When in the course of the life of a human being the moment comes when one has the right of independence and to make their own decisions, it is good to give our reasons openly so that the whole world can see the rightness of our reasons for declaring independence.
>
> God has given us rights that no one can take away from us and that everyone should respect. That right is liberty to live our lives as we see fit. We were all created equal, and therefore we should all treat each other with respect. But when the abuses are many that parents have inflicted on their children, it is our right to ask for justice and to take the liberty to make our own decisions without our parents obliging us to do what we don't want to do. To prove this, here are some facts:
>
> My parents have prohibited me from spending the money that I earn from my work.
>
> My parents have prohibited me from going out with my girlfriends.
>
> They do not allow me to buy the clothes I want.
>
> They do not allow me to listen to the music I want.
>
> They do not allow my girlfriends to come and visit me.
>
> They do not allow me to go anyplace that is not school.
>
> They do not allow me to talk on the telephone.
>
> They do not allow me to drive their car even though I'm already 16 years old and have my driver's license.
>
> They do not let me watch television.
>
> They force me to do everything by myself.
>
> They force me to wash all the dirty clothes.
>
> They do not give me money to spend on things I want; they choose things they like.
>
> I have tried to speak with my parents but they will not listen to me. I have tried asking them to let me make my own decisions, but instead of listening to me and acknowledging the rightness of my reasoning they punish me. Therefore, my parents have violated my right to live my life as I wish to.
>
> I declare myself independent from my parents and that I am a young person free to make my own decisions and free to do with my life what best appeals to me. With the support of God and the help of the government I can at last be an independent person.

Lydia's essay holds together logically. She has followed the format of the Declaration of Independence very well while making this her own declaration. Her claims may be exaggerated, but then so are some of the claims in the original document. Again, the importance is the connection that makes fundamental principles and documents of our government come alive for students.

The "My Life Is a Political Statement" assignment comes toward the end of the academic year. Again, extensive prewriting activities are necessary. This activity also is an opportunity to do some cross-curricular work with math. As a former math teacher I am comfortable with helping students work through the math required to compare two washing machines that use radically different quantities of water and energy, commuting by bicycle versus by car, and other lifestyle issues. All of these comparisons contain subjective as well as objective elements. I always gave my algebra students the assignment of writing an equation that compared the cost of commuting by bicycle with the cost of commuting by car. I do not make my government students work through the equation, but I show them the savings the algebra classes came up with as an introduction. I hold an open house at my home, which was built to conserve water, gas, and electricity. About 20 percent of the students visit and get to see how my family cuts natural resource use in half without sacrificing quality of life. My students also know that my two high-school-aged children and I commute to school by bicycle.

I share with the students the facts about low wages in other countries where many of the consumer products and brands they favor are produced. Invariably there is usually much information available about some organization trying to raise consciousness about a particular international corporation, so there is plenty of material on the subject. We have the geographic advantage that we can talk about the many assembly factories just across the Mexican border, one hour's drive away. I do everything I can to make students aware of how the simple choices they make in their everyday lives have economic and therefore political consequences. Students share their hopes and dreams for their personal future, and we discuss the accompanying political and economic ramifications.

I ask them to write simple paragraphs to explore just one of these connections. They can use the paragraphs as prewriting activities for a more formal essay. Further support is given by the use of leading questions to stimulate their thinking. Questions I ask usually include the following:

1. Do you work after school, and if so what do you spend the money you earn on?
2. What other choices for spending the money would be possible?
3. Planning to be an employed, productive person has what effect on society in comparison to living on welfare?
4. What volunteer work do you do and whom does it help?

Over and over again I ask them to multiply the results of one person or one family's choices by thousands and millions of people to get a sense of what the impact on society might be.

These activities take up to two weeks preceding the writing of the essay. After they write rough drafts, I ask students to review them to make sure that they have explicitly shown how an action or way of doing something has economic and political effects. I ask that the essay cover both current and future lifestyle choices. Two pages, at least, are necessary to cover the subject.

In the work turned in last year many statements indicated that students were seeing the connection between individual action and the world around them. Take this example from the essay by Araceli Tiscareño, a fluently bilingual Chicana:

> I knew that in some actions I was taking I was wrong, but never really stopped to
> think about it. For example, I used to take thirty-minute showers with a strong shower

head. A couple of weeks ago we got a new bathtub and remodeled our bathroom and without thinking about it we installed a less powerful shower head. Now I am taking faster showers to make the political statement that I do care about our water.

Others begin to realize that aspects of their lives are important in larger senses. Edmont Aguirre writes:

I was lucky enough to grow up the right way, raised by both of my parents. I believe one of the things wrong with today's kids is that they weren't brought up by both parents and/or weren't at least taught good morals. Two parent homes are political statements because they provide stronger financial and emotional stability.

Or take this selection by Nannette Pierson:

My main pair of shoes are Birkenstocks which are made in Germany by hard working Germans who make at least minimum wage, not in some sweatshop in Thailand where the workers put up with very little pay, abuse, and poor working conditions.

As for the future, many students already have strong ideas about what they want. Typical is this statement by Belinda Urbina:

One of the most important political statements that I plan to make in the future is the number of children I am going to have, and at what age. I definitely plan on being married, graduating from college, having my career in progress, living in a permanent home, and being financially secure.

Although I wish the students would write more explicitly about the political statement they plan to make with their actions and dreams for the future, it is clear to me that they understand that there is a connection. They see that how they live their lives now and in the future affects the economics and politics of the society they are part of. The classroom readings and discussions have helped the students begin to think about these subjects. However, it is in the personal writing that they individually make and develop the connection between their own lives and societal issues affecting economics and government. That is critical thinking. That is my goal.

EXTENSION ACTIVITIES

1. List five writing activities that you use in your classes to help students make connections between your subject area and real life. In other words, how do you make the learning in your subject area applicable to students' lives?

2. List five writing activities that you use in your classes to help students think critically about your subject area. Are there any relationships between this list and the list in the preceding question? Why or why not?

REFERENCE

Krashen, S. (1998). *Under attack: The case against bilingual education.* Culver City, CA: Language Education Associates.

5

LA VOZ LIBERADA: WRITING TO LEARN IN A SHELTERED ENGLISH CLASS

SALVADOR GABALDÓN
TUCSON UNIFIED SCHOOL DISTRICT

If we teach in isolation,
we cannot learn from each other.

ABSTRACT

No single teaching technique is the answer to the many challenges teachers face. Proposed in this chapter, however, is the notion that an effective way to develop students' literacy skills is to engage them in a structured program that combines multicultural literature and writing-to-learn strategies. Gabaldón describes several writing-to-learn strategies he has used in his sheltered English classroom.

Let me tell you a classroom story before I begin speaking about writing to learn. It is a story that may sound familiar to some of us—a story of one student's triumph. Teaching 150 to 200 students each year to read and write skillfully often seems like an overwhelmingly complex task, demanding more than a mere flesh-and-blood teacher can possibly accomplish. But stories about the many students—students such as Arcelia—who succeed not because of our flawed efforts but despite them help us maintain perspective and remind us that learning involves the spirit even more than the mind. In my twenty-five years of teaching high school English, first in Los Angeles and then in Tucson, Arizona, I have learned to believe in the power of stories.

Arcelia's Story

The young woman, about twenty-three years old, was poised and confident. As a college student who had lived nearly all her life in the community, she had been invited to speak that Saturday to a group of parents and teachers about a subject that had caused her a great deal of pain: her experience in the public schools. Although I had not seen her in several years, I recognized Arcelia immediately as the student who had struggled valiantly to earn a D in one of my junior English classes. A Chicana who now spoke English more fluently than her native Spanish, she represented the kind of student that American schools historically have not educated very well and the kind of student who will become a majority in many states during the next few decades (Banks, 1997; Bennett, 1995; Cummins, 1996).

Arcelia addressed the group with the respectful forcefulness that she had always used in class. She gave the following account of her experience in U.S. schools:

> I started school a little late for my age, but by the time I entered fifth grade, my scores on the Language Assessment Scale [a commercially available test used to determine levels of fluency in English and several other languages] indicated that I was speaking both Spanish and English fluently enough to be placed in a bilingual education program. According to my report cards, my teachers noted that I was intelligent, sociable, and hard working. They recognized early on, however, that I was having unusual trouble learning to read and write in either English or Spanish. A special education teacher determined that my trouble was due to a learning disability, but my parents refused to allow me to enter the special education program. Neither of my Spanish-speaking parents speaks English; both are illiterate. My older brother had once been placed, with disastrous results, in a special education class; understandably, my parents were determined to give me a chance in a regular classroom.

Arcelia struggled in middle school with reading and writing, even as she continued to develop her proficiency in oral English. Despite her disability, Arcelia was a survivor. She compensated for her illiteracy with highly developed verbal and social skills, a self-deprecating sense of humor, a polite manner, and excellent attendance. She even managed to make honor roll status in middle school. When she entered high school, of course, the facade began to fall apart. "My grades plummeted, and though it was becoming increasingly obvious that my difficulties stemmed from a reading problem, my high school English teachers were unprepared to teach me basic reading and the school offered no remedial reading classes."

More troubling to Arcelia, however, was the fact that her parents seemed to have given up on education and were putting pressure on her to leave school and help out with the family business, selling handmade tortillas on the city streets.

Arcelia seemed destined to become a dropout statistic—except that she needed to fill an elective class period and was assigned to work as a library aide. Through good fortune and the strength of her personality, she impressed the school librarian, who took a special interest in her. The librarian contacted special education again, but members of the department explained that "it was too late" and there was nothing they could do for Arcelia. The librarian then, at her personal expense, paid to have Arcelia tested and placed in a literacy program, the adult vocational training project run by the county. In just a few months, Arcelia's reading level improved by several years, and she graduated reading at an average adult level before going on to a community college.

What is the point of this story? It is a cautionary tale against pointless guilt. Of course, I wish I could say that I had been that librarian. Instead, I was one of those teachers who had recognized Arcelia's trouble but who did not know how to help her. Why had I not done more? It is the kind of question that haunts teachers all the time, even as we coach, tutor, sponsor, and take university classes after school. I knew that she was reading, at best, at a perhaps third-grade level. I do not know how any particular teaching strategy—other than the one-on-one tutoring and concentrated instruction she eventually received—could have helped Arcelia in her circumstances. High school English teachers are generally at a loss when a student is too far behind in reading level. Many of us teach classes with thirty-five students of varying abilities and high transience rates. Moreover, the majority of English teachers are not trained to teach reading; in my estimation, we are primarily trained to teach literary criticism and expository writing. And yet I discovered that I was not alone. The librarian was there. The county program was there. Most of all, Arcelia's amazingly resilient spirit was there. As long as a community of learners exists, our weaknesses as individuals do not necessarily doom our students. Our responsibility is to learn from our mistakes, to tell the public about such stories, to point out the flaws in the system, and to push for improvements—not to beat ourselves up about our imperfections as teachers. That way lies cynicism, depression, and burnout.

MULTICULTURAL LITERATURE AND WRITING TO LEARN

If teachers can agree on one thing about literacy, it is probably this: There is an inextricable link between reading and writing. The more students read, the more they will develop their writing skills. Before my students take a reading assessment (Tests of Achievement and Proficiency [TAP]), I can make a fairly accurate estimation of their reading ability by examining their initial writing assignment. For instance, here is one of Veronica's focused writings, describing her first day as a ninth grader at Pueblo Magnet High School:

> The fear twists my stomach into knots, but I continue walking down the seemingly endless hallway. I clutch my notebook in my sweaty palms, thinking to myself, I hate this place! The room numbers don't make any sense. I see an occasional familiar face, but I'm too afraid to ask for directions. Somehow everyone else seems to know exactly where to go. Comfortable and relaxed, they just seem to belong. Tears build up in my eyes. What should I do?

It was no surprise to me that Veronica scored at the eleventh-grade level on the TAP, which is administered to all ninth graders at the start of the year. Her decision to write in the present tense, thereby intensifying the emotional effect on the reader, indicated an advanced degree of sophistication. Nevertheless, I can no more take credit for Veronica's skill than I can take the blame for Arcelia's lack of skill. What teachers can take credit for is our own growth as lifelong students: expanding our knowledge of multicultural literature, attending in-service workshops and graduate courses, and learning to employ new techniques.

Clearly, no single teaching technique is the answer to the challenges that teachers face. But I saw that a growing number of my students found only a tenuous connection between their lives and the traditional reading and writing lessons they studied in school. In response, I searched anxiously for new ways of reaching the young men and women who entered my classroom each year. Eventually, I collected a number of strategies that I had not been taught in the school of education. Of course, the approaches I describe here serve some teachers better than others—personality is always a consideration—and they will not solve every student's learning difficulties, but they have worked capably with the majority of my students. At any rate, I can say this with some confidence: in my experience, the most effective way to develop the reading and writing skills of language minority students in high school is to provide them with a structured program that combines multicultural literature with writing-to-learn strategies.

Multicultural literature is a godsend to contemporary English teachers. Classic works such as *Beowulf, Romeo and Juliet,* and *Tale of Two Cities* should always have a place on high school bookshelves but never to the exclusion of new and vibrant voices. Contemporary literature such as Ernest Gaines' *A Lesson before Dying* (1994) and Victor Villaseñor's *Rain of Gold* (1984) can serve as a doorway to the classics, but most importantly it is literature that can stand on its own. It is critical for students to understand that writers live among them in today's world and that these writers seek to shape the world in some way through the use of language. I want my students to see that contemporary writers can provide insights not only about universal human concerns but also about specific, contemporary issues that our students face day to day, such as guns in the schools, the effects of immigration policy, and the accelerating rate of technological and societal change.

Throughout my teaching career I have given lots of thought to the question of developing more skillful writers. My classroom instruction has evolved into a personalized writing-to-learn style over many years, even before I had ever heard the term *writing to learn*. The theory behind writing to learn is that the very process of writing, when used as a tool for reflection, can help to develop our ability to think (Gere, 1985). Although certain techniques are associated with the process of writing to learn, the techniques do not define the process. Writing to learn is defined by its intent. Any technique that is intended to have students learn by writing—to have them write about how they learned, to have them reflect on their own understanding, to have them examine how their learning has affected their worldview—is writing to learn. I suspect that most of us can remember a time when we discovered how our beliefs change as we attempted to articulate them. In writing an essay about heroes, for example, Darius discovers that he does not see all of his older brothers in quite the same way:

> Finally, the last one of the men that I look up to is my brother Maurice. He's going through a difficult time right now. He doesn't have as much heart and wisdom as my brother Lonnie or as much strength as Ray, my other brother, but I think he can learn from his bad experiences. Maybe it's not so much that I look up to him. It's more like I have faith in him. Just like Peter asked Jesus many hard questions and became one of the wisest and strongest disciples, Maurice will learn from his hard experiences and become wiser and stronger in his own way.

In describing his brothers, Darius at first categorized them as a group—his brothers, equally loved and respected. However, by the fourth sentence, as he identifies the specific qualities they have, he discovers that he will not be able to talk about Maurice in the same way he did about Lonnie or Ray. He may love his brothers equally, but he recognizes that the first two are heroes to him because they have demonstrated qualities such as wisdom and inner strength. Maurice, on the other hand, is in the midst of a struggle—perhaps even a heroic struggle—to develop such qualities, but he has yet to demonstrate them successfully.

Writing to learn is a style of learning that is as far removed as possible from the "memorize and regurgitate" tradition (Gere, 1985; Zemelman & Daniels, 1988). Because reflective writing is part of a process that depends heavily on discussion and brainstorming, it is, in several ways, especially adapted for the type of cultural and linguistic diversity found throughout America. Specifically, it allows for two-way communication, for time to examine and reject ideas before they are committed to a formal paper, and for consideration of others' views in relation to our own. Best of all, it places the focus of instruction on higher-order thinking skills, such as comparing and contrasting, analyzing, extrapolating, and illustrating with metaphors.

A few general principles—most of which would appear basic and that I suspect are practiced by effective teachers throughout the country—serve to define the writing-to-learn classroom as I understand it:

1. The teacher creates an atmosphere of trust. Students write best when they write honestly and openly.

2. The teacher uses the knowledge base that students bring into the school—then builds on that base (Freire, 1989).

3. The teacher thematically connects the writing and the reading, focusing on contemporary multicultural literature.

4. The teacher inspires students to take responsibility for their own learning.

It may be useful at this point to offer a description of my own classroom and my teaching style, not as an ideal, of course, but as a case study that can lead to constructive discussion and a critical analysis of writing to learn. My ninth-grade English classes have been designated as "sheltered instruction" courses, meaning that the instruction includes a special emphasis on cooperative learning, media, and visual aids to communicate content. On occasion I even use a second language (Spanish) to communicate a literary concept. The classes are typically composed of about thirty students: perhaps sixteen Chicanos and Chicanas who are dominant in English, another eight or so Mexican immigrants who have completed advanced English-as-a-second-language (ESL) courses, and the remaining group composed of African American, Asian American, European American, and Native American students. The school's community is made up of working-class families, primarily employed in construction and service industries. On standardized tests of reading comprehension, our ninth graders typically enter high school with grade level scores ranging from fourth to eighth grade, as measured by the TAP.

THREE WRITING-TO-LEARN STRATEGIES

As I noted earlier, writing to learn is more a philosophical approach than a collection of techniques. However, educators have identified a group of approximately two dozen assorted teaching strategies that they label as writing-to-learn techniques, ranging from admit slips to unsent letters and from dialectics to role playing. No one teacher should expect to use them all. I have tended to concentrate on the following three: dictation, listing/focused writing, and metaphorical questions.

Reflective Dictation

The ancient writing activity of taking dictation takes on a new vitality when it is paired with reflection. Initially, I am the one to select short passages that use language in unexpected ways or contain striking images or present controversial ideas. But once we have completed a few examples, I delegate the task of selecting appropriate passages to individual students. While I first read the whole passage and then repeat sections as necessary, the students take dictation as accurately as possible. Afterward, students pair up and I write the passage on the board or show it on an overhead. We check each other's work and we discuss common errors, suggest alternative constructions that the author might have used, explore the meaning of the passage, or examine its diction. The students then write a reaction to the piece. Was it a good selection? Which words were new to them? Which sentence parts seemed awkward? Which seemed most effective? What details were enhanced by their imagination as they read? This activity allows for an intensive study of language aided by the multicultural nature of the material we investigate. Here, for example, is an excerpt from *Two Badges: The Lives of Mona Ruiz:*

> You have a questionable background, your family is questionable, your friends are questionable. If you want to do something with your life, you've got to stay away from them. No one will take you seriously until you distance yourself and create a life away from all that.
>
> (Reprinted with permission from Ruiz, M. [1997]. *Two badges: The lives of Mona Ruiz.* Houston, TX: Arte Público Press.)

The passage suggests some interesting questions regarding its construction (parallel structure and the intentional use of repetition), but it also refers to a struggle that my students know well. How much of our identity are we willing to give up to win acceptance from society? The brief comments that students might make during this activity can easily generate into a fully developed essay at a later time. This is how Patricia initially responded to the Ruiz passage:

> There is a saying in my family: de tal palo, tal astilla. From that kind of wood comes that kind of splinter. It means that people in some ways are like their parents, for good or for bad. The important thing, I believe, is to know which is the good and which is the bad. That way, you can practice the good and try to hold back the bad, no matter what other people may think about your family.

The aphorism that Patricia uses to introduce her paragraph serves a multitude of purposes. It is a chance to display her knowledge of a language other than English. It bespeaks of a certain degree of pride in her parents and her culture. Most of all, it indicates that she has made a connection in her mind between the written word and her life experience outside of school.

Listing/Focused Writing

Listing/focused writing is similar to the activity described in the preceding section, but instead of focusing on a dictated passage, students focus on writing about a single assigned topic after generating a list of related subtopics. I call these focused writings "sketches," and I challenge my students to write 250 to 500 words on the assigned topic. It is a way of developing fluency and confidence in their ability to respond to a variety of subjects. Students learn to rely on their experiences as a source of knowledge and are often surprised by how much they know about a given topic. One example of a subject I assign is sleep. Rudolfo Anaya's novel *Zia Summer* (1995) opens with a dream, and the idea of controlling one's dreams during sleep becomes a recurring theme. When I first ask students to write 500 words on sleep, they think I have lost my mind. How can I ask them to write about something that they cannot see or even remember doing? It is such a boring topic; there is nothing they will be able to say. But then we start listing—generating the list of possible subtopics:

- The time they go to bed
- The number of hours of sleep they need
- The longest they have slept
- The longest they have gone without sleep
- The rituals they follow before going to bed (saying prayers, getting clothes ready, brushing one's teeth, etc.)
- How soundly or lightly they sleep
- How they arrange to wake up on time
- The kind of mood they wake up in
- The conditions that allow them to sleep most comfortably (white noise, open window, night-light, teddy bear, pillows, etc.)
- The irritations that most trouble their sleep
- How much they dream and how often they have nightmares
- The habits of sleepwalking or talking in one's sleep

Suddenly, they discover a world of possibilities, and meeting the 500-word goal seems more reasonable. Just as important, they are eager to communicate the newly discovered details of their own sleep habits and thus are motivated to write.

Metaphorical Questions

Metaphorical questions as a writing-to-learn activity are featured in Gere's (1985) *Roots in the Sawdust.* I use metaphorical questions primarily as a tool for revision. Once students have written a complete essay, they are often reluctant to change anything beyond making "a neater copy." Another problem that students often face is shallow writing, writing that lacks details or intellectual depth. Metaphorical questions allow students to generate depth and see alternative ways of structuring parts of an essay that they thought had been completed (Elbow, 1998). For example, if students have written a couple of drafts of an essay on the subject of sleep, yet have not developed the second copies very much beyond the first, I might assign them the task of answering the following metaphorical questions (Elbow, 1998):

1. How would you define sleep, using your own words?
2. What words are synonyms for sleep?
3. What words are antonyms for sleep?

4. What word is more powerful than the word *sleep?* (For example, *jealousy* is strong but can be overcome by *wisdom.*)

5. If sleep had a color, what would the color be?

6. If sleep were a place, what would the place look like?

7. What plant or creature would be a good symbol for sleep?

8. What other word might *sleep* marry and what would be the offspring? (For example, if *wealth* married *wisdom,* they would have *prosperity.*)

9. What does sleep look, taste, feel, smell, or sound like?

10. What objects do you associate with sleep?

Once they have responded to the questions, they must choose some of the responses to add to or replace parts of the existing essay. The activity often leads to a flurry of revisions. This is how Joaquín originally composed one passage from his focused writing on sleep:

> After I crawl into bed, I just lie there for a few quiet moments before I drift into sleep. It's almost like getting ready to enter another world.

After Joaquín answered the metaphorical questions, he chose to revise that particular passage by inserting part of the responses he gave to questions five and six:

> After I crawl into bed, I just lie there for a few quiet moments before I drift off into a deep-blue sleep. It's almost like getting ready to enter another world, a world of shadows, like a moonlit forest full of unseen magic.

The paragraph is not much longer; Joaquín added only fifteen more words. Yet the quality of the writing has improved significantly. The images—a deep-blue sleep, a world of shadows, a moonlit forest—add a poetic dimension that the original passage lacked.

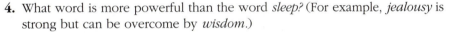

ARE GOOD WRITERS BORN THAT WAY?

Do any of these activities really help to develop better writers? Consider this comment: "I don't know how to make any of you into good writers. I'm not even sure that anyone can be taught to produce good writing. Frankly, I'm convinced that you either know how to write well or you don't. But, since this is a writing class, I suppose we have no choice but to take a stab at it."

With those words, an English professor welcomed me to my first college class in writing. It was a surprising start to what turned out to be an excellent class, and it took me a while to figure out why he would make such a statement. It was a "grab line," an attention-getting device based on hyperbole. And it worked. Though he continued by explaining that the "good writing" he was talking about was more accurately "great writing," the kind that is recognized in a gifted author, he had shocked us into focusing intently on his words. Then he concluded his point by observing that, whether or not we had a special talent for writing, he believed that all of us could become more skillful writers. I have come to the same conclusion about my students.

It would be wonderful for us to discover that one of our students had become a great writer—another Sandra Cisneros or Walter Mosley. Yet we are more likely to face classrooms that contain a number of students needing the kind of help Arcelia needed. And the number of great poets or novelists we produce is not a measure of our effectiveness as teachers of writing. Our immediate task is to help students become as skillful as possible and, just as importantly, to develop in them an appreciation for the pleasure and power of writing.

EXTENSION ACTIVITIES

1. The number of students developing proficiency in English is increasing in our classrooms. Do some research to find out how many such students are enrolled in your local district or your school. Discuss writing strategies that you could you use in your classroom to help your students develop proficiency in English.

2. Gabaldón discusses three writing-to-learn strategies that he uses in his classroom—reflective dictation, listing/focused writing, and metaphorical questions. Try these strategies with your own students and compare the results. Which strategies were most productive? What problems did you discover in implementing them?

3. Assign a short multicultural selection for your students to read; then have the students write a journal entry in response to the reading. Use the strategies described in this chapter to guide students in moving their writing from private to public discourse. Reflect on your process and your students' efforts and prepare a summary of the experience.

REFERENCES

Anaya, R. (1995). *Zia summer.* New York: Warner Books.

Banks, J. (1997). Preface. In J. Banks & C. Banks (Eds.), *Multicultural education: Issues and perspectives* (3rd ed.). Needham Heights, MA: Allyn & Bacon.

Bennett, C. (1995). *Comprehensive multicultural education: Theory and practice* (3rd ed.). Needham Heights, MA: Allyn & Bacon.

Cummins, J. (1996). *Negotiating identities: Education for empowerment in a diverse society.* Ontario, CA: California Association for Bilingual Education.

Elbow, P. (1998). *Writing with power* (2nd ed.). New York: Oxford University Press.

Freire, P. (1989). *Pedagogy of the oppressed.* New York: Continuum Publishing Company.

Gaines, E. (1994). *A lesson before dying.* New York: Vintage.

Gere, A. R. (1985). *Roots in the sawdust: Writing to learn in the disciplines.* Urbana, IL: National Council of Teachers of English.

Ruiz, M. (1997). *Two badges: The lives of Mona Ruiz.* Houston, TX: Arte Público Press.

Villaseñor, V. (1984). *Rain of gold.* New York: Avon Books.

Zemelman, S., & Daniels, H. (1988). *A community of writers: Teaching writing in the junior and senior high school.* Portsmouth, NH: Heinemann.

6

WRITING TO LEARN AS A WAY OF MAKING SENSE OF THE WORLD

MARYCARMEN E. CRUZ

CHOLLA HIGH MAGNET SCHOOL

ABSTRACT

Multicultural education is presented in this chapter as a way for all students to have an equal opportunity to learn. An essential feature of multicultural education is that it promotes learning about the world from multiple perspectives. Writing fosters the kind of reflection and exploration so critical to learning from different viewpoints. Therefore, included in this chapter are writing-to-learn activities that can be used to help students examine issues from diverse perspectives, and, in the process, expand their knowledge.

"Cada cabeza es un mundo" ("Every head is a world"), my grandmother would tell her children to remind them that people do not all think the same or act the same. As a teacher who enjoys working in a school with a culturally and linguistically diverse population of students, I recognize that we also do not all learn the same. The works of Luria, Gardner, and others speak to the ways that we perceive and process information—in essence, the way that we learn. Each of us sees the world from a different frame of reference, depending on our experiences, values, and assumptions about the world. Viewing situations from different perspectives not only helps us to understand our own world but also can inform us about improving our community. If our goal in education is to produce literate, thoughtful citizens who will participate actively and responsibly in society, then we want to teach our students to examine their worlds and identify their roles in creating positive changes within the community.

Transforming society is the result of a productive education, one that helps students to examine social issues critically—issues such as prejudice, racism, and discrimination. When students carefully study the conditions of society, they can then learn to take action on those problems (Banks, 1996; Berman, 1990; Sleeter, 1996). Multicultural education is one movement that proposes this kind of transformative thinking in the curriculum in order to reduce prejudice in our society and create a more just democracy (Banks, 1996, Banks & Banks, 1997, Hillis, 1996). This transformation occurs one step at a time, beginning with gaining knowledge from diverse perspectives.

CHANGING DEMOGRAPHICS AND WORLDVIEWS

We know that by 2020, approximately 40 percent of the U.S. population will be from culturally, racially, and linguistically diverse homes (U.S. Bureau of the Census, 1996). Many schools already exceed that percentage, but that does not mean that we are offering a multicultural education to students. An education is multicultural not because students are from diverse backgrounds but because its approach to the students and their learning encompasses learning about the world from diverse perspectives. A multicultural education teaches students to expand their thinking and become aware of the knowledge they need to create a truly democratic community. It provides students with "opportunities to investigate and determine how cultural assumptions, frames of references, perspectives, and the biases within a discipline influence the ways that knowledge is constructed" (Banks, 1996, p. 21). Banks goes on to say that we should also provide students with opportunities to not only construct knowledge themselves but also to show how this knowledge is influenced by their own limited assumptions, positions, and experiences.

A multicultural education provides an equal opportunity for learning for all students. Providing equitable access, then, means knowing our students, all of our students, whatever their backgrounds, whether they sit individually in our own classrooms or attend our schools collectively across the country. It means being aware of whose worldviews are being presented and learned. Sleeter (1996) reminds us that traditionally the voice and knowledge of students of color, students from low-income housing, language minority students, and females who have learned not to assert themselves are most often disregarded in classrooms. Therefore it is crucial that we provide in our classrooms empowering education that is constructivist in nature, education that "evolves as one digs deeper and deeper into issues of social justice and cultural diversity, and as one pays closer and closer attention to the thinking of children" (p. 197). Multiculturalism provides the opportunity for students and teachers to learn from each other and to incorporate each other's viewpoints as they interact. A goal of multicultural education is to strengthen students' ways of learning—to understand various ways of perceiving the world and even adopt new, restorative ways of thinking in order to take action toward a more democratic, harmonious society.

Expanding Comprehension: Writing and Thinking to Sharpen Learning

When I talk with colleagues about ways of learning from different viewpoints, I mention learning experiences that help students not only to reflect on what they know but also to explore new avenues of thinking. Writing to learn promotes this kind of reflection and exploration. It is a way to help students sort through and express their ideas. The writing becomes a means for thinking and understanding; it becomes part of the learning process rather than, as often used, only a vehicle for demonstrating knowledge collected. Through writing-to-learn activities, students make inquiries and wonder aloud about what they are learning. They analyze ideas, verify assumptions, and make connections to new information. This kind of processing leads to comprehension of concepts and material. More than that, it fosters critical thinking and reflective learning (Caine & Caine, 1994; Emig, 1983; Luria, 1979). Students ponder what if and what could be, but they do not ponder in isolation. What the students write must be shared, for it is through the discussing, sharing, and rethinking that learning occurs.

Learning is social (Applebee, 1996; Goodman, Smith, Meredith, & Goodman, 1987; Vygotsky, 1978). To make sense of the world, we must test our assumptions and check our knowledge with others. We negotiate meaning as we interact with others and our environment. Writing to learn helps students to look at an issue from different lenses in order to create a vision for themselves and the world. Perhaps that is the most powerful reason I use writing-to-learn activities. They provide experiences in which all students have an equal opportunity to learn.

Writing to Learn: Fostering Multicultural Thinking and Increasing Cognition

In my high school, diversity is strong. Approximately 76 percent of our students come from culturally and linguistically diverse backgrounds—57 percent of our students identify themselves as Latino, 23 percent white, 10 percent African American,

9 percent Native American, and less than 1 percent Asian or Pacific Islander. We have students whose families have been in the United States for three, four, or five generations and whose family values and traditions are blended from their ethnic heritage and the dominant society. We also have students classified as developing proficiency in English, or limited English proficient, because they come from homes where two languages are spoken and because the students' literacy test scores are low. In addition, our school has students who are recent arrivals to this country, English-as-a-second-language (ESL) students who are learning survival English language skills. And although we have students whose families cover all income levels, as well as students living on their own, 60 percent of our students are eligible for free or reduced-price lunches. My high school, and consequently my classroom, is a reflection of the growing changes in demographics in our nation. The classes I teach are as varied: a ninth-grade English course whose roster shows a random sampling of the school population; an English-as-a-second-language class, made up only of students in grades nine through twelve who are recent arrivals to this country and learning to speak, read, and write in English; and a Latino literature class, a combination sophomore through senior English credit course whose focus is on literature by and about Latinos in the United States. With such diversity, I, like so many others, want to find ways to tap equally into the knowledge of my students and help them make connections to new learning.

The writing-to-learn activities I describe in this chapter aim to get to the thinking, beliefs, and assumptions of the learners. I offer samples of particular activities to suggest how writing can open the door to learning for students. What I recognize is that any activity in isolation loses its point. Writing-to-learn activities must be part of a whole way of teaching and learning to promote awareness and critical thinking. Once students write and share their reflections, they can use their writings to look at issues from diverse perspectives and expand their knowledge.

Think-Pair-Share

One of my favorite writing-to-learn activities is **think-pair-share.** This activity, which also fosters cooperative learning, is quick and can be used to introduce a lesson, check for comprehension, or review material. In think-pair-share, students individually respond in writing to a question or prompt, then pair up with another student to read or discuss their responses; finally, the whole class regroups to share knowledge or insight from the question or prompt. A useful tool, think-pair-share not only taps the previous learning of students but also serves as a barometer for the teacher. It indicates the collective knowledge of the class on the topic and can point to areas that may need clarification or reteaching. In an introductory discussion of human rights in my ninth-grade English class, we mentioned people who stood up for what they believed—from contemporary and historical figures such as Martin Luther King Jr., Mother Teresa, and Martin Luther to everyday citizens such as the participants of the Million Man March. In one think-pair-share, I asked the students in my ninth-grade English class to reflect on what they knew about any of the people we had mentioned or why working for human rights was important. One of my students, Blanca, wrote the following:

> I really don't know who Martin Luther was. I heard things about him right now, but I don't have a sure explanation in my head. I'm pretty sure he had something to do with Martin Luther King Jr. He was probably someone important to everything that went on during the time people were fighting.
>
> I think MLK Jr. was very important. Maybe if he hadn't done what he did, there would still be all that racism. I mean there is still some today, but it has improved since those days. I really think what they used to do was very dumb and unfair to everyone. And in someway, it was even unfair to white people. They really never got to know everyone the way they really were and so they just learned to judge by what others would say. Also they missed out on all the culture and all the things they could accomplish with them.
>
> To me MLK Jr. didn't only help black people, he also helped many other races. He helped the community be what it is today. All people have a chance to do something they really want without having to worry about getting in some kind of trouble. You were talking about some kind of March. I didn't know about it.

After the class sharing, we clarified information such as the identities of Martin Luther and of Martin Luther King. We also categorized the information to look at myths and facts. This activity became the springboard for later discussions and investigations on topics of heroes, discrimination in society, and community involvement. Because think-pair-share prompts the student to make connections between prior and new knowledge, it is an effective learning strategy in most content areas. Moreover, it is a successful tool in moving students to work cooperatively and to collaborate on ideas. Gregarious students take advantage of this opportunity to dialogue, and quiet students are usually open to sharing in the personal setting of the pairs. Think-pair-share is also beneficial to second-language learners, who need time not just to process information but also to adjust to hearing that information in a new language. Once they have formulated their thoughts, they need to test out their ideas and express them to others in the second language. Think-pair-share gives second-language learners time to think and the opportunity to negotiate meaning so that they can develop language skills while building knowledge. In reality, this process of reflecting, expressing, and elaborating is a means of building schema or a framework of knowledge.

Response/Remembrance

Another activity that helps students sort through new information is one I call **response/remembrance.** Like think-pair-share, response/remembrance can be used during or after teaching a lesson. In this activity, students respond to questions that are meant to draw out the strengths of different kinds of learners. Some students learn by finding out facts and asking "How does this work?" Others need to analyze key points and question "Why is this?" Still others need to look at possibilities or solutions and wonder "How many different ways can I view this?" Finally, some students learn by intuition and relating to their feelings and must ponder "How can I interpret this?" After a lecture, video, or some other type of presentation, I ask students to respond to the material by answering any of the following questions:

What do you remember?
What did you learn?
What surprised you?
What intrigued you?
What do you wonder about?
What impressed you?

Providing options allows students to choose the question or questions they feel comfortable exploring. Answering the questions causes students to elaborate on the material and helps them to move ideas into long-term memory. It also provides an opportunity for students to express insight. After viewing a short slide show about ancient indigenous civilizations in Mexico, students in my combination tenth-, eleventh-, and twelfth-grade Latino literature class responded in writing to these questions. Here are responses from Alejandrina and Michele, respectively:

Some things I remember were all the temple's the tribes built for their gods and pyramids they made. They also made statues for the gods, there were gifts. What surprised me was that the temples, pyramids or statues were very old, big and in somewhat good shape. It surprised me because this is the first time I seen pictures of this before. Something I learned would be all the stuff I said and how the people gave up there lives or others lives for their gods. Something that stayed in my mind would be how they did things for their gods. What I wonder, is what would happen if they did not want to give there life up for a god?

What surprised me was the birth of the children how the mother would squat down if she was working in the fields. Things have really changed and I'm not too sure some has been for the best. I wonder if there is more than this. If we are missing a big part of our ancestors' past, and if there is, will we find it? I learned that it was harder then and that even though there wasn't a lot of technology they managed to build things we would never be able to (by hand).

I ask students to share what they have written with the class. Sometimes they read the entire piece; other times they read only a sentence. Sometimes they offer only a key word or phrase. Whatever the students offer, the class respects the sharing and discusses the concepts. Whether students respond to all the questions, a few, or only one, the point is to help students make connections from their own experiences and to reflect on the content. It is the reflection first and the elaboration next that helps the writing from questions turn the path to learning. Some of their wonderings will be the basis for future research, and their response/remembrances become the touchstone for other connections to learning.

Collaborative Note Taking

A variation of response/remembrance is **collaborative note taking.** We first preview an article by discussing the topic. Then we agree to read only one section of the article at a time. As we read the section, we discuss its main ideas and examples. Next, I give the students five- by seven-inch index cards and ask them to write the points or issues they remember from the reading. Some students refer back to the passage; others do not. After only a couple of minutes of writing, we share aloud our notes, discussing the ideas and copying the new "remembrances" of each student onto our cards. We continue this process until we have finished the article. By the end of the piece, we have literally collected our thoughts.

After reading one section of a *Time* magazine article about lengthening the school year, my advanced-level ESL students contributed these notes:

180 Days Are Not Enough

- People think that more days means better skills.
- Two elementary schools in New Orleans go to school for 220 days.
- Kids admit that if they weren't in school, they wouldn't be doing anything.
- Teachers say that their students don't read the way they are supposed to.
- One obstacle to the change is money. It costs $121 million to change K–12.
- Parents think their children are learning and are safe.
- Teachers like the $.
- But some people say more isn't better if what you have isn't doing the job in the first place.

After we had completed the reading and note taking, the students had enough fodder to move on to an expository writing or speaking assignment. In my students' case, they had the choice of writing a persuasive essay or giving a persuasive speech about the number of days they suggested school should be in session. Their suggested audience was the school board, the parent-teacher organization, the principal, or another interested adult.

Through the process of reading, discussing, note taking, and discussing again, the students comprehended the material more richly than if they had stumbled through the article in its entirety. This process, called chunking—a strategy from second-language theory (Cummins, 1996; Krashen, 1996) and from brain-based research (Caine & Caine, 1994)—breaks the article or piece to be studied into manageable parts for the learner. Having students write after they have discussed a topic helps to reinforce ideas for the learner. To ensure that concepts move from mere discussion to the learner's memory (or learning), students need to apply the information. Response/remembrance and collaborative note taking call for clarification and elaboration, which we know from brain-based research are processes that help information move from short-term to long-term memory. We know that what is stored in short-term memory is not permanent. To be stored in long-term memory, information must be hooked to existing networks of previously acquired information. That hooking occurs when learners clarify for themselves or when they explain or expand information. Moreover, the sharing of their remembrances helps students expand their web of knowledge.

Narrative as Writing to Learn

Narrative is another effective tool that I have used as a writing-to-learn activity to hook into new material. By tapping students' previous experiences, the narrative draws learners toward the concept to be studied. It also serves as an application of the material. Narratives do not always have to be retellings of direct personal experience. They can also be written role plays; for example, students can assume the persona of a major figure in history or a character in a novel and tell her or his version of an incident, or they could relate a day in the life of a common element—a cold virus or an amoeba, for example. As introductions to a lesson, narratives help to focus learners' attention and experiences. They become the bridge from the personal to the abstract. As conclusions to a lesson, narratives help learners move beyond the immediate. They help students to find meaning in the concept and to make connections out to the world. As part of a unit on family stories, my advanced ESL class read excerpts from Victor Villaseñor's *Rain of Gold*. I asked students to reminisce with their families about events and incidences in their family history that needed to be retold—stories that should live on from generation to generation. Following is the work of Isaias, one of my ESL students who had been in this country for only two and a half years when he wrote this story:

> Let me start by saying that my grandmother told me this particular story that took place at Sonora Mexico in the village by the name of San Nicolas. There's this one very interesting story that involved my grandmas grandparents. We were known to have powerful psychic powers. My ancestors were known to also save lives. It was a dark black night when this one pregnant young lady was trapped in this very deep hole, she had accidentally slipped in, on her way from work, my grandmother had said that the road was very dangerous for woman and especially children's to even think about crossing though at night. Anyway my ancestors lived in the middle of that danger zone village. My ancestor by the name of Guadalupe felt this fear and something told her to check-out the village, she immediately screamed out her husband's name which was José and urge him to please give a quick look outside. So José indeed rushed to get he's knife and lantern and he kissed Guadalupe and started walking. When he got tired of searching and proceeded home he heard a soft voice mumbling, "Help! Help! Please somebody help me!" José was near home, he told the pregnant young lady to calm down that he will be right back. José didn't know much about delivering a baby so he went to call his wife which delivered baby's for all the little villages near by. When everything turned out to be good, the young lady did indeed have a beautiful healthy baby boy that was named after both of them "José Guadalupe" of course the girl was

grateful forever. And that's the end of this story that my grandmother told me, there's others but are a lot more complicated to tell.

After we shared our stories with each other, we discussed their significance. What qualities or values did we appreciate, what made this story timeless, what similarities did we see among the stories, and why did we like the story? The sharing of narratives enriched our understanding of the content and of each other and broadened our world perspective as well.

Summary

Summary is another writing-to-learn strategy that aids student comprehension. Summarizing is a kind of review; it calls for students to put in their own words what they have just read or understood. It is more than just recall; it requires that learners make sense of the facts or details before writing them down. To encourage students to think carefully about their summaries, I often like to suggest audiences for their writing to learn: another student who is interested but unfamiliar with this piece, a principal who is checking on our process, and so on. Having an audience in mind helps learners sort through the information as they summarize the material. When I am reading the students' summaries, one strategy I like to use is marking with a colored highlighter the words or phrases that state key concepts from the text. This is an effective visual cue of the concepts the learners are acquiring. Here is a summary written by a student developing proficiency in English in my ninth-grade English class. Although her literacy skills are weak, her summary indicates her understanding of the chapter from *The House on Mango Street*.

The First Job

This chapter is about Esperanza first job. One day Esperanza needed money because the Catholic high school cost a lot of money. And her papa say that the public school it's bad influence. So she thought to find an easy job like working in stores or in a hot-dog stand. When she went to her house that afternoon, her mom called her to the kitchen and her aunt Lala was sitting there drinking coffee. Her aunt Lala told her that she found a job for her at the Peter Pan Photo Finisher on North Broadway where she worked and her aunt Lala told her how she was and to show up tomorrow saying that she was one year older. So the next morning she put on her navy blue dress that makes her look older and she borrowed money for lunch and for the bus because there were paid her next Friday. So she started to work; and later on when lunch time came, she was scared to eat alone because everybody was looking at her, so she ate fast, and she had time left over so she went back to work early and then break time came and she know where to go. So she a coatroom, and she meat an older Oriental Man. They talked for a while about her just starting, and a while more the man say to her that they could be friends and while more he asked her do you know what day it is and then Esperanza say no, he told her is my birthday and he asked her for a kiss and she kissed him on the cheek. And he grabs her face with both hands and kiss her on the lips and doesn't let her go.

Summaries have been helpful learning assignments for my students of all ages. They demonstrate at a quick glance what students have gleaned, and they suggest what still needs to be reviewed.

Letters, Letters, Letters

One of the best ways to incorporate writing that helps the learner make connections and that helps the teacher check for comprehension is **letters,** sent and unsent. Letters that are drafted to a real audience have much impact on the students. For example, after reading excerpts from Victor Villaseñor's *Rain of Gold* and then hearing the author speak at our school, my advanced ESL class talked about his words. Eventually, the discussion settled on what the students believed was Villaseñor's message. After our discussion, students drafted letters to the author thanking him for his presentation and highlighting what they considered the salient points of his talk. Although the letters were brief, the insights of the students were mature. Weeks later my students still referred to the points they had connected.

A variation of the letter assignment is to have students write a letter to a friend or relative explaining a particular issue or topic we have studied. This assignment allows for clarification, elaboration, questioning, and predicting. After writing their letters, the students read them once to a partner or two to get feedback. Then I ask the partners to read the letter again, this time looking for information that might be introduced or explained in more detail. With these kinds of responses to their initial writing, the students then change the genre of their piece to a draft of an analysis paper or a research report, for example. They use the information or premise in the letter to offer the same information to a more academic audience. This activity prepares students to make the transition from informal to formal writings. For example, in my ninth-grade English class, my students were reading *The House on Mango Street*. I asked the students to write a letter to a friend or a relative who might be interested in what is happening in the book but did not have much information on it. Here is a sample from one student:

Dear Michelle,

Hi! How are you doing. You wouldn't believe it at school there's a new person. His name is Darius. When I first saw him I thought he was cute. When I meet him he was a jerk. He doesn't like school at all and he's really stupid. He's always daydreaming. He's like in the clouds or something. He acts so immature. He still chases girls. Yesterday he had made an intelligent comment. He was looking up at the clouds and he pointed to a fat one and said that was God. I believed him.

There's also another new person. Her name is Marin. She thinks that she's all that and a bag of Doritos. She claims to have a boyfriend in Puerto Rico. Nobody believes her. She has nice eyes. There green. She always wears dark nylons and lots and lots of makeup. She also sells Avon. She thinks that she's gonna get married. Well that's all of the new news. Write back soon. Bye

Love you Cousin,
Bridgett

What the students focused on in their letters became the touchstone for their expository writing. They highlighted the main ideas raised in their letters and used them to organize a preliminary outline for their formal writing. I also gave the students a prompt to help them move their letters into formal writing. I asked them to consider these questions: What is the character you are focusing on like on the outside? (What are her or his qualities as they appear to others?) What is the character like on the inside? (What are qualities that the character may not reveal to others but that we as readers can see?) What are the fears or anxieties of the character? What are her or his hopes and dreams? If the character had a motto, what would it be? Here is Bridgett's genre change:

Darius

My character analysis is about Darius. He's a character that's in the *House on Mango Street*. He has a chapter about him. I did my coat of arms on him and I also wrote him in my letter to a relative. The motto I thought fitted Darius was Don't Worry Be Stupid. I found the motto on a poster. It seemed to fit him. I'm not calling Darius stupid. It's that he acts ignorant and doesn't really worry about it. He also doesn't worry about anything. He doesn't have a goal in education. Soon he's gonna realize how much education is worth to him. He's gonna wish someday that he listened in school.

Darius in the inside I think is a happy person. I think that he has fun in his own way. People may think that the fun he has is immature but it's fun to him. His fun is to chase girls with firecrackers or a stick that touched a rat. People think that the inside of Darius is ignorant and that he doesn't have any common sense, but in the inside he's a great person.

In the outside of Darius is a shy person and in the darkness of everybody. The outside looks like a fool and an immature person. He doesn't like school and does not care for it, but deep, deep, deep, deep, deep, deep, down inside he's really a neat and intelligent person. He's one day gonna like school. In the book Darius makes an intelligent comment about the clouds in the sky. Esperanza and some other people were trying to figure out what the clouds were. Darius comes to them and points to a fat, fluffy cloud and he said that cloud is God. He can be intelligent when he wants to.

Darius fears to be intelligent. He really doesn't like school at all. Darius is out in space somewhere. I think he fears many things besides being intelligent. He fears it because he's afraid he's gonna change. He's not gonna change no matter what he does.

Darius has many dreams. One of them is to be famous. You don't need to be smart to be famous. I think that he wants to get out of the darkness of everybody and in the light in front of everybody. He doesn't want to be known as the little immature boy in school but as famous person who accomplished many things. He wants to do a lot in his life. Lastly, I think that this character Darius was living in the nineties he would make a great friend and a human being.

I chose Darius because he seemed very interesting. When I read the chapter about Darius I really liked him. He seemed like an interesting person to write about. Even though there's was only one chapter about him it provided myself the writer a lot of information about him.

Instead of having students moan "I don't know where to begin" or "I don't have anything to say," I found the students ready to try the change. They recognized that their letters were only a first step in the process of drafting a formal character analysis, but in writing the letters they realized that they had acquired knowledge. However, they were not merely finding out what they had learned; they were seeing what they still needed to know. They saw exactly where they had to do more research to fill in the "holes." That is writing to learn.

Another variation of this letter writing is to change the identity of the writer—that is, role play. Rather than write as themselves, students assume different personas, say, that of a homeless mother of two, a young banking executive, a mayor, an engineer, and so on. The letter can be written then to an audience such as a school board, readers of the local newspaper, credit agency, and the like. This kind of writing helps learners to look at the material from a different perspective and make new connections with the information.

One of my favorite kinds of letters, though, is the letter of reflection that students write to the readers of their portfolios. Unlike for the other letters described in this chapter, for this assignment I usually offer a detailed sheet (Figure 6.1) to prompt students;, the evaluation is always students' personal reflection, though. The insights students provide are powerful tributes to their learning. At the end of his first semester in high school, one of my ninth-grade students wrote the following letter of reflection:

Dear Reader,

In this portfolio I have included several examples of my writings from this semester. These writings will show how I have progressed throughout this term. I have tried many different styles or types of writing. I have written a review of a movie, an analysis of a character in a book, a reflection of a speaker, a personal narrative, and a proposal. I have learned to self-edit my papers and use peer critiques as a way to enhance my writing. The content of my writing is deeper and more thoughtful than before. My spelling and grammar are still not as good as they should be, but I am picking up on it more. The most important things I have been able to do are to write with more feeling and thought in my papers. As a reader I am learning to look more carefully at the ideas in the books. As a student I am becoming more organized.

My personal narrative, "Water Balloon Friday," is one of my best pieces. I found it easy to write because I like to write about enjoyable past experiences. One of the changes I had to make was to narrow it down to one specific Friday. By being able to rewrite a memory so well, it gave me a lot of confidence in further writing.

I did not enjoy writing the character analysis on Esperanza in *The House on Mango Street* as much as because the writer jumped around a lot and never really focused on one point. It took a lot of thought and patience to get through the book and the paper. No matter how many times I wrote and revised this piece, I still didn't get it right because I never really understood the book. Making the coat-of-arms was difficult but enjoyable. What I mean by this is it was difficult to find pictures that describe the character's personality, but it was enjoyable searching for them and putting together the final product.

Writing reflections usually comes easy to me, especially when I am writing about something I feel strongly about. In my piece called "Mr. Kenny," I found it easy to write about him even though I didn't like listening to him. By reading this reflection it may seem that I'm just insulting him, but it was really hard to write positive things about such a negative man.

My proposal, "Youth Empowerment," was written with others. Because we were writing to meet a deadline, we did not write as carefully as we should have. The project did not turn out as well as we had hoped. Even though we knew our project wasn't put together all that well we were really hoping that it would get funded. If we had had more time to edit and make a second copy of what we had done, our writing would have been stronger and there would have been fewer mistakes in the grammar and spelling. I cleaned up some of the mistakes for the portfolio copy.

I wrote a review on the movie, *The Indian in the Cupboard.* This turned out to be a very enjoyable writing experience. Although to most people writing a review may seem like a very difficult task, I seem to like it even though it didn't turn out as well as I had been aiming for. Each draft I did made the review a little bit better. It seemed to be every time I re-read it I found a better way to re-phrase something.

I think I have developed more as a writer, a tiny bit more as a reader, and a lot more as a student this past semester. The peer critiques really helped because you could see your writing through other people's eyes. Points I thought were clear were not so clear.

For example, in "Water Balloon Friday," I could see that people understand what fun I had, but they needed me to focus on just one specific event to avoid confusion. I wish I could spell better, write clearer, and type faster. If I had these skills, I think it would improve my writing and overall performance and help me in my future classes. For example, I could keep ahead of the class and get done sooner so I could have more time to study for other classes. Also, I would not have to stay up such late hours trying to clean up my mistakes. I also wish I could read faster and have a wider vocabulary so I could get through interesting stories a lot faster. In this next semester, I hope to read more and by doing this I hope to improve my vocabulary. I would like to read some kind of adventure story and try to write a review on it.

Sincerely,

Ben

I am always inspired by the quality of the letters of reflection. And the students themselves express their own amazement at what they have accomplished and learned over a course of time. These letters of reflection are a required component of the students' end-of-the-term portfolios, which are graded. As a requirement they provide the opportunity for students to reflect on their progress and express insight about their work. They are an appropriate part of the portfolio, but they can also be used at the end of any unit as a means for personal evaluation.

Writing letters, whether they are actually sent or not, provides feedback to students about what they are learning. Through letters, they can review information, elaborate on ideas, and express insight about relationships they see and applications they can make with this new knowledge. Letter writing clarifies comprehension for the learner, and sharing letters helps students expand their perception.

Learning Logs

Maintaining learning logs or journals is another writing-to-learn strategy. I have kept learning logs with my students as a way to stimulate the students' thinking. Following Nancy Atwell's lead, (Atwell, 1998) I like to compose in front of my students.

Portfolio Self-Evaluation Letter

Date

Dear Reader,

1. In this first paragraph, talk in general about what this portfolio shows about you as a writer, as a reader, and as a student.
   a. List all the kinds of writing you tried (essay, narrative, analysis, poetry, reflection, etc.) that worked.
   b. Talk about what you have learned to do or are able to do in terms of your writing process, the content of your writing, and the mechanics of your writing.
   c. What do you think are the most important things you have been able to do well this semester as a writer, as a reader, and as a student?
2. In the middle paragraphs, talk about each piece of writing or work you include in your portfolio.
   a. What is the title? How would you rank this piece in terms of quality (or in terms of most to least effective)? Why?
   b. In what ways is this piece different from the others?
   c. As you wrote, what were some of the things you changed, or decisions you made, from one draft to the next?
   d. Looking at your first draft and the final draft of the piece, is there anything you notice that shows how you changed as a writer? Or are there things you are able to do that you never knew you could do?
3. In the final paragraph, discuss your plans overall as a writer, reader, and student.
   a. How have you changed this semester as a writer, reader, and student? What have you discovered about yourself as a writer, reader, and student?
   b. What have you discovered about your writing? (Cite examples from your writing to show what you mean.)
   c. What are some things you wish you could do better as a writer, reader, and student?
   d. What kinds of writing, reading, listening, or speaking activities would you like to try next year?

Sincerely,

Your name

Your signature

Maybe the students are working on their entries or maybe they are pausing because of writer's block, but while we have the quiet time in the classroom made wholly for their thinking and writing, I put a blank transparency on the overhead projector, pull the screen down, turn the machine on, and write. I have noticed that I need to do this kind of modeling very few times before my students pick up on the freedom of expressive writing. Soon the students settle into the comfortable ritual of entering the classroom, opening their notebooks, and responding to a prompt. Variations occur. Sometimes we enter summaries in the learning logs after we have discussed an issue or read a passage from an article or work of literature. Other times the elaboration takes shape in the form of a letter. Sometimes we jot down our remembrances. Other times it is just a freewrite. Students can wonder about the day's assignment, express fatigue over the work, ask for assistance, or offer other thoughts related or seemingly not related to the class or school. The point is that the journal or learning log becomes an active, nonthreatening account of learners' progress. It documents for the students and the teacher the thinking that has occurred (and that is developing). Rather than have isolated bits of information floating on separate pieces of paper, the learning log is a visual representation—a kind of graphic organizer—of students' learning. It is a convenient place for many students to hold the pieces together. What is important to remember about learning logs as journals is that the entries are rarely final products. The purpose of these assignments is to help students develop their thinking and learning, sort of an incubator of parts. Actual entries themselves or the ideas expressed in them can be used later on as the springboards for more formal assignments that require revision and polished final drafts.

Maintaining a journal requires that it be used regularly in the classroom, one to three times a week, for example. It is also important to have students share what they have written, although students should have the option to pass. Sharing allows not only for modeling but also for comprehension.

An Integrated Social Studies–Language Arts Unit

Just as learning logs are useful measures of students' learning, so, too, do we see students progress when we use writing-to-learn activities carefully throughout a unit. In fact, writing-to-learn activities by themselves may be meaningless for students. The power of writing to learn becomes apparent when the activities are seen as part of an approach to learning. I learned that lesson through an integrated social studies–language arts unit investigating customs around the world that I did with my ESL students. I wanted the students, who were Spanish speakers and mostly from Latin American countries, to learn about lifestyles around the world. A wonderful introduction had been a very small article in the newspaper describing how a small delegation of teenagers from Russia was traveling to various cities in the United States on an educational tour. I brought the article in for my students, and we discussed what they would have asked the Russian students if they had had the opportunity to meet them.

This was the hook I needed to get the students to open the door to a unit of global study. If they could talk or communicate with students from anywhere in the world, what would they like to find out? In a modified think-pair-share, the students individually brainstormed a series of questions they would like to ask. Then I had them form groups to complete two tasks: First, they shared and discussed their lists of questions, reviewed them for similarities, and added other questions. Each group wrote all its questions on a sheet of butcher paper and posted it in the room. Once all groups had posted their sheets, we reviewed the questions as a whole class. Some were the same, some were related, and others were completely different. How could we make sense of so many different ideas? The host of questions needed some type of organization.

The students recognized that the questions were falling into categories, which led to the next task—reordering the questions and placing them in appropriate categories. Each group determined the category titles—for example, education, family life, economy, religion, entertainment and recreation, government, holidays, and traditions. Once the groups had determined and discussed their categories, identifying each question falling under the category, they posted their results around the room. We again reviewed as a class, clarifying ideas or modifying categories. Now that we had an organized set of questions, we were ready to use them.

After deciding on countries to investigate, we were faced with another dilemma: How would we find the answers to these questions? We brainstormed again. On butcher paper, students listed ways they could research the desired information. The responses of the students proved that they knew about using primary as well as secondary sources. They proposed a plan of action: Locate and interview people from the countries, write letters, and gather information from books, encyclopedias, and so on. Of course, these were methods that I would have recommended for research; that the students suggested them, making them their own, made the ideas more meaningful. We had community buy-in.

Ultimately, the students used all these resources and more. They sent letters to American embassies in their chosen countries; they interviewed people from the countries (after drafting and revising the interview questions); they read various texts: encyclopedias, magazine articles, and books. They viewed films, took notes on the material, and shared their information from the notes with each other. They wrote and shared summaries from some sources, and they wrote narrative scripts for their culminating activity. For this activity, they presented their information in a panel format, with each member of the panel role-playing a particular figure—for example, a government official, a peasant parent, a wealthy business owner, or a university student. A chief investigator who asked questions of the panelists and facilitated their conversation on the topics they had studied led the panel. The panels were overwhelmingly successful. They demonstrated collaboration at its best. Moreover, the whole experience involved writing to learn, but it integrated listening-, speaking-, and reading-to-learn experiences as well. For some of our disenfranchised students, this strategy of writing to learn gives ownership for learning because the process allows for personal negotiation of meaning. By participating actively in this unit, more than merely acquiring information, my ESL learners acquired knowledge. There is a difference.

FINAL RECOMMENDATIONS FOR PROVIDING AN OPPORTUNITY TO LEARN

As the ethnic and linguistic makeup of our classrooms change, we must find ways to ensure academic success for our culturally and linguistically diverse students and ensure that all of our students experience an equal opportunity to learn. The National Council of Teachers of English (NCTE) (1986) offers suggestions for teaching reading and writing to ensure the academic success of culturally and linguistically diverse students. Although writing-to-learn activities are not mentioned by name, they correspond perfectly with these NCTE recommendations:

When teaching writing,

1. incorporate the rich backgrounds of linguistically and culturally diverse students by introducing classroom topics and materials that connect the students' experiences with the classroom;
2. provide a nurturing environment for writing by introducing cooperative, collaborative writing activities which promote discussion, encourage contributions from all students, and allow peer interaction to support learning;
3. provide frequent, meaningful opportunities for students to generate own text;
4. replace drill and exercises with frequent writing by assigning topics for a variety of audiences and purposes;
5. recognize that second-language acquisition is a gradual development process and is built on students' knowledge and skill in their native language;
6. respond supportively to the writing of students by acknowledging and validating their experiences, feelings, and ideas; and by evaluating students' writing in a way that fosters critical thinking.

When teaching reading,

1. incorporate the rich backgrounds of linguistically and culturally diverse students by introducing classroom reading materials that celebrate the students' cultural richness; connecting the readings with the students' background knowledge and experiences; encouraging students to discuss the cultural dimensions of the text;
2. recognize that first and second language growth increase with abundant reading and writing;
3. use classroom writings as valid reading material;
4. increase students' understanding of reading materials by encouraging student-central activities and discussions recognizing that experiences in writing can be used to clarify understanding of reading.

The practices outlined here capitalize on the reciprocal relationship between reading and writing. These recommendations not only focus on the academic success of culturally and linguistically diverse learners but also speak to providing equal access to the curriculum and the opportunity to learn from diverse perspectives. That is what multicultural education offers.

As part of a multicultural curriculum, writing to learn provides the opportunity for students to actively gather information and analyze it through their own eyes and the eyes of others. It helps teachers and learners to get inside each other's heads and make connections from one world to another. Writing to learn can awaken an awareness in our students of the knowledge they need to not just make sense of the world but to be able to make positive contributions to the community.

EXTENSION ACTIVITIES

1. In this chapter, Cruz has presented a number of writing-to-learn activities that she uses with her students, from native speakers of English to learners developing proficiency in English. Which of these activities can work in your classroom? Why?

2. Look at the recommendations of the National Council of Teachers of English for working with culturally and linguistically diverse students. Make a list of literacy practices in your classroom that fit these recommendations.

3. How do you see writing-to-learn activities helping you to develop a multicultural curriculum in your classroom? How can you use writing to learn to awaken an awareness of diversity and expand the knowledge of the learners you teach?

REFERENCES

Applebee, A. N. (1996). *Curriculum as conversation: Transforming traditions of teaching and learning*. Chicago: University of Chicago Press.

Atwell, N. (1998). *In the Middle: Reading and writing with adolescents*. Portsmouth, NH: Boynton/Cook.

Banks, J. (Ed.). (1996). *Multicultural education, transformative knowledge, and action: Historical and contemporary perspectives*. New York: Teachers College Press.

Banks, J., & McGee Banks, C. A. (Eds.). (1997). *Multicultural education: Issues and perspectives* (3rd ed.).Boston: Allyn & Bacon.

Berman, S. (1990). Educating for social responsibility. *Educational Leadership, 48*(3), 75–80.

Caine, R. N., & Caine, G. (1994). *Making connections: Teaching and the human brain*. Alexandria, VA: ASCD. Association for Supervision and Curriculum Development.

Cummins, J. (1996). *Negotiating identities: Education for empowerment in a diverse society*. Ontario, CA. California Association for Bilingual Education.

Emig, J. (1983). *The web of meaning: Essays on writing, teaching, learning, and thinking*. Upper Montclair, NJ: Boynton/Cook.

Goodman, K., Smith, E., Meredith, R., & Goodman, Y. (1987). *Language and thinking in school: A whole language curriculum* (3rd ed.). New York: Richard C. Owen.

Hillis, M. (1996). Racial attitudes: Historical perspectives. In J. Banks (Ed.), *Multicultural education, transformative knowledge, and action*. New York: Teachers College Press.

Krashen, S. (1996). *The natural: Language acquisition in the classroom*. Englewood Cliffs, NJ: Prentice Hall.

Luria, A. R. (1979). *The making of mind: A personal account of Soviet psychology.* Cambridge, MA: Harvard University Press.

National Council of Teachers of English. (1986). *Expanding Opportunities: Academic Success for Culturally and Linguistically Diverse Students.* Position Statement No. 16469-1450.

Sleeter, C. (1996). *Multicultural education as social activism.* Albany, NY: State University of New York Press.

U.S. Bureau of the Census. (1996). *Resident population projections of the United States: Middle series: 1996–2050, by sex, race, and Hispanic origin, with median age.* Washington, D.C.: U.S. Government Printing Office.

Villaseñor, V. (1984). *Rain of gold.* NY: Avon Books.

Vygotsky, L. (1978). *Mind in society: The development of higher psychological processes.* Cambridge, MA: Harvard University Press.

7

REAL LIVE AUDIENCES FOR REAL LIVE COMMUNICATION: WRITING TO LEARN AND THE POSSIBILITIES OF TECHNOLOGY

LORAINE CHAPMAN
TUCSON UNIFIED SCHOOL DISTRICT

ABSTRACT

Purposeful writing for real audiences is one way to engage adolescents in meaningful learning. Technology, although not a panacea, has many facets that can be harnessed to help students write successfully. Included in this chapter are writing activities and suggestions for incorporating technology as a writing-to-learn tool.

WORKING WITH CHALLENGING STUDENTS

I love a good challenge. It is those out-of-the-ordinary situations that force me to stretch and try new things. That means I have had opportunity to remind myself that challenging students are truly blessings in disguise.

I remember a year when I felt especially blessed. I was working with a ninth-grade class whose members had lots of interests, but school was not one of them. If an activity was associated with reading or writing, they would rather pass, thank you very much. I pulled all the tricks out of my teacher's magic bag, tried a variety of projects, but nothing ignited their interest and the year progressed with only occasional success. They were a challenge!

Finally near the end of the year, I decided to give a special project one more try. I contacted retired members from our community. In pairs, students met with, interviewed, and wrote biographical sketches about their retired subjects. The final product was a collection of the biographies the students had written. We received grant money to publish the book, and everyone, retired subjects and students alike, received a copy.

At the beginning of the project, much time was spent discussing the kinds of questions that would result in the type and amount of information students would need to write an interesting biographical sketch; after the information was collected, much time was spent writing the sketches. In our computer writing lab, each pair of students composed a biographical piece about their retired subject using word-processing software. They were excited about the ability to affect the appearance of their writing using various fonts and formats, especially because they knew their writing would be in an actual published document with a real audience. I can still hear students collaborating on word choices—*word choices,* for heaven's sake—these students who did not want to write anything, period, let alone discuss the best *word choices.*

After the project was completed, the students saw the results of their work, a published book with a cover designed using computer software. The book contained the written biographical sketches as well as photographs of students with their subjects involved in the interview process. They were extremely proud!

During the class period when they received their books, students asked if I was going to repeat the project with my ninth graders the following year. I replied that I had not decided and asked what they thought. Would that be a good idea? They assured me it would. One student said others needed to have an opportunity to do this kind of project because it made writing important and fun. Wow! Did she make my day!

REASONS FOR SUCCESS

The project was successful for my students for many reasons. One reason was having a real audience to write for. I had found that I could talk about the concept of audience for a specific writing assignment or even define a specific audience, but students knew their writing was really for me, the teacher. Having an authentic purpose for the writing and knowing that people, in addition to the teacher, were honestly interested in the final written product was powerful for my students. The quality of their writing became truly important to them.

Two important elements in writing, theorists and writing teachers claim, are audience and purpose (Graves, 1983; Kirby & Liner, 1988; Lindemann, 1995). In the "real" world, people make writing decisions based in part on their analyses of audience expectations and the purpose of the writing. Morrissey (1983) states that students are also aware that audience and purpose for writing outside the classroom vary, and composition teachers, then, need to create tasks that require students to reflect on target audiences. Researchers such as Lynn Dianne Beene (1987) have also noted that people learn to write when they have something to write about, when there is an immediate need for the writing, and when they have a real audience for the communication. The concept of audience, then, is an important consideration that can impact the success of a writing project.

Another reason for the success of the project was technology. Technology helped my students create documents that had a professional appearance, and the process of creating those documents appealed to students with a variety of learning styles and intelligences. Technology, I have found, is not a silver bullet for producing wonderful writers—what can be done with technology can usually be done without technology—but technology can often help do the work more quickly and efficiently. With word-processing software and a scanner, students easily created clean, professional-looking documents that they were proud to share with others.

TECHNOLOGY MEETS AUDIENCE AND PURPOSE: POSSIBLE PROJECTS

Projects that include a real purpose, an audience for the writing, and access to technology can provide many opportunities for students to be successful writers. Publication is at the core of most of these activities, and examples of some projects I have used successfully include published newsletters, books, and magazines.

Newsletters

Creating newsletters can be powerful for students. A newsletter can be written for any group whose members have a common interest. One strategy for using newsletters is for the teacher to create a newsletter template using word-processing and graphics software and then have students write the articles to fit the newsletter template. Different groups of students can be responsible for the newsletter content throughout the school year. The audience for the newsletter may be, for example, parents or a particular grade level of students.

One year when I taught ninth graders, my classes created a newsletter for feeder school eighth graders. Students preparing for the transition from middle school to high school were interested in what their previous classmates had to say about their experiences as ninth graders. A textual dialogue was established between the two groups, with eighth graders asking the questions and my students, being the authorities, supplying the answers. What a win-win situation! The fears of middle school students moving to high school were somewhat abated, my students received the benefits of being "the experts," and writing for a real audience made the product important. Students were concerned about their newsletter being the best they could make it; after all, their "reps" as members of the high school community were at stake. And the computers, scanners, and word-processing software made a polished product possible.

Several writing-to-learn activities helped prepare my students to create their newsletters. For example, shortly after I introduced the project, we looked at well-constructed newsletters that could serve as models, then in groups students analyzed the newsletters and, based on student-generated criteria, listed the best features of each newsletter. Another day, at the end of a class spent drafting articles and laying out the design for the newsletter, students were given back their list of best features and asked to relate at least one item from the list to their own newsletter. The activity took only a few minutes but reminded students of the best qualities a newsletter should include.

Books

Writing books for younger children was an exciting project for my students one year when I taught in a middle school. Because the campus included two schools, a middle school and an elementary school, I was able to connect with a first-grade teacher. We assigned teams made up of first- and eighth-grade students, and my eighth graders had the opportunity to work often with their first-grade "buddies." The younger students sometimes dictated and my students wrote. Together they made peanut butter and jelly sandwiches and listed the sequential steps. First-grade recess became a time for sharing new games my students had created. After spending much time together, for an end-of-the-year project, my students wrote books that starred their first-grade buddies as the main characters. By that time, my students knew the first graders well and could write a story that included a super-hero, a ball player, a pilot—whatever would appeal to the buddy. After they wrote rough drafts, students used computers to create the final books. They designed and made covers, sometimes with computer technology, sometimes with paper and markers. Finally, they read and presented the books to the first graders at the end of the school year. The younger children were delighted, and the eighth graders were thrilled to see that their efforts were appreciated, even though several students were so proud of their efforts, they really would have liked to have kept the books themselves.

My students learned many things from this project. One thing they learned was that the end product of the act of writing is valuable. That means, they realized, that the *process* of writing must be valuable also. Because they attached value to their written products, being able to do a good job of writing became valuable also, and the process of writing, therefore, took on new importance. And their products, the books, were again made more professional looking because of the technology we had available.

Writing-to-learn activities were the thread that provided much valued continuity to this project. One day, early in the project, on entering the room students had five minutes to write a short profile of the first-grade students they worked with. Next, based on the student profile, each student wrote a list of possible starring characters who might be appropriate for the book. This process helped my eighth-grade students examine a variety of possible roles before making that important decision of who the main character would be.

Magazines

Sometimes peers can be an important audience, as they were to my twelfth graders who created magazines. The purpose of the unit was to explore the concept of defining and writing for an audience, and the final product was a student-created magazine that appealed to a student-defined audience.

During the first part of the magazine unit, students analyzed a number of magazines to determine the types of features, articles, and advertisements different magazines include. The school librarian saved copies of a variety of magazines for us, and, in pairs, students completed a worksheet for each magazine they analyzed. Using the worksheet, students explained how each magazine set and developed the content to appeal to a specific audience. After their analyses, students as a class developed a list of characteristics that they considered to be common to successful magazines.

During the second part of the unit, groups of students selected a target audience. They planned their magazine using the list of characteristics as guidelines and divided the tasks for creating the magazine among group members. Then it was time for students to put their plans into effect. It was during this part that technology was most utilized, particularly scanners and word-processing and graphics software. After the magazines were completed they were enjoyed by fellow students.

Students saw the magazines as an authentic writing experience, and peers became a real audience because each group used the list of characteristics developed earlier as the benchmarks for rating the success of each magazine. We developed a rating form that each group filled out for each magazine. It was obvious that the opinions of their peers were important. Each group was eager to receive its feedback and see its ratings.

Students commented on how enjoyable the unit was, but I knew how much time students had invested in writing, revising, and editing the contents of their magazines. Once again, the early stages of the project were filled with writing-to-learn activities such as the magazine analysis sheets, which helped students learn a great deal about the hows and whys of magazine construction. It was a successful educational experience because students learned about the concept of writing for a specific audience and found that the process of learning was exciting.

INTERNET OPPORTUNITIES

Technology can provide not only the means for students to create professional-looking documents for real audiences but also the connection to those real audiences. When my students produced their book of biographical sketches or their newsletters, I located their audiences; however, today, unlimited opportunities exist for students to connect with real people by using the Internet. Through e-mail, students can communicate with others anywhere the Internet exists, and by displaying their work on Web sites, students have the ability to publish their writing for the whole world to read.

Web Sites

School Sites

Numerous schools have Web sites on the Internet. Often a section of a school site is devoted to displaying student work. The posted work can be related to any content area or any topic the school selects. Some pages exhibit poetry or short fiction selections written by students. Other pages may exhibit artwork or the results of student research. There are also student-written histories of neighborhoods that may include historical and contemporary photographs. Some schools change the writing posted on a regular basis, and students submit work judged by teams of teachers and/or students. Selected writing is published on the Web page for not only the school but the world to view and read. Announcements are made about the winners of the Web selection, and students scramble to see their work on the school page. Parents become as excited as students about seeing their sons' and daughters' writing on the World Wide Web. And some students become the creators of the Web pages, not just contributors to the content of the pages.

Some schools post student writing on a site and ask others to critique or offer suggestions to improve the writing. This approach can be used on an intraschool network, available to only those at the school, or on the Internet, available to anyone worldwide. Guidelines about the type of suggestions desired or a form for feedback can also be posted and used by the individuals responding.

Additional Sites

Other sites on the Web ask students to submit their writing for contests, for publication in electronic magazines, or to readers who will read the work and reply with suggestions and comments. All these uses of the Internet provide students with real audiences.

Sites change often, and an Internet address that is active today may be gone tomorrow, but to find the addresses of presently active sites where students can submit their writing, do an Internet search. To get ideas of how various schools are providing publishing opportunities for their students, visit some school Web sites.

E-mail

Another avenue for student access to real audiences is e-mail. E-mail is the instant, electronic pathway to reach experts, peers, or classmates in the room next door or any country around the world. There are several ways to find e-mail addresses of people for student communication. Go to the Internet and do a search for pen pals. You will find organizations that provide addresses for student pen pals. Or, if you want to connect with experts in astronomy, cycling, and kite making—just about any topic—the Internet is at your service. Many projects provide student e-mail access to scientists, sports experts, or writing tutors, for example—real people for student communication!

E-mail Projects

Projects using e-mail can be simple or complex. For example, I could locate a teacher across town who has students in a class or grade similar to mine, perhaps a group of ninth-grade English students. The teacher and I can agree on similar writing assignments, a personal narrative to begin with, perhaps, that gives information about the students. We can establish pairs, one member from each class. Students can exchange the writing via e-mail and comment on their partners' narratives. For opening comments, I might have students list something they enjoyed about the written piece and ask two questions that the personal narrative prompts. The comments can be exchanged, again by e-mail, and the writers can revise their pieces to include the information that answers the questions. As the students become more comfortable with the process of e-mail and with their partners, the types of feedback readers are asked to provide can become varied.

All types of documents can be exchanged by e-mail. If another class in another school, town, or country is studying the same content as my class, students can create games or puzzles about the content and attach these documents to e-mail messages. Each class can complete the game or puzzle and send back the results for scoring. Creating the game or puzzle will be as helpful to learning the content as completing or scoring the exchanged documents.

Another source of e-mail connections can be found in the multitude of projects on the World Wide Web designed for students. There are projects related to all subject areas, from mapping parts of the universe to communicating with explorers bicycling across Africa. These projects provide opportunities for students to participate in electronic field trips and ask questions via e-mail of the experts leading the field trips. One project has math students working with fractals. Another project has students creating virtual travel brochures about their community and adding their brochures to a Web collection. To locate such student projects, again, do an Internet search.

Student-Created E-mail Projects

Although participating in structured projects can be exciting, students may find creating their own project, posting the project on the Web, and asking for students around the world to contribute to their project even more exciting. One example of such a project is the creation of an electronic bilingual magazine. The magazine in-cludes student writing in two languages, English and a second language, and stu-dent artwork related to specific cultures. It is on-line, is available for the world to see, and includes an invitation for students to submit their own work. The host stu-dents review the submissions and make decisions about what to include in their magazine. The development of the magazine becomes a wonderful learning experi-ence because it involves students making judgments about what constitutes good writing, which translates into improvement of their own writing.

Again, such projects can be simple or complex. Posting a simple science experi-ment and asking other students to duplicate the experiment and e-mail the results can be an exciting way for research to come alive for students. After receiving results, stu-dents can analyze the data, create spreadsheets or databases using computer software, and contact those students who participated in their project, informing them, by e-mail, of the results. Again, this project provides real-life work with real-life audi-ences. Some sites on the World Wide Web exist for teachers to post just such projects.

Web site and e-mail projects can focus on anything, from science experiments to short story publication. Writing-to-learn activities, therefore, can be an important vehicle to help students understand the content of a project as well as the appro-priate conventions and styles of writing for various purposes and audiences.

This is an exciting time for teachers and students. Opportunities for students to have access to a real audience and do real work continue to grow at an increasing rate. The Internet is, today, a tool for teachers to make the connections with those real audiences. What technology will bring us tomorrow can only be dreamed about, but I certainly do not want to miss it. It is bound to be exciting.

EXTENSION ACTIVITIES

1. What are some ways that you provide an authentic audience for your stu-dents' writing in your content area?
2. Describe the ways in which you have integrated technology into your con-tent area, particularly the writing aspect.
3. Try some of the ideas in this chapter and write a reflection. Any insights?

REFERENCES

Beene, L. D. (1987). *Writing assignments: What we know we don't know.* Paper presented at the annual meeting of the Conference on College Composition and Communication, At-lanta, Georgia. (ERIC Document Reproduction Service No. ED 280 085)

Graves, D. (1983). *Writing: Teachers and children at work.* Portsmouth, NH: Heinemann.

Kirby, D., & Liner, T. (1988). (2nd Edition). *Inside out: Developmental strategies for teaching writing.* Portsmouth, NH: Boynton/Cook.

Lindemann, E. (1995). *A rhetoric for writing teachers.* (3rd Edition). New York: Oxford.

Morrissey, T. J. (1983). *Audience, purpose, and persona in student writing.* (ERIC Document Reproduction Service No. ED 240 581)

8

A WRITING TEACHER LEARNS

MICHAEL ROBINSON

UNIVERSITY OF ARIZONA

ABSTRACT

In this chapter, Robinson uses his own experiences teaching Native American high school students to illustrate the anxieties—and rewards—of writing with students of a different cultural background. Participating with the students in writing-to-learn activities helped the author come to terms with issues of his own identity, pedagogy, and writing. He argues that writing as exploration offers as much for teachers as it does for students.

> My shield is the Yaqui flag, my culture. The stars mean our ancestors. The sun is our father, the moon, our mother. The blue is the sky, white purity, and the red is the blood shed when our ancestors fought the Spaniards. I put the heart for the heart that beats inside of me, the rose for the Sewa Ania (flower world). This is what I am and will be for the rest of my life and I'm proud of it.
>
> —Ande

The student texts quoted in this chapter are reprinted from the booklet *Native American Literacy Camp, Anthology of Writing, Summer 1995,* comprised of writing that each of the twenty-eight students who participated in the camp selected to represent his or her work. The pieces excerpted here are the products of Patricia M. Cordova, Andrianna Cecelia Escalante, Peter V. Flores III, Jeremiah Juan, Sky Lewis, and Tina Lisa Cordova Molina. The author expresses his gratitude to these and all the students who have participated in the camp over the years, and to Epiphanio Guerrero who created and has guided the program.

WHAT CAN TEACHERS LEARN BY WRITING?

I argue that writing to learn works best when the students are not the only ones practicing it. Teachers have as much to learn from their own writing as students have to learn from theirs—perhaps more. When teachers write as a way of learning, they model for students how writing can operate in people's lives. Writing also allows teachers to explore the questions arising from their own experiences inside and outside the classroom, in the past and in the present. Writing engages us in what composition theorist Ann E. Berthoff (1981) calls "the continuing audit of meaning," that activity which is the engine of learning (p. 42).

Parker Palmer's (1998) work linking spirituality to teaching makes, I believe, a similar point. He emphasizes the importance of opening ourselves as teachers, of making ourselves vulnerable, of beginning again. He reminds us that when we really teach, we make ourselves available to change. Entering into writing with our students and into the writing of our students can accomplish this transformation in powerful ways.

STEPPING INTO OTHER CULTURES

The students I taught during three summers of a Native American Literacy Camp took me back to this beginning place in a variety of ways. When my friend Anne-Marie, who advised teaching assistants and codirected the writing project I attended, first approached me about teaching Native American high school students from the Tucson area, the idea excited me. As an African American, I wanted the chance to work with another minority population, to work to perhaps make possible for others some of the opportunities that had been made possible for me. As the opening day of the camp approached, however, and as I met with the other teachers, I wondered if I was in over my head.

Beth, my teaching partner the first year and an adviser for graduate teaching assistants, had lived in Arizona for decades, had worked with Native American students, and had used Native American literature in her courses. Ann, my partner during my second and third summers and a graduate student in literature, also had read and taught Native American literature. Our fourth colleague—Chris my first year and Sal during my last two years—was an experienced high school teacher and had worked with Native American students in the past. I, on the other hand, had no high school teaching experience, had little experience with Native American students aside from the one or two I had encountered in my first-year composition courses, and had read virtually no Native American literature.

I did a good deal of smiling and nodding during our meetings in preparation for the camp, afraid to betray my ignorance out of fear that I would be unceremoniously dumped from the program. As my colleagues tossed over my head the names of authors and texts we might have the students read during the camp—Sherman Alexie, N. Scott Momaday, Leslie Silko, Louise Erdrich—I felt like the rawest of beginners. I feared that my colleagues, and more importantly my students, would see through my ignorance and read it as insincerity. These kids, many of them categorized as at risk, would quickly strip my thin veneer of racial identity bare, would uncover the Anglo in minority clothing that I had feared myself to be since my days at a virtually all-white Catholic high school in Kansas; they would see that I was intellectually "passing." So I had no choice but to go back to the beginning as teacher and as minority.

RECAPTURING THE MAGIC OF BEGINNING

As a rule, we who live the academic life tend not to hold a very high opinion of beginners. Introductory courses—courses for beginners—are often the ones we least like to teach. We shunt them off to less-experienced teachers, or we handle them grudgingly ourselves but long for the opportunity to show what we can really do, to teach at the "higher" level.

The elementary and secondary teachers I have known manifest this disease of hierarchy in a different way, but the symptoms persist. I discovered the insidiousness of this hierarchy when I participated in a writing project a few years ago. Most of the participants taught at the elementary and middle school levels, and they were, quite clearly it seemed to me, excellent teachers: intelligent, imaginative, energetic, devoted to their students. I still envy them and try to steal techniques from them whenever I can. Even in many of them, however, I noticed a certain deference to those who taught high school and college students. This hierarchy reared its ugly head in graduate education courses I took during my doctoral study. Often the other graduate students had several years of experience in public school classrooms; some arrived at our class straight from a day of wrestling with the material realities of interacting with students. Yet rather than place theory and practice in dialogue, many deferred to the theoretical training—or defensively resisted the theory talk—of those of us who were full-time graduate students. I sense in them a belief that we who teach adults and adolescents must somehow know more than those who teach young children. Certainly a number of factors might account for these attitudes. The continual denigration of public schools, accompanied with the low pay and little respect teachers receive, does nothing to contradict the notion that teaching in lower grades calls for less knowledge ability. In addition, the attitude of many in higher education toward colleges and departments of education helps communicate the message that however elementary and secondary teachers may think of what they do, the academy often looks on the classroom as a place not worthy of study.

We tend to forget, in our professional hurly-burly, the magic of beginnings, the joy of stepping into the thin air of new experiences. In her book *Writing down the Bones* author Natalie Goldberg (1986) talks about "beginner's mind" this way:

> When I teach a beginning class, it is good. I have to come back to a beginner's mind, the first way I thought and felt about writing. In a sense, that beginner's mind is what we must come back to every time we sit down to write. There is no security, no assurance that because we wrote something good two months ago, we will do it again. Actually, every time we begin, we wonder how we ever did it before. Each time is a new journey with no maps. (p. 5)

> From *Writing Down the Bones: Freeing the Writer Within* by Natalie Goldberg, © 1986. Reprinted by arrangement by Shambhala Publications, Inc., Boston.

Of course, the need to return to the beginning is one of the secrets of writing, and, like all of the most important secrets, we must be reminded of it again and again. Being in the presence of these students over three summers drove me back into myself. To be sure, we had our differences: of generation, of race, of education, of class. Their struggle to place themselves in society, however, reminded me of my own. Ultimately I came to admire and envy their honesty and the courage they brought to the crises of adolescent minority life.

Pete Guerrero, a teacher at Tucson's Cholla High School, began the literacy camp when, in the summer of 1993, he took twelve students camping in Arizona's Chiricahua Mountains, where they also did work for the National Forest Service. The next summer Pete obtained funding to expand the program to five weeks, including one week of English classes at the University of Arizona. The group then spent two weeks working at New Pascua, a town on the Pascua Yaqui Reservation just southeast of Tucson, and two weeks camping in northern Arizona. During the summers of 1995 and 1996, the writing component of the camp was expanded again, this time to two weeks.

In each of the three summers I taught in the program, from 1994 to 1996, we four teachers broke into teams of two and divided the thirty students into two groups of fifteen. Each team of teachers worked daily with the same student group for the entire camp. My partner the first year was Beth, a longtime Tucson resident and the mother of two teenagers. Beth is dark haired, bright eyed, relaxed, and quick to laugh, and these characteristics provided a helpful counterpoint to my more anxious and talkative nature. She is also a talented and experienced teacher, is well read in Native American literature, and was supportive both of the students and of me.

ANXIETY ABOUT IDENTITY

Much of what I recall about that first summer is about how extremely self-conscious I felt in front of the students. In part, this self-consciousness stemmed from the fact that I had never dealt with high-school-aged students before. As I had progressed toward a career in teaching, in fact, I had deliberately excluded any consideration of teaching high school. I could picture myself in my imagination dealing with elementary and even prekindergarten children, kids not yet victims of school weariness and cynicism. But high school students had always in some sense frightened me, perhaps because I had disliked them even when I was a high school student myself. In Kansas, in the overwhelmingly white school I attended—about four African Americans and a handful of Hispanics in a school of about 250—I managed to succeed academically and even in official positions of leadership. My peers elected me president of the student council, and I performed as the drum major for two years, but I never felt truly embraced by my white classmates. They seemed to make a place for me in spite of, not in addition to, my race, seeing me as an exception that proved the rules they believed about African Americans.

Race also complicated my relationship with the students in the literacy camp. On the one hand, I felt a certain affinity with them because I also came from working-class origins and because they and I had lived the experience of minorities in a majority world. I wanted to be careful, however, of making too much of those commonalities. I knew that the Native American experience was distinct from my background, and I did not know what judgments they would make about the distance I had traveled from that background. Would they see me as someone who had sold out, who had been co-opted? Would I appear to them as a token in an ongoing effort to remind them of what they could not do?

I had never before had to deal with these kinds of concerns. Working, living, and teaching in predominantly white settings had allowed me, in a strange way, to manage the issue of race. Being the only minority, or one of a few, made me something of an expert in those settings. My response could cut short discussions on race; my status gave me authority that made it difficult for whites to challenge my point of view. But teaching Native American students was different. Suddenly someone else's minority expertise trumped mine.

During my second and third years teaching in the camp, I worked with Ann, a slim, wry, and edgy redhead whose New England accent would occasionally creep into her speech—sometimes intentionally (she enjoyed pronouncing her Massachusetts hometown of Worcester "Wista" for us), sometimes not. Ann and I had much more the relationship of peers, though she, too, was more versed in Native American literature than I was. Perhaps because of our common status as graduate students, perhaps because we were closer in age than Beth and me, but perhaps most of all because of a certain anxiousness we shared, Ann and I developed an almost sibling demeanor in front of the students that I very much enjoyed and still miss.

Especially in that second year, writing with the students helped me to come to terms with my own past and ethnic identity. Because we had the students for two weeks in 1995 rather than the one week in 1994, I produced more writing with the students and saw more of their writing. They created poems and stories about families, wrote about violence, about dreams, and about ambitions. We asked them to write found poems in which they stitched together various lines culled from different poems, advertisements, and other texts. They wrote pieces about their identities as Native Americans, as adolescent men and women, as residents of "the rez." They listened to rap or "oldies" from the 1970s or 1980s. Their words displayed, by turns, an optimism and a frightening degree of sadness and the possibilities for their destruction. As one student wrote:

> My past-time hobbies are writing, drawing, and kicking it with my family or my homies. I try to spend all the time I have with my family and friends. I don't know what life will give for me to get by each day. I do know that a life can easily be taken away. This is why I take life so seriously. I make each day worthwhile and fun, and I hope that tomorrow will be better or the same. My past-time is to take time to show my family and friends I love them.
>
> After I finish school, I plan on going to college. I would like to become a children's doctor. If I don't want to be a children's doctor, I want a job dealing with children. I love children. Children are people who I can trust. They are easy for me to get along with because they will never hurt me. This is the person I am.

In the midst of such difficulties, however, and counter to the expectations I had before I taught in the camp, the students possessed a great deal of pride in their tribes and heritage. Several of them knew some of the songs and stories we read in our texts for the class. Several regularly attended tribal celebrations, festivals, and dances and were steeped in the mythology and spiritual traditions of their tribes.

I began to reconsider my own identity and past: racial, religious, and familial. I found myself telling stories about my experiences, about growing up with my four brothers in a household full of tension and conflict between my parents. I recovered memories of my family, memories of the love that had sometimes passed between us even in the midst of that conflict. I recalled the devoutness of my Roman Catholic youth. And all of these insights flowed through the students in the camp and the writing I did with them. This entry in my journal illustrates that movement:

> Two confirmations today, Mia and Patricia. I wonder, do they wear those white gloves? Do they know what it's supposed to mean, becoming soldiers of Christ? I sure never did. Thought I did at the time, red I was with the fire of holiness, the tongue of flame flickering over my head.

ANXIETIES ABOUT TEACHING

Those revelations, however, came slowly. In my first year teaching in the camp, I recognized that the situation in which I found myself demanded that I justify what we were doing. I saw that in attempting to get these students to engage with writing, I would have to persuade them that their writing might speak to them, and I could not accomplish this goal without thinking at least conceptually about the way writing engaged me. I attempted to grapple with this issue in the writing I read to them early in my first camp in 1994:

> Why write? Why paint or draw? Why sing or dance? Why play basketball? They are all ways of getting to know and show others who we are. For me the starting point in

writing is who I am and where I am right now. What do I see when I look around me? What does it remind me of? How does it make me feel. . . ? And remember that *everything* you write, everything, is really about you and who you are. You're in the words you choose, the ideas, the sentences. In the way you move your pen across the paper. Something in each word portrait is you.

I also became, in a new way, conscious of my experience of the classroom, conscious of what it felt like to be a teacher and honest about the fear that experience engendered. My fear came out during one period when we asked the students to write a complaint:

> I wish I was better at dealing with these students. They bitch, bitch, bitch, but do they want to do anything? No. It drives me crazy. I don't know what to do with them.

As I wrote in class on the first day of the 1996 camp, with Ann and the students scribbling away beside me:

> I was nervous coming in this morning the way I always am on the first day of class. I never know what the students are going to be like, whether they won't say anything and just look at me like they died about three hours ago and nobody told me.

Certainly the camp involved difficulties and struggles both between the students and my sense of what I should be doing and within me. Perhaps the most productive struggles surfaced in this latter sense. The students did not always respond as I wanted them to or even read the material or participate in class in the ways I wished, as I began to reflect on in the middle of this freewrite:

> but I'm really thinking about who's not writing instead of who is—thinking about what people are doing; some people most maybe all are at least writing something they clearly either read something from the book last night or glanced at it this morning but some haven't—I guess we all have our things we're afraid of—we all have our weaknesses and things we want to avoid—maybe that's just where some people are—does it bother me more this year or do I just forget during the year how annoying it can be, how much it can piss me off sometimes?

In the very act of this writing, I moved from my anger and frustration at the fact that a few students were not writing to some attempt to understand their resistance. I also learned about the different experiences literature can convey, experiences I had undergone but had rarely found in traditional literature. One of the texts we read was a passage from Rudolfo Anaya's *Bless Me, Ultima* (1972) and I wrote this in my journal in response:

> I picked *Bless Me, Ultima* because I like the dream sequence and the conflict between the father's side of the family and the mother's side. It reminded me of my father, who is wild and likes to do what he wants, and my mother, who was always strict and proper and made us act respectable. I could identify with the struggle for the son's destiny. And I liked the setting, which is the llano, the plains. I come from the plains of Kansas, and I like things that remind me of it. My favorite line is, "They were an exuberant, restless people, wandering across the ocean of the plain." The plains remind

me of the ocean, going on as far as you can see—feeling blown by the wind—feeling really small—feeling the power of the weather over you and your life.

I remembered being struck by the landscapes in Luci Tapahonso's *The Women Are Singing* (1993). In response to it, I recalled the natural spaces of my youth and childhood. I recovered the Panamanian jungles I explored as a boy; I returned in my writing to the open, dusty spaces of the California and Utah desert that provided the backdrop for my earliest memories.

A MULTICULTURAL WRITING STUDIO

I have discovered that I am the kind of writer who needs writers around him. Their presence releases me to pursue the writing life as well. I have not decided whether to categorize this quality in myself as a strength or a weakness; I suppose it has elements of both.

My students in the Cholla Native American Literacy Camp reminded me how wonderful the place of beginning can be. They also taught me that beginning is not merely for novices, the uninitiated, and the inexperienced. Beginning is that place to which we must all return when we want to grow, when we want to learn. The beginnings to which they returned me have as much to do with my origins as a person as they do with my origins as a writer. Indeed, the more I recall my experiences with those students, the more I realize that those two senses of myself cannot be separated.

As I wrote in my journal that second summer:

And remember that *everything* you write, everything, is really about you and who you are. You're in the words you choose, the ideas, the sentences. In the way you move your pen across the paper. Something in each word portrait is *you*.

Whether intentionally or not, the students in the literacy camp demonstrated that, at least in their case, I was right. They placed themselves in their writing in ways I did not expect when I began teaching, even in ways I did not expect while I taught them. But nothing I write can speak as powerfully as their own voices. Voices like that of Peter writing about the shield drawing he made, which he dubbed the child of the mad face:

The shield with the mad face was made for me because when I was ten years old, I was always mad at school and at the teachers. I was always mad because they would always get me mad. And I would always go to the office and teachers would always call home and tell my mom or dad that they would have to come pick me up at school 'cause of the way I would act. Then one day a Medicine Man came to my house and asked me why I was always mad. I told him I didn't know. He then said that he was going to spend time for me to make me a shield that looks like me when I get mad. Then a few days later, he came back with the shield and showed it to me. And when he gave it to me, he said that the story on the shield was about me when I got mad. And now every time I get mad, I go to my room and look at the shield to remind me if that is the way I want to look for a while. So that's why it is hung up in my room.

This story, coming from a student who wore Dallas Cowboys jerseys and spoke of his desire to be a professional baseball player, surprised me because it demonstrated the heritage that Peter could draw on and make use of, given the opportunity.

Another student, Jeremiah, showed me that these students possessed strength of character that I could never have imagined:

> I felt different when my brother died. I felt a change in my life because he had died. In my mind, I always pictured us together, growing up, going our separate ways, but still visiting, then dying in our old age. As I looked at him in his casket, I saw how cruel life could be. Every time someone dies, I'm reminded and it pisses me off. (Life is full of shit and you just to shovel it out of the way but it still hurts.)

The stark power of his prose, and courage of his perseverance to go on living in spite of life's pain, startles me even as I read it now, years later.

Then there was Sky, a tagger who dreamed of being "the graffiti king." Here is his found poem:

> lost in a world of confusion
> confused by the ruled
> destroyed by modern society
> the strive for cultural survival
> side by side are hung
> as I am standing
> not wanting to die, dodging through the wilderness
> exhausted from running, you are walking
> distant earth I am
> on the light blue earth I am.

And finally there was Patricia, whose "I am" poem probed the complexity and divergent currents of her life:

> I am sleeping, listening to the radio.
> I am with my little nephew, buying him clothes.
> I am getting things for his room
> I am in my room because I have a lot of things on my mind and I'm watching TV
> I am remembering my brothers always getting into trouble.
> I am remembering when I used to be shy, now I'm straight out blunt, I speak my mind.
> I am having happy happy joy joy days now.
> I am scared when my family and I have problems.
> I am scared for my little cuzzin Melina, a baby with leukemia.
> I am worried my tio might drink himself to death.
> I am complaining now that there's people getting hurt for stupid reasons.
> I am complaining because friends are back-stabbing friends.
> I am more into being a lawyer.
> I am frustrated with people who don't mind their own damn business.
> I am me, a teenager in a crazy world AKA Mi Vida Loca.

So perhaps the most important thing this teacher learned from writing was the echo of my own message to the students. In their writing, they talked about using their heritage to help them deal with the difficulties they knew they would have to face in the future: the fight for survival, the attempt to fulfill their dreams, the desire to preserve their culture, and their connections to family even as they sought better ways of living.

I learned that teaching, like writing, requires an investment of the self. Consequently, we can only truly teach when we come to accept ourselves, and we can only accept ourselves when we are able to articulate our identities to others without fear or shame. The honesty and courage of my students helped me to do this better than I had done it before, and now, years later, I reread their pages for inspiration and insight, and for acceptance.

EXTENSION ACTIVITIES

1. Describe your experience writing with your students. What insights have you gained from this experience?

2. Robinson talks about the magic of beginnings. Relate an experience you have had beginning—beginning the school year, teaching a new class, teaching a new subject, or the like. What are the advantages and disadvantages of beginning?

3. Generate some writing topics or strategies that you could use in your classes to have students use their heritage to deal with difficulties at school.

REFERENCES

Anaya, R. (1972). *Bless me, ultima*. Berkeley, CA: Tonatiuh International Inc.

Berthoff, A. (1981). *The making of meaning: Metaphors, models, and maxims for writing teachers*. Upper Montclair, NJ: Boynton-Cook.

Goldberg, N. (1986). *Writing down the bones: Freeing the writer within*. Boston: Shambhala.

Palmer, P. (1998). *The courage to teach: Exploring the inner landscape of a teacher's life*. San Francisco: Jossey-Bass.

Tapahonso, L. (1993). *Saanii dahataal/The women are singing*. Tucson, AZ: University of Arizona Press.

9

"FOREVER ON THE MORNING WIND": EXPANDING THE CANON OF AMERICAN LITERATURE

EDITH BAKER

BRADLEY UNIVERSITY

ABSTRACT

Featured in this chapter are strategies any instructor can employ to develop thinking and writing activities in an American literature course. These strategies are based on the following assumptions: (1) for a student to make meaning he or she must care about the topic and (2) a connection of the personal concern with a history of others who have shared that concern may engage students to learn about a tradition of similar responses throughout history. Journals or learning logs are used here to integrate students' personal lives and knowledge bases with a tradition of American writers. These journal or learning log entries are eventually developed into more formal essays.

Every year, I become more humble in the classroom as I collaborate with a number of first Americans: Yavapai-Apache, White Mountain Apache, Navajos, Zuni, and Hopi. I have learned from them that the four directions in Leslie Silko's collection *Storyteller* and novel *Ceremony* are symbolic in many cultures. I have also learned from A-Jay, a nontraditional student, that the significance of the "morning wind" is that the Navajos believe that the spirit of their deceased family member watches over them in the morning wind. To teach students to listen to and discover their own voices and place themselves in a tradition of American writers is to help them prepare for making meaning throughout their lives.

From the Outside In

I was not always so wise. Armed with sophomoric sociology, good intentions, and a master's degree in American literature, I went to the Navajo Reservation in Indian Wells, Arizona, in 1967 as a Volunteer in Service to America (VISTA) volunteer. I knew more about Navajos from Gladys Reichard's book *The Navajo* than from cultural experience. I soon learned what it was like to be the nonnative in a remote area. Everyone else spoke another language; I was the outsider. When they laughed, I knew they told a joke. I quickly learned to read nonverbal cues, pointed lips, and averted eyes. I was neither despised nor welcomed—I was ignored and invisible. After surviving the snow of 1967, the members of the community decided I might stay, although they suspected that I was still there to write a book about them. That I have never done, but the lessons that I learned in being the outsider have stayed with me in my teaching career. Too many students are outsiders to the reading and writing processes.

Thirty years later, I have learned much about overcoming invisibility, a knowledge that has helped me to teach students from many backgrounds, from Vietnamese Americans to Mexican Americans and Native Americans. I have taught in public and private institutions in the Southwest and Midwest. By integrating students' personal lives and knowledge bases with a tradition of American writers—and contemporary ones not yet in the tradition—an instructor in a multicultural classroom can spark all students' enthusiasm for learning, reading, and writing. To engage students in a dialogue becomes the challenge, no matter how silent or weak the voices may be. Journals or learning logs provide the vehicle for students to challenge their private worlds in collision with public worlds.

Overcoming Invisibility with the Journal

For the purposes of this chapter, journals refer to unedited student writings that develop ideas and reflect thinking; shaping and editing into more formal essays is not necessarily a requirement, but specific content related to the subject matter of literature is. Some topics are assigned and some are selected by students, but all journal writings are expected to show thoughtful consideration of the content of American literature, the broad topic of the American dream(s), and inductive hypotheses about the American character. My classroom is a writing-to-learn classroom, and many of the activities are designed to elicit responses that help students write their way to understanding and knowing, as well as demonstrate mastery of the content of the reading.

Students need to be asked to respond in writing to questions that stimulate their imagination and learning—then, their fluency abounds. If instructors can design effective writing assignments, there is no containing students' engagement with classroom texts or their own creations. However, trial and error of thirty years of developing assignments still makes me as vulnerable as a beginning teacher when I initiate any new writing assignment. Often I fail. I fall back on a few very successful assignments—for example, a profile of an influential character, an initiation paper, revision of fairy tales, and definition of a community problem and proposal of a solution. Nevertheless, I have learned some strategies that any instructor can employ in developing thinking and writing activities in an American literature course. Some assumptions, attitudes, and specific journal-writing activities follow.

WRITING AND THINKING TO MAKE MEANING

One underlying assumption is that for a student to make meaning, he or she must care about the topic. As instructors stare out at a classroom of students whose clothing may mock, imitate, or defy our 1960s and 1970s clothing styles, we may wonder what today's students care about. Yet some universals prevail; the creation of self and construction of identity are universal concerns and confusing rites of passage. Although most of these assignments have been field tested with beginning college students (developmental as well as reentry and traditional age), these activities would probably work with students from seventh grade through college, because the making of meaning is a universal concern.

Whereas in tribal cultures people celebrate adulthood with puberty rites, today our students have shifting moments of maturity. Identity, development of self, and assumption of adult roles in society are stages along a continuum, as the psychologist Erik Erickson (and any parent) points out; the preteen and teenage years are prolonged into the ambiguous (and sometimes static) zones of being a student. Thus, an anthropological approach of studying cultural universals usually engages students, whether aged twelve years or twenty-two or seventy-two. Wissler (1929) defined certain concepts universal to all cultures, including socialization of the young, initiation rites, governmental organization, religion, and rituals for death. After Wissler studied many Native American cultures, he abstracted these universals and argued that all cultures respond to these general patterns. Whenever I receive excellent student work, I frequently notice I tapped into some universal and cultural concern, such as initiation rites or socialization into adult society. Thus, it is important to discern what students care about.

To attempt to foster students' connection and engagement with the course is the fundamental premise that all these thinking and writing activities are built on. For a student to make meaning, he or she must be passionately interested in the topic. Finding those topics is our challenge. We are not trying to teach grammar, but we are trying to excite students to communicate their message so that they will learn the grammar and realize its importance in reaching their audience. We are not trying to teach students biographies of authors, but we are trying to teach them that their life matters and that they are able to create their own autobiographies. Finally, we are not trying to teach a litany of American values, but we are trying to teach students to read and analyze the language of the Declaration of Independence, for example, and to see how those ideas relate to their lives and beliefs today. The friction and resistance to the ideas—or congruence—may be what defines them as Americans.

The next assumption is that a connection of the personal concern with a history of others who have shared that concern may engage students to learn about a tradition of similar responses throughout history. Life choices can be overwhelming for students, but a tradition of writers in American literature—from Cabeza de Vaca to a contemporary Navajo or Laguna—provides guideposts. Notice that the authors and voices come from many centuries. Fundamental to this approach is the assumption that all students are writers with ideas to express: they just need to be asked the right questions to stimulate their thinking and interest. I stress frequently in my class that although we are studying American writers, students also belong in that great tradition of writers as they wrestle with what their contemporary definition of their American values might be. I give them options for topics that allow them to explore their own creativity and development. Often a student cites his or her own poem as a favorite journal entry.

For example, how do students see nature in relationship to their lives? Is it worth a poem? Do they identify with the monolithic or spiritual nature of Emerson or do they believe they can control the natural forces in their lives? Does Barry Lopez's (1988) chapter "Gone Back into the Earth" (from *Crossing Open Ground*) remind them of being in enclosed spaces? Do they enjoy Walter Mosley's description of the desert or Rudolfo Anaya's descriptions of New Mexico? One activity might be for students to read selected passages of Thoreau (or any of these other writers) and then immerse themselves outside in nature to write their piece. For this activity, I stress that anything is acceptable; students are just to sit for forty-five minutes and observe their surroundings closely. They can write descriptive prose, wander in their thoughts with musings about their career, and observe some aspect of nature closely. These are the usual directions I give; they have produced everything from a detailed explanation of dead rats to oak trees to playgrounds and children to the wild waves of Lake Michigan.

Following a practice encouraged by whole-language specialists, we take time to publish student writings by having students read and share their work in class. I usually try to do this activity soon after the semester starts, because it generates enthusiasm for writing as well as the literature; the energy usually carries on throughout the course and establishes my classroom manner of listening to students' ideas. I stress repeatedly that students are all writers, and everyone in eight classes over three years has produced something worth sharing. To solve the problem of length, I ask students each to select one paragraph from their work to read aloud; this usually ensures a well-written piece of prose. The atmosphere in the reading is nonjudgmental and praising—perhaps I comment on a metaphor, a well-written line, or an excellent vocabulary choice. I also allow time for other students to respond freely to writings, but I am careful not to permit negative comments or rejections; a supportive environment is essential at the early stages of the course. I find something positive to say about every paper.

Such positive reinforcement of students' ideas and the instructor's belief in the possibility of everyone refining his or her writing are assumptions the instructor must stress often. Some students will say that they cannot write or have nothing to say; such ideas need to be challenged with examples from previous discussions. Ample time must be given, and points may be awarded for students to read selected passages from their writings to the class. Having students select one paragraph from their journal writings is an effective tool; most students can find something they are proud to share.

Early in the semester, the instructor needs to develop a pattern of listening to students and their ideas, because many will have come from classrooms in which the teachers have all the answers. Students have learned to endure instructors' pauses; if they wait long enough, instructors will finally say what they want. The classroom milieu must be encouraging, so the reluctant voices have a chance to be heard. By writing, even the reticent ones construct a response. Thus, the assumption is not only that engagement with the self will lead to engagement with a tradition of letters but also that all students can be writers and have something to say. Although the primary audience is the self, students become aware that their peers and the instructor are also an audience.

To that end, many of these writing activities are sequential and build to a more formal paper. Early in the journal writing (or writing log), students summarize ideas in texts (by stating some principles from the Declaration of Independence or Martin Luther King's "Letter from a Birmingham Jail") or demonstrate through plot summary that they have read the assignment. Twice a week for thirty to forty-five minutes (or one sitting), they need to respond with specific comments about the readings. (This activity could be adapted to daily papers of plot, character, and thematic analysis; I have heard of one instructor who requires students to keep note cards on every story, which ensures that they have read the text before class and are ready for discussion.)

In the first evaluation of the journals, it is imperative for the instructor not to give credit for any digressions unconnected to the content of the course (such as discussion of the previous weekend). Most instructor comments will be supportive and encouraging, such as "give more details." Grammar is not marked at this time, but flow of ideas and wrestling with course material should be praised. Descriptions of places on students' nature pieces are often outstanding. I stress discussion of tone, character, point of view, and other literary elements until I am certain that students can recognize them. I do not give credit for writing about girlfriends or boyfriends; students must refer to their readings and prove to me that they have read the assignments, one of the purposes I state in my overview of journals. Sometimes I simply comment, "I like this piece very much." They appreciate the praise, and it is frequently warranted. Many experiment with poetry.

DEFINING THE AMERICAN DREAM

A sample assignment might be for students to abstract apparent characteristics of Native American writings, after they have read a variety of chants and songs from people in many different tribes. Another might be to ask them to note characteristics of creation stories and compare and contrast them with any they might know. Once again, I attempt to have students articulate their explanations for their origins and nudge them to connect new information to existing schemata.

Because this is a course in American writers that serves a general education audience by a discussion of American values, I begin early in the semester by eliciting a group brainstorm on the board about characteristics that make up Americans. (Ideas such as rugged individualism, ethnic pride, Puritan work ethic, and so on can be used to provoke discussion if it stalls, but the students usually have lots to say, and I act as a scribe to write all their contributions on the blackboard.) This activity usually follows a diagnostic writing done on the first or second day of class: their definition of the American dream. Before much times passes, I want students to express in writing what they personally believe is the American dream. At the end of the course, many students refer to this initial piece as their favorite writing for the entire semester. I quickly review the pieces, primarily for idea flow but also note sentence and organizational skills and focus on paragraphing abilities. I often make suggestions for revision and allow that in their journal.

When giving the specific writing directions on this topic of the American dream, I attempt to make them nonthreatening. I tell students to express anything they want—how they interpret the phrase *American dream,* what it means to them personally, how recent immigrants may define it, what they want it to mean, or what established Americans or Native Americans think it means. This prompt often produces pieces with cynicism about everyone not being able to achieve an American dream because of prejudice, gender, class, and so on; however, it also shows students that no two people in the class have the same definition. Discussion is always lively as students in small groups share several sentences of a paragraph and then contribute to the larger group discussion. As an instructor, I read many platitudes about "being the best one can be,"—but the American dream is an accessible topic, and everyone has something to say. As a writing instructor, I can quickly comment on the content of the diagnostic writing and determine how much extra work must be done on grammar and sentence structure. At this time I also ask for specific details to back up generalizations and provide a good entrée into future journal writing.

Soon after this writing on the American dream and the brainstorm on the board, students develop a writing habit of producing two journal pieces a week, supported by specific examples and textual references. Irrelevant writing must be eliminated; I tell them one or two typed pages must say something about the content and general topic of the course. In three or four weeks, I collect the writings. I might ask students to compare and contrast the ideas, themes, or writing styles of two authors (one traditional and one contemporary), for example. One choice that works well here is a comparison of the writings of Cabeza de Vaca and Equiano. I might also ask students to summarize major points of an introductory chapter on the history of a period, such as the eighteenth century. I ask them to generalize about styles, topics, authors, concerns, voices, women's roles, and so on in the works of various authors. A comparison of the concerns of Louise Erdrich and Charlotte Perkins Gilman might be fruitful. What choices did the narrator of Kate Chopin's *The Awakening* have? Are any of these similar to writers or individuals of today? The primary purpose of these assignments is to stimulate divergent thinking and connect pieces and periods to existing concepts.

I also allow students to include one poem or autobiography (in the style of Equiano, DuBois, Bradstreet, Wheatley, or Ben Franklin), but I restrict this personal writing, because there is a tendency for many writers to submit pages of poems that are extremely difficult to comment on. Nevertheless, there is pride in individual work and the fact that these students are "American authors." Although students have some choices of assigned topics, they must respond to a minimum number of journal entries. (I provide possibilities but allow them to digress if the entry is text based and they support generalizations with specific examples.) My decision about how many of these entries can be freewritings depends on the quality of work I have received. I make this decision after the first three or four weeks and the initial review of the journals or learning logs. I can always become less regimented in the writing prompts later. Many students may do additional writing and submit more pieces than required; the journal is the only place I allow extra credit.

Early on I stress that this inductive approach will help us develop a theory about how certain American values, such as the desire to maintain cultural identity, have changed over time. Sometimes I even tell students that the final examination (essay question) will be a take-home assignment in which they will take one American value (idea, concept, or belief) and show the evolution of this idea over at least three centuries, documented with specific textual references. I stress that they must explain the concept—at a second or third level of thesis analysis—and not simply state something as simplistic as "God is mentioned in Anne Bradstreet and Emerson, but Crane writes about a universe without a God." What is the connection and evolution of the place of religion and God in Americans' lives? To write that Southerners justified slavery to God or that Navajos saw God as father and mother—earth and sky—needs a connection to a larger thesis.

For example, students might be able to support a thesis that the early Puritan writings were about a vengeful God, who was an omnipotent father; the naturalists constructed a universe in which God was synonymous with nature and the oversoul, and writers such as Crane created a universe in which a pagan god of chance rules humans' lives. An outstanding thinker might even be able to speculate about contemporary writing and discuss possibilities about how ideas or beliefs in God have changed, with reference to writers such as Alice Walker, Equiano, Martin Luther King, and so forth.

All of these theories about American literature must be supported with specific textual passages from the readings, so students learn quickly that they can be writing parts of their final exam as they write short pieces throughout the semester. I allow them to use journal materials, as well as their texts, in the in-class or take-home examinations; diligent students have many portions written in smaller papers throughout the semester to help in compiling the final examination. This method allows for the final paper to be a collection of portfolio pieces, revised and expanded as the semester continues.

Making Meaning through Writing

As is evident, much student choice is involved in this class. Students also choose one novel to read, which many of them tell me is the first time they have ever been able to do that in an English course. The novel must be one about which a body of literary criticism exits. After they find something they would like to read, I make certain that it is a novel by an American author (or have students check) and then tell them to read freely, especially before they are overwhelmed with deadlines for other courses. Often a freewriting on themes they notice in their novel will lead them to an idea for a theme to trace throughout the semester; subjects such as the roles of women, evolution of the concept of family, race relations, spirituality, and the individual and society have been recent topics.

When students have a broad category, pattern, or theme, it helps them to organize the vast information from multiple authors. For example, one female student decided to write her final examination on emerging identity and the changing roles of women. Jenny read poems of Anne Bradstreet that focused on traditional roles in a family, yet hinted at irony; she also read the works of Harriet Jacobs, Charlotte Perkins Gilman, Zora Neale Hurston, Ann Beattie, and Denise Chavez. Her conclusion was that writers in the seventeenth and eighteenth centuries "focused on roles in family life and Christian values. In the nineteenth century, there were more choices and a search for identity in African American, as well as Caucasian women." Finally, in the twentieth century, women attempt to fulfill a more equal role in achieving their individual American dreams. Although this may not be the most earth-shattering thesis, for Jenny it was original, and she supported it with examples of the literature she read and remembered. She was writing about her own dreams and identity in the process.

Another student, Rachelle, wrote about the concept of beauty in American culture. Her work was informed by reading Toni Morrison's *The Bluest Eye,* as well as Emerson's essay "Beauty" and the poems of Anne Bradstreet, Phillis Wheatley, and Emily Dickinson. Her work required much close reading and citation of texts, but she also was wrestling with the contemporary culture's concepts of beauty. She might also have included the writings of Sandra Cisneros (*Woman Hollering Creek*), Ana Castillo (*So Far from God*), or Denise Chavez (*Face of an Angel*).

Finally, Sarah wrote about the evolution of the faith-reason dichotomy in American literature. She applied ideas in the writings of Rowlandson, Franklin, Paine, Edwards, Thoreau, and Emerson to the thesis that by the end of the nineteenth century, America was no longer at either "end of the [faith-reason] continuum and was floating somewhere in the middle. Faith had changed from a supernatural faith to a more self-centered faith. Human reason was not sufficient, but human feeling was." Sarah's own clarifying of faith and values was occurring in her journal coincidentally. To suggest that she consider which America (Barbara Kingsolver's *Another America* would work well here)—Catholic Texas or Southern Baptists in the African American community—would be an excellent way to broaden her traditional understanding.

Much of the rationale for this course design comes from Toby Fulwiler's (1987) stress on journals and Peter Elbow's (1987) concept of freewriting. Fulwiler (1987) elaborates on his method by detailing a case history of a classroom, in which he kept a journal while teaching an American literature class at the University of Vermont. In 1987, at the Conference on College Composition and Communication, I heard Fulwiler discuss teaching an entire course in American literature using only journals; at that time, I decided that students needed to do some freewriting, but they also needed direction in writing a thesis-based essay.

To that final end, in my American literature course, students produce a documented essay on some particular aspect of the novel they have selected (eight to twelve pages, or 1,800 to 2,400 words). Many students are at the beginning stages of literary criticism, and producing an analysis of one character is all they can manage. Some students are great readers, and they may have read other material by the author, in addition to much literary criticism. I try to avoid traditional novels, which they have already read and developed a Cliffs Notes approach to, such as *Huckleberry Finn, The Great Gatsby,* or *To Kill a Mockingbird*. Although these novels are readily available and might be appropriate for some middle school or high school classes, I require students to select something more contemporary or multicultural; a great range of choices exists. Even a collection of short stories by an American author (such as Sandra Cisneros, Rudolfo Anaya, or Bobbie Ann Mason) will work for this assignment, if students can focus on one aspect or unifying theme. The essays of N. Scott Momaday, Anaya's *Bless Me, Ultima,* David Rice's *Give the Pig a Chance,* or Dagoberto Gilb's *The Magic of Blood* might also be effective choices.

Before students read any literary criticism, I suggest they freewrite about their own observations on the novel. I call this a "creative research paper," and, once again, I stress their original interpretations, grounded in the text. Then we visit the library and learn about researching authors' lives and critical interpretations. In that first collection of journals, I give students space to write about their novel. I spend time discussing writing processes and invention and provide access to sample papers from previous classes.

One student wrote about his theory of two cycles of nature in Leslie Silko's *Story-Teller;* another discussed the unity of effect in James Dickey's *Deliverance.* As is evident from the latter example, I present literary theory and assign Poe's essay with a definition of the unity of effect; then I ask students to apply his theory of the unity of effect to either Crane's short story "The Open Boat," Sandra Cisneros's "Woman Hollering Creek", or Gilman's "The Yellow Wallpaper." As the semester progresses, we also continue to speculate about where today's novels and short stories are headed, with respect to the unities.

All the Components of the Language Arts

Students also present a five-minute oral report on their novel to the entire class, and discussion continues on general topics of themes and unities, with representative passages of the author read. I provide a criteria sheet for evaluation (when I assign the oral report) and guidelines for preparing the speech, thus connecting the reading, writing, speaking, and listening skills of the language arts. To ensure quality oral reports, I make this activity worth 5 percent of the grade (the written paper is 30 percent of the course grade). By the time these more formal speaking and writing and research activities begin, the shorter journal writing has been discontinued. A semester breaks down roughly into half the time for journals and half for the documented essay (about seven weeks for each component).

Students who want the instructor to supply all the answers find this is a frustrating course. But students who are curious and tentative in finding their voices (and I have many such students) begin to soar. They like reading and writing and developing a stronger voice. The pieces on the American dream at first are sophomoric, but students are forced to define abstract terms and generalities (What is "freedom"? What is "family"?), principles any composition instructor embraces. Because the Scholastic Aptitude Test II is now being marketed in promotional literature from the Educational Testing Service as a way for students to achieve the American dream, students suddenly see how pervasive these concepts are. To find the embedded origins of contemporary thought is perhaps the greatest challenge of this course. Revisions of students' initial diagnostic pieces on the American dream are more thoughtful than the original drafts and are supported by numerous details and examples.

The ultimate purpose of this course is grounded in the symbolic processes of language making:

> To think in the first place, human beings need to symbolize, for in using language they represent, come to know, and understand the world. We actually do much of our learning through *making* language; or, another way, *language makes thinking and learning possible.* (Fulwiler, 1987, p. 4; italics are Fulwiler's)

Donald Murray (1985) writes that "The act of writing is an act of thought (p. 3)." He continues: "Writing is one of the most disciplined ways of making meaning and one of the most effective methods we can use to monitor our own thinking (p. 3)."

Language helps us articulate that connection to the past—the voices of our ancestors "on the morning wind"—and define our American dreams, even as we move toward them. This epistemic integration of knowing and being and discovering and creating produces a powerful way of learning and making meaning—with and through writing.

Finally, the following are guidelines that not only undergird the activities described in this chapter but also form the foundation on which my classroom practices rest.

Foundations for Learning in a Multicultural Classroom

1. All students are capable of becoming good writers; they just need to be asked the right questions.

2. For students to make meaning, they must care about the topics discussed. For most students, writing about the self or personal topics creates engagement.

3. When an instructor designs questions that stimulate students' creativity and imagination, students become fluent.

4. Subjects that relate to universal concerns, such as construction of identity, are usually effective in engaging students' interests.

5. Topics of universal concern not only engage students' self-interest but also connect to a tradition of American writers who have voiced similar concerns.

6. Engagement in thinking, reading, and writing activities is fundamental to students' developing interest in learning to communicate their message; grammar becomes an editing and revision tool rather than the subject matter of the course.

7. When grammar is taught in context, students remember its purpose.

8. All stages of writing processes must be encouraged, from invention to publication. Reading students' writings (always with permission) to the class is final confirmation of their worth. Oral presentations are integral to the reading, writing, thinking, and listening processes.

9. A sequence of journal (or learning log) activities, produced throughout the course, allows students to refine their thinking and develop parts of their portfolio, which may culminate in a revised paper at the end of the semester.

10. Students, when given choices of texts or topics, become loquacious. Often they tackle projects far beyond minimal requirements.

11. When student thinking is sparked, writing becomes a trail of those thought processes.

12. Whenever possible, read materials written by contemporary and nontraditional writers; a wealth of choices exists. Such choices encourage not only the diverse background of student authors but also student reading choices.

13. Finally, students will enjoy discovering their own voices as they define their dreams. They will read, think, write, speak, and listen to multicultural voices as they find their own voice in the din of contemporary culture.

Extension Activities

1. Baker takes her students through a series of writing-to-learn activities. Can you use these activities in your classroom? What kinds of modifications would you have to make to apply these activities to your content area?

2. Baker relies much on the journal as a writing-to-learn tool. How important is the journal in your classroom? How do you keep the notion of using a journal fresh for students?

3. Describe your experience in your classroom using writing-to-learn strategies as invention activities and then going through the writing process to produce more formal writing.

References

Elbow, P. (1987). *Writing without teachers* (2nd ed.). New York: Oxford.

Fulwiler, T. (1987). *Teaching with writing.* Upper Montclair, NJ: Boynton/Cook.

Murray, D. (1985). *A writer teaches writing* (2nd ed.). Boston: Houghton Mifflin.

Wissler, C. (1929). *An introduction to social anthropology.* New York: Holt.

The American Indian: An introduction to the anthropology of the new world (3rd ed.). (1938). New York: Oxford.

10

PLACE POETRY: A FORM OF SELF-EXPRESSION

AMY RUSK-FOUSHEE

TUCSON HIGH MAGNET SCHOOL

ABSTRACT

Writing poetry is one of the finest tools of self-expression. In this chapter, Rusk-Fousheé describes the place poetry unit, which employs writing-to-learn strategies to teach students the mechanics of poetry writing. The student samples show that through these strategies the students not only learn to write poetry but also discover much about themselves.

WRITING POETRY: AN OPPORTUNITY FOR SELF-DISCOVERY

Writing poetry is a process of falling in love with language and discovering one's own voice. High school students are instinctively receptive to poetry because of its brevity and emotional emphasis and because they identify so strongly with music. One of the ways that American youth have traditionally sought to separate themselves from previous generations has been through musical and, by extension, poetic expression. Writing poetry provides students with the opportunity to investigate their personal identities and to learn from their revelations, a process that is not encouraged by mass-market culture. The majority of high school students dress alike, talk alike, and act alike largely to hide their differences. Poetry writing is a means of writing to learn about and appreciate these differences.

PLACE POETRY: THE UNIT

Place poetry is the collaborative effort of a teacher and a librarian. It was designed for freshman classes at Tucson High Magnet School to capitalize on the ethnic and cultural diversity of the student body, which is approximately 60 percent Latino, 30 percent European American, 7 percent African American, 3 percent Native American, and 1 percent Asian American. In the unit, students are encouraged to show where they live or feel most comfortable through their writing. They may take a concrete approach to the assignment by choosing to describe their neighborhood or home or an abstract one in which they depict a person or mood that creates a sense of security or place. In either case, the goals of the unit are to help students develop some comfort with writing poetry, to grasp and articulate aspects of their individual selves, and to see beyond the pressures of conformity.

Students are strongly encouraged to write a poem as their final project. However, it may be desirable to provide an alternative, such as presenting a poem by an author who expresses a sense of place similar to the student's own. Writing-to-learn activities to introduce students to the myriad of poetic devices and terms are incorporated into the unit. In addition, students are required to maintain a journal folder that includes the various handouts, exercises, and poems to use as reference. Their individual compilations serve as a means of self-evaluation. The objectives of the unit are that students will (1) experiment with language that is culturally and linguistically relevant; (2) identify poetic elements such as personification, rhyme, repetition, and alliteration; and (3) produce a class glossary of current slang terms.

One of the pitfalls of teaching poetry is presenting students with a barrage of examples before they get the opportunity to write. It is essential to build in time for students to document their reactions to the unit in their journals, as well as to experiment either by imitating the different poets' diction and writing styles or by exploring their own. David Burk (1992) in his article "Teaching the Terrain of Poetry," argues that we shortchange students by emphasizing products over process. He comments that without guidance, students tend to reproduce generic cloud and season and friend poems—simple, safe wordplay that fails to connect with their own perceptions and feelings. The following straightforward principles Burk offers should be displayed prominently in the classroom:

1. Poets make decisions about rhyme.
2. Poets arrange their words on the page to suit their own purposes.
3. Poets say things in ways they have never been said before.
4. Poets revise.

   (Reprinted with permission from Burk, D. [March, 1992]. Teaching the terrain of poetry. *English Journal,* 81(3), p. 27.)

Burk also cautions against relying too heavily on prompts, patterns, and recipes. Frameworks are easy to use and "generate good-looking products quickly," but they rob students of the choices that make unique what they have to say (Burk, 1992, p. 27).

Two weeks, or ten class periods, is a reasonable estimate for the duration of the place poetry unit. Following is an outline of the daily activities:

Day One
1. Post Burk's principles for writing poetry.
2. Brainstorm slang words on the board.
3. Pass out and read aloud Andres Carranza's poems "Ganga Slanga" and "Cruisin' the Boulevard," accompanied by a glossary of slang terms.
4. Discuss Carranza's use of language (e.g., code switching, vernacular, and so forth).
5. Solicit definitions for the slang words on the board to create a class glossary.

Day Two
1. Pass out and read aloud Jimmy Baca's poem "Forced by Circumstances."
2. Discuss Baca's identification with the place where he grew up.
3. Introduce or review the use of simile, metaphor, and descriptive language, using examples from Baca's poem.
4. Journal entry: Students practice using simile, metaphor, and specific adjectives to describe sounds and smells in their own neighborhoods.

Day Three
1. Pass out and read aloud "The Sacred," by Stephen Dunn.
2. Discuss the meaning of *sacred* in the poem.
3. Pass out and read aloud "In the Inner City," by Lucille Clifton.
4. Journal entry: Students write about which poem they liked the most and why.
5. Homework: Students bring in musical selections, including lyrics, with themes of place.

Day Four

1. Copy and pass out lyrics and listen to songs selected by students or pass out lyrics and listen to the following songs:

   a. "This Must Be the Place," by the Talking Heads

   b. "The Regular," by the Replacements

   c. "Under the Bridge," by the Red Hot Chili Peppers

2. Discuss devices, such as personification and repetition, and highlight the effect of a loved one's presence on sense of place.

3. Optional activity: Students work in pairs to compose an additional verse for any of the songs presented.

Days Five and Six

1. Pass out and read aloud Gary Soto's "Ode to Mi Parque."

2. Explain the significance of an ode.

3. Have students compose class poems.

4. Pass out and read aloud Sandra Cisneros's "Good Hotdogs."

5. Discuss line breaks in both poems.

6. Revise class poems as a group.

Day Seven

1. Pass out and read aloud Rokhl Korn's "On the Other Side of the Poem."

2. Introduce the concept of stanzas.

3. Discuss the difference between literal and figurative language.

4. Journal activity: Students write a four-line stanza with figurative language, using "On the Other Side of the Poem" as a prompt.

Days Eight through Ten

1. Have students begin writing final poems.

2. Confer with students about their progress.

3. Have students revise poems.

4. Have students present their poems orally and/or display them in the classroom.

PLACE POETRY: THE PROCESS

Within every high school there is a mixture of "crews," or social circles, so we begin the unit by brainstorming slang words on the chalkboard to develop a class glossary that will reflect the orientation and interests of the various student groups. The glossary also reveals where the students live specifically (i.e., what part of town or neighbor-hood and, more generally, city or region of the country). It is surprising the degree to which the class glossaries change from year to year; examples from the previous years provide an excellent way to demonstrate the organic, transitory nature of language. Students become very animated when they realize how many idiomatic expressions and terms they can think of and how many have to be explained to the instructors. It seems that each generation has the desire to recreate itself through language.

Definitions in academic English are added to the list of slang words on the board to help students differentiate between formal and informal language and connota-tions and denotations. Many students associate poetry with formal language because their exposure has been limited to the traditional canon of Wordsworth, Dickinson, and Whitman, so it may take some coaxing for them to see that slang, although in-formal, is poetic and metaphorical. In this unit, students are exposed to various con-temporary poets who use the language of the times because, like other artists, they want their work to reflect the historical setting.

Examination of "code switching," the linguistic expression for switching from one language to another within the same sentence or conversation, and the use of a hybrid of two languages is a natural outgrowth of the class glossary because, like slang, both phenomena place a poem historically and geographically. Code switch-ing is a trend that students generally take for granted until it is pointed out to them. Because code switching between Spanish and English is a routine way of speaking in cities along the United States–Mexico border (and in most places where there is an emergent immigrant population), it can make a poem more appealing because of its familiarity. There are many words or idiomatic expressions in languages that can-not be directly translated without some loss of meaning. For example, the Spanish construct *tener ganas* literally means "to have an inclination," but it is used to ex-press a combination of desire, drive, and general chutzpah. In her article "Palabras de la Frontera," which appeared in Tucson's fall 1997 *Border Beat: the Border Arts Journal,* a relatively new publication that addresses life along the United States–Mexico Border, Susana De La Peña provides historical context for the crossbred na-ture of language. She cites many examples that students can appreciate, such as the Texas Tornados song, "Hey, baby, que pasó? Won't you give me un besito."

Various poems that use slang, code switching, and/or a mix of Spanish and Eng-lish are read aloud to illustrate the effectiveness of using a specific vernacular. The poetry of Andres "El Gato Rebelde" Carranza is a good choice because he uses some of each, in addition to providing a glossary of terms that students can compare with their own. Following is a sample from his poem "Cruisin" the Boulevard"(1993):

Cruisin' the boulevard al estilo muy loco
con tu Brylecream hair y dinero poco
It's a Friday night buscando rucas
    Get closer! Don't lose them están chulas
They wave to you y como flirt las sigues. . .

    (Reprinted with permission from Carranza, A. [1993]. Cruisin' the boulevard.
The Bilingual Review/ La Reviste Bilingue. Phoenix, AZ: Hispanic Research Center.)

On day two of the unit, the following selection by Jimmy Santiago Baca (1986) is recommended to introduce the concept of place and acquaint students with descriptive language. Baca refers to the South Valley, the predominantly Mexican American area of Albuquerque, New Mexico.

> Forced by circumstances
> to live in this Heights apartment—
> how strangely clean and new
> these white walls are,
> thin orange carpet
> that sprawls through every room
> like a rat's
> red faded wrinkled brain
> pulsating noises
> from tenants below.
> The ceramic faces of women
> who live here,
> and buddha-cheeked men
> who all wear straw hats
> to walk their poodles,
> manicured and clipped elegant
> as heirloom dinnerware
> glittering beneath chandeliers—
>   I don't want
> to live here
> among the successful. To the South Valley
> the white dove of my mind flies,
> searching for news of life.

(by Jimmy Santiago Baca, from MARTIN AND MEDITATIONS ON THE SOUTH VALLEY. Copyright © 1987 by New Directions Publishing Corp.)

The instructor leads a discussion about where Baca is living in the poem and asks students how it is similar to or different from their own neighborhoods. The instructor reviews the concepts of simile and metaphor before asking students to give examples of descriptive language from Baca's poem. He or she then asks students to write their own similes and metaphors to use in their place poems. It is more challenging and thus more valuable for students to describe what they smell and hear rather than only what they see, because they generally have more experience with visual description. Examples of precise adjectives are provided, such as *Mariachi* or *Ranchera* in place of *Mexican music*.

Students need to hear many voices and many perspectives to help them find their own. They are more likely to get hooked on poetry if they are exposed to a range of poems in which they can see or hear themselves. This personalization is necessary before students are bombarded with terms and techniques. Stephen

Dunn's poem "The Sacred" (1998) sets the stage for day three of the unit. The theme of the poem, which follows, concerns high school students' notion of a sacred place. For many of the students, it is where they feel the power associated with independence. For others, *sacred* connotes a spiritual location. In either case, students are generally eager to discuss the poem after it is read aloud.

The Sacred

After the teacher asked if anyone had
    a sacred place
and the students fidgeted and shrunk

in their chairs, the most serious of them all
    said it was his car,
being in it alone, his tape deck playing

things he'd chosen, and others knew the truth
    had been spoken
and began speaking about their rooms,

their hiding places, but the car kept coming
    up, the car in motion,
music filling it, and sometimes one other person

who understood the bright altar of the dashboard
    and how far away
a car could take him from the need

to speak, or to answer, the key
    in having a key
and putting it in, and going.

Finally, no longer able to abide the sacred
    so defiled,
a young woman said it was God

and only God who filled her with awe,
    And how sad it was
that a dumb car could replace church

in someone's life. The class grew silent again
    As if a hypnotist
had spoken one of those deep, simple words

that jerk people into the past. Maybe a place
    wasn't sacred, one of them said,
if it didn't make you feel uplifted

and small, a little afraid to be in it.
    There were murmurs and nods.
The teacher was pleased that the sacred

seemed disturbingly loose in the room,
     the class divided, alert
Through the window he could see students

lying on the grass, a Frisbee hovering
     In numinous flight, but in fact
his mind was drifting even farther

to a place he loved where the bartender
     knew his name
and what he liked. The sacred was finished

now, he joked, class was over and everyone
     should think
about what it really meant. The serious student

already knew, and was the first out the door.
     Some lingered a bit
to pursue what had been said, though this

was their way of connecting with others
     who might love them
and invite them places they'd never regret.

    (Reprinted with permission from Dunn, S. [1988]. The sacred. In
P. Janeczko [Ed.], *The music of what happens: Poems that tell stories*. pp. 23–24.
New York: Orchard Books.)

    Students more comfortable with concrete examples of place may prefer to model
their poems after Lucille Clifton's "In the Inner City "(1996), which is read aloud by
a student volunteer. It makes an apt contrast to Dunn's poem in content and style:

In the Inner City

in the inner city
or
like we call it
home
we think a lot about uptown
and the silent nights
and the houses straight as
dead men
and the pastel lights
and we hang on to our no place
happy to be alive
and in the inner city
or
like we call it
home

    (Reprinted with permission from Clifton, L. [1996]. In the inner city. In
J. Yolen [Ed.], *Sky scrape/city scrape: Poems of city life*. p.21. Honesdale, PA:
Wordsong/Boyds Mills Press.)

During the rest of the period, students are instructed to write in their journals about which poem they like more and why. They should be encouraged to use some of the terms mentioned previously in the unit.

On approximately day four of the unit, we incorporate music to maintain student interest and provide more examples of what makes a particular place special or like home. Very often it is a person or the people associated with a location who make it unique. There are countless songs of all musical genres that portray a positive or uncommon sense of place. Students are encouraged to bring in their own selections, in addition to those provided by the instructor. The song "This Must Be the Place," by the Talking Heads, a pop band of the 1980s, is a perfect example of one's "home" being wherever a loved one is. Another suggestion is "The Regular," by the "pregrunge" band the Replacements, because it depicts a sense of belonging, with which students can identify.

"Under the Bridge," a ballad by the Red Hot Chili Peppers, an alternative rock band, introduces students to the concepts of personification and repetition. It is a love song written about Los Angeles that could be used as a prototype for other cities. Time permitting, students may work in pairs to compose an additional verse for any of the songs presented.

After reading Gary Soto's poem "Ode to Mi Parque," from his book *Neighborhood Odes* (1992), students compose class poems to edit as a group the following class period. The teacher explains the significance of an ode and then writes two lines from the poem—"On Sundays. . ." and "I often think. . ."—on the board. Students are asked to finish each of the lines on separate pieces of paper (keeping their own neighborhoods in mind)—for example, "On Sundays everyone on my street plays basketball" or "On Sundays we go to my Nana's house for dinner." The lines are collected, and a volunteer puts them in order to create a class poem. The teacher points out how the repetition of statements holds the poem together like the refrain of a song. Customarily, the students who are interested in putting the lines into some order have a natural sense of rhythm. For instance, one student systematically left out the elliptical construction "I often think" and, without guidance, created the following class poem in stanza form:

I Often Think. . .

I often think that the moon is a faraway place, but the sun is nearby

I often think, why is high school so hard?
Going to school isn't important
The world will come to an end

I often think the sun will burn the mountains to ash as it sinks to sleep

I often think black people aren't accepted
It's harder for black people to get jobs
I want to be a professional break dancer

I often think of being dead

I often think of what life will be like in five years

Men should do all the housework
The streets are dangerous, but I'm not scared
I often think a lot!

"Ode to Mi Parque" also lends itself to a lesson on line breaks. Students have a tendency to want to make each line of a poem a complete thought or sentence. Soto uses enjambment, or run-on lines, to move the poem forward.

Another neighborhood-oriented poem that appeals to students is Sandra Cisneros's "Good Hotdogs" (1987). Like Soto's poem, it is stichic (organized line by line) as opposed to strophic (organized by stanzas). The line break decisions Cisneros makes in the poem reflect her knack for reproducing natural speech patterns. She uses a syllabic meter pattern as well to make the poem more musical.

Using "Ode to Mi Parque" and "Good Hotdogs" as models, students work together to revise the class poems so that the line breaks contribute to the movement and music. Conservation of language, or getting rid of any word that does not enhance the poem's meaning, should be stressed. Following is an example of a poem before and after the group editing process:

Before
I. "On Sundays. . ."
On Sundays I get up and go to church and hear all the wonderful old ladies
    sing to the Lord.
On Sundays I perform at church with my Mariachi group.
On Sundays I wake up to the sounds of Gospel music.
On Sundays I practice break dancing.
On Sundays my mom listens to oldies.
On Sundays I watch the Cowboys beat the 40-Whiners.
On Sundays I thank God for being alive.

After
II. "On Sundays. . ."
I wake up to Gospel music
All the wonderful old ladies
Singing to the Lord
On Sundays. . . I perform Mariachi
Practice break dancing
Watch the Cowboys beat the 40-Whiners
On Sundays. . . my mom listens to oldies
Thank God for being alive.

Besides rehearsing some of the technical aspects of poetry such as line breaks, students need practice using figurative language. They have a strong tendency to rely on literal images because of lack of exposure and the fear of taking risks. The focus of day seven's activity is to inspire students to stretch their imaginations to create vivid imagery. The Yiddish poet Rokhl Korn provides a perfect prompt for creative thinking in his place poem "On the Other Side of the Poem" (1987). The poem is organized into stanzas, a style that many students find easier to imitate than free verse.

On the Other Side of the Poem

On the other side of the poem there is an orchard,
and in the orchard, a house with a roof of straw,
and three pine trees,
three watchmen who never speak, standing guard.

On the other side of the poem there is a bird,
yellow brown with a red breast,
and every winter he returns
and hangs like a bud in the naked bush.

On the other side of the poem there is a path
as thin as a hairline cut,
and someone lost in time
is treading the path barefoot, without a sound.

On the other side of the poem amazing things may
    happen,
even on this overcast day,
this wounded hour
that breathes its fevered longing in the windowpane.

On the other side of the poem my mother may appear
    and stand in the doorway for a while lost in thought
    and then call me home as she used to call me home
    long ago:
Enough play, Rokhl. Don't you see it's night?

> ("On the Other Side of the Poem" by Rokhl Korn, translated by Seymour Levitan, from THE PENGUIN BOOK OF MODERN YIDDISH VERSE by Irving Howe, Ruth R. Wisse, and Khone Shmeruk. Copyright © 1987 by Irving Howe, Ruth Wisse, and Khone Shmeruk. Introduction and Notes Copyright © 1987 by Irving Howe. Used by permission of Viking Penguin, a division of Penguin Putnam Inc.)

Beginning with the elliptical construction "On the other side of the poem. . ." each student is charged with coming up with a four-line stanza using figurative language, which they will add to their journal or folder. Following are samples of students' writing:

On the other side of the poem
I see another poem
where there are no trees
and we have to live in a bubble.
On the other side of the poem
are mounds of ice cream

hills of candy
and a tag with my name on each.

On the other side of the poem
I wonder when the world is going to end
and how it's going to be sucked
into the sun and explode.

At this point in the unit, students have had experience with the elements of poetry and the writing process. They are ready to demonstrate and reinforce what they
have learned by writing the first draft of their own poems. Revision during class time
and as homework is a requirement. The instructor, peers, and the journals or fold-
ers are all necessary reference tools during the writing process. Furthermore, students are required to confer with the instructor about their poems. As a culminating
activity, students are encouraged to read their poems aloud or display them in the
classroom. Following are Ian's, Michelle's, and Joe's poems, respectively.

My Place

There is a place
Where we can kick it

Like it's 1999
Play video games

Neto, Carlos, and Mary—
You beat the game

When the music
Starts, everybody

Gets jiggy with it
And the players

Start to play
The freaks get freaky

It turns crazy
That groovy place.

A Haven

We stand again in this haven
and now I've found a soft red light.

You say that you behold a sunset in
my face and silver stars in my smile.

I try to calm my heart which trembles
like the wings of a sapphire hummingbird

About to fly away into
the vast blue above us.

"Da Joint"

I know a place
where the dank ain't laced
it's the place to be
by yourself or with a young lady

Every night the party's
all night long
and you know it's gonna be hittin' strong
so get yo boogie on

It's been going on
for 3 hours long
and there's not a damn thing wrong

we got black, white, and brown
who came to get on down
ain't no need to clown

so keep yo gang shit back
cuz tonight
we gonna dance track after track.

Writing poetry is one of the finest tools of self-expression. The place poetry unit, because it employs writing-to-learn strategies, is successful in teaching students the mechanics of writing poetry while providing them with the equally important experience of discovering something about themselves.

EXTENSION ACTIVITIES

1. What writing-to-learn activities does Rusk-Foushee use in the place poetry unit? In what ways can you use these activities in your content area?

2. What is the place of poetry in your classes? In what ways can you use poetry to help students hone their understanding of the subject matter in your classroom?

REFERENCES

Baca, J. S. (1986). *Martin and meditations on the south valley.* New York: New Directions.

Burk, D. (1992, March). Teaching the terrain of poetry. *English Journal,* 81(3), p. 26–31.

Carranza, A. (1993). Cruisin' the boulevard. *The bilingual review [La revista bilingüe.]*, 18(1), p. 58.

Cisneros, S. (1987). Good hotdogs. In *My wicked wicked ways.* Berkeley, CA: Third Woman Press.

Clifton, L. (1996). In the inner city. In J. Yolen (Ed.), *Sky scrape/city scape: Poems of city life.* Homesdale, PA: Wordsong/Boyds Mills Press.

De La Peña, S. (1997). Palabras de la frontera. *Border Beat.* 7, p. 48–49.

Dunn, S. (1998). The sacred. In P. B. Janeczko (Ed.), *The music of what happens: Poems that tell stories.* New York: Orchard Books.

Korn, R. (1987). On the other side of the poem. In I. Howe (Ed.), *The Penguin book of modern Yiddish verse.* New York: Viking Penguin.

Soto, G. (1992). Ode to mi parque. In *Neighborhood odes.* San Diego, CA: Harcourt Brace Jovanovich.

11

PERSPECTIVES ON THE THREE-VOICES NARRATIVE

CARL C. ANDERSON

PALO VERDE MAGNET HIGH SCHOOL

ABSTRACT

As the U.S. population continues to become increasingly diverse, it is essential to be able to look at events from multiple perspectives. N. Scott Momaday's *The Way to Rainy Mountain* (1969) is the story of a journey told in three voices (mythical, historical, and personal), allowing the reader to see the journey from multiple perspectives. Described in this chapter is a unit plan that combines the reader response approach and writing to learn to allow students to produce their own three-voices narrative.

INTRODUCTION

The unit and lesson plans I present in this chapter rely on a narrative style based on N. Scott Momaday's book *The Way to Rainy Mountain*. This book is an autobiographical journey that is at once historical, personal, and evocative, moving from the past to the present. The journey becomes a vehicle for myths and stories that have been told and passed down through the oral tradition. Oral tradition, according to Momaday (1969), is a way of preserving, passing down, and recording by word of mouth the myths, legends, stories, and lore of a group of people. The story of this journey is told in three voices, showing three different perspectives.

THE ORIGIN OF THE UNIT

At an annual spring conference of the University of Arizona English department, I attended Dr. Anne-Marie Hall's presentation on oral tradition. She discussed a unit based on *The Way to Rainy Mountain* that she had taught her college students. I liked the way she used a reader response approach to help students connect with the text even as she guided them toward two goals: (1) to explore how myth and reality interact to create or define a culture, and (2) to discover the places of literature and history in our cultural lives. Reader response theory has its roots in the work of Louise Rosenblatt, who argued in her book *Literature as Exploration* (1983) that readers bring much to the literary work. She asserted that meaning is not embedded in the text; instead, readers use their experiences to construct meaning as they read. In this approach, as they read, students use expressive language to explore and construct meaning. Because of my interest in Native American cultures, because of my belief that multicultural literature has an essential place in actualizing the dimensions of multicultural education, particularly the knowledge construction dimension (Banks, 1997), and because I consider Momaday's epic journey to be one that many students can identify with (at various levels) and learn from, I adopted and adapted Hall's unit for use in my sophomore English classes. My adaptation became the three-voices narrative unit.

The three-voices narrative unit is a writing-to-learn activity prepared as an extension to a sophomore-level English survey of world folktales. Dr. Anne Marie Hall's handout "Oral Tradition" is used as the primary model for the design and methodology of the unit. Following the steps outlined in her handout, I use the reader response approach and the essay assignment she describes to help my students achieve the worthy goals that she has delineated. In the lessons that follow, I attempt to create conditions for students and teachers to read and respond to and through storytelling voices and folktales. Those responses, personal experiences, and the stories read and heard are then transformed into public writing. This public writing, an end product of the writing-to-learn process, becomes a narrative in which students relate three different stories in three different voices.

MULTICULTURAL CONSIDERATIONS

The presentation of folktales and the creation of the three-voices narrative in a literature study course can provide unlimited opportunities to teach multicultural perspectives. How one person or group may perceive things is culture bound. As models, Hall's handout and Momaday's book provide the framework and structure to relate creatively the interaction of culture, discourse patterns, and language registers. Kaplan (1984) describes the intimate relationship between language and culture—that language is a manifestation of a particular cultural worldview. In a study he conducted on the discourse patterns of second-language learners of Arabic, Asian, and Latino descent, he noted the existence of other ways of paragraph development aside from the more "normally desirable" one in English. In English, paragraph development in expository writing follows a linear inductive or deductive pattern. On the other hand, paragraph development in Romance languages tends to be nonlinear and digressive. In Asian languages, paragraph development in expository writing is mostly circular and indirect. It is important for students to have background information on discourse patterns as they begin reading *The Way to Rainy Mountain,* because the book does not follow the linear pattern typically found in English texts. Likewise, a discussion about the way the book is written and the worldview portrayed is necessary.

Another multicultural issue that needs to be addressed in the course of this unit is language registers. Joos (1967) delineates five language registers: frozen, formal, consultative, casual, and intimate. Frozen register is used in prayers, rituals, and legal and historical documents. Formal register is the language of textbooks and most lectures, used for a one-way transfer of information. Consultative register is the register of the classroom—polite, interactive communication. Casual register is used among friends, peer groups, and so on. Intimate register is used in very close relationships—the register of couples, twins, husbands and wives, and so on. The register or style used in speech or written communication depends on the audience, the topic, and the purpose. The three voices used in *The Way to Rainy Mountain* are of differing registers. The choice of register is indicative of the narrator's stance toward the audience, the topic, and the purpose for communication. When the students are ready to write their three-voices narrative, they, too, will make decisions about language registers.

The seemingly nonlinear aspects of reading, responding, and creating in three (or more) voices provide students with the opportunity to see, reflect on, and react to literature from many different cultural perspectives. While guiding discussions, answering questions, and writing with the class, I seem to gain more insight into each student, into each student's culture, and into our school community in general.

CHAPTER GOALS

One goal of the three-voices narrative unit and this chapter is to view the relation-ship of the oral tradition, folktales, and writing to learn from multiple perspectives. This lesson is part of a larger multicultural unit that relies on reader response for the creation of background knowledge and as an anticipatory set for the writing of three stories at once. In this chapter I present a response-type narrative discussion of my own experience, student voices (short samples of student writing), and Hall's im-portant handout. Another and probably the primary goal here is to provide teachers with the material to create a lesson using *The Way to Rainy Mountain*. Momaday's storytelling style is an excellent model for students to use to enhance their aware-ness of their own unique heritage and storytelling voices.

THE WAY

The way this chapter and the unit's lessons are written is directed toward reflective thinking in a multiple-voice narrative. The ability to hold three concepts simultane-ously on the same plane and the weaving of these concepts into a story are the way of this lesson. On a more formulaic level, this chapter is one part how-to discussion told in a chronological sequence; the second part, the student voices section, reflects the original intention of the three voices on the same plane or facing pages. Fonts are used in this chapter to replace certain layout techniques. The student writing section is an illustration of the students' inchoate understanding of the notion of multiple per-spectives. Relatedness, unity, thematic qualities, and the emotional impact of student writing reflect the way things went in class. Students read, responded, and created. Meanwhile, I weave in various methodology and pedagogy to parallel the reader's ex-perience of the way the narrative is woven in *The Way to Rainy Mountain*.

DETERMINING THE THREE VOICES: WEEKS ONE THROUGH THREE

I assign the book *The Way To Rainy Mountain* as outside reading to my sophomore English class, and in class we discuss aspects of the reader response journal. Hall uses the reader response approach in this unit to allow for "positive and negative reader's reports to be explored relative to non-Indian/Indian, 'literary,' and 'social science' attitudes about defining and communicating contemporary literature by and about Indians." Students have one class period to begin reading and writing their re-sponses. Most of their reading is done outside of class, and students are reminded to do the reader response journal as a *during-reading* activity. My expectation is that the reader response journal as a writing-to-learn activity will mediate the students' understanding of the text being read. It is a particularly useful tool for this unit because of the unique format of the book *The Way to Rainy Mountain*. The juxtaposition of the three voices and the discourse pattern (Kaplan, 1984) are elements of the book that might prove confusing to students. In the course of reading this book, it is not unusual for students to get lost and to find that comprehension of the story does not occur until they have read twenty or thirty pages. The reader response journal is a way for students to record their grappling with the text.

I briefly explain to students the three-voices narrative of *The Way to Rainy Mountain*. Momaday relates his journey in three voices, each with a different origin, format, and methodology. The first voice is that of the storyteller relating narratives that have originated within the family or tribe. The second voice is that of the objective historian relating facts, definitions, and description gathered from written sources. Finally, the third voice is that of the reflective poet, who tries to use memory, association, and imagination to connect to the other voices. We discuss the idea of three voices telling three different but related stories and how the use of different registers (Joos, 1967) serves to distinguish each voice. I explain to the students that while they are reading the novel they should also reflect on personal, family, and culturally related stories. They will be asked to write a three-voices essay for the final assignment of the unit.

In class I provide background information on the oral tradition, multiple perspectives, and N. Scott Momaday's reputation as a writer, professor, narrator, and historian. I remind students that Momaday did not necessarily invent or create all of the "voices" in *The Way to Rainy Mountain* and for that reason they are encouraged to ask parents, grandparents, and other relatives about some family-related oral traditions. During this period of outside reading and reader response writing in their journals, I ask students if they have any questions regarding their experiences of these first few weeks. Most students like and want to know more about the questioning aspects of the response journal. They seem to like asking questions of the characters and the author.

The students also begin to wonder about the essay. The term *essay* seems to make them a bit apprehensive. In an attempt to alleviate their anxiety, I remind them that they will be reading, discussing, and analyzing folktales from the sophomore anthology during the time of their outside reading and that there will be plenty of time to discuss the essay. They need to understand that the form and style of the final project will appear in the various folklore we will study and they will have a variety of choices to use as models.

At the start of most class periods I read a folktale from the book *Classic Folktales from around the World* (Nye, 1996). I read orally and then we briefly discuss the folktale. These discussions generally deal with the elements of folktales and common themes from the reading. Students' understanding of these elements provides them with more choices for their own writing. Most students enjoy the daily oral readings and often ask to borrow the book so they can look for a voice.

I provide some background information on Native American literature and culture. Primarily, Native American literature is thematic. Themes commonly found in Native American literature are also values basic to many indigenous peoples: needs, values, culture, self, and environment. I also provide background information related to the four directions: east, south, west, and north. Native peoples begin with east, unlike the dominant culture's preference for beginning with north. I encourage students to find such cultural focus in their own writing. "Follow the direction the sun travels," I urge.

I also share for students' potential use the American Indian literary and storytelling reliance on pairings of words, ideas, animals, and expressions. Some of the most interesting background information that students enjoy and relate to is the use of visions as messages in dreams, dream songs, and the traditional reality that a living thing, an object, a physical force, or abstract quality has spirit that personifies it. A common value in my Finn culture that directly relates to Indian culture is the understanding that poetry and stories are not owned. Instead, they flow through us from a higher force. The spoken word is the most powerful use of words. Therefore, one must use extreme caution when committing the word to paper. From an American Indian point of view, folktales, myths, and legends are referred to as oral history and as oral tradition.

My hope is that the students will learn that they themselves are oral tradition, that they are history, and that they are symbol makers. I have learned after more than twenty years of working with and for various Native American studies programs that the words *myth* and *legend* imply something gone or in the past. The students in this class are to take the Native perspective that the oral tradition is living. With this understanding many students seem to take more interest in the meaning of the stories read and shared. Also during this third week, in the course of our discussion, we replace the anxiety-laden term *essay* with a more palliative term, *narrative*.

DETERMINING THE THREE VOICES: WEEKS FOUR AND FIVE

In the fourth week it is finally time to begin our discussion of the reader response journals. Initially, the students, generally quiet, appear to be confused, and perhaps even somewhat embarrassed to share their responses. I state, "You know, most people who read this book don't quite put things together until they've read twenty pages or so. The first time I read this book I didn't know what was going on until I got about halfway through it—and I was a senior in college when I first read this book." This seems to ease their apprehensions. Soon students are saying that it is page twenty-six, thirty-two, or the description of the narrator's grandmother's house that put things together for them. It is apparent that the three voices in the story begin to weave for them at different times in the story. The discussion is very wide ranging. However, there are many questions related to Kiowa tribal culture and Indian culture in general, and students ask questions about the times, places, events, and symbols. They offer many of their own understandings and possible explanations for their discussion questions. This is writing and talking to learn.

Many students rely on my experience in Native American education for answers to the culturally and ethnically related questions. Armed with the background examples and explanations that I provide, together with their knowledge of oral tradition and folklore, students cull ideas from their responses to form their own interpretations. Highlighting this free-flowing discussion are many reasons and extension examples from the anthology, from the oral readings, and from personal experiences.

Students also have particular questions that they would like to ask the author, Momaday: Why did you want to write this story? How did you come up with one voice or the others? Why do the Kiowa believe in the stars, a mountain, horses, and nature? Note that the questions are primarily how and why, which would indicate that some higher-order thinking is taking place. I always wish afterward that I had audiotaped this discussion because it reflects a growth of learning and realization. This book, this story, these voices are things that these students know, care about, and want to emulate.

The discussion lasts the entire ninety minutes of the "flex" period (we depart from the traditional schedule two days of the week and meet with only three classes in ninety-minute blocks) and ends with a review of Hall's handout (see appendix). We discuss what is on the sheets regarding voice, perspective, and the oral tradition. I put some of these ideas on the board and discuss many others with the class. Many students agree with the concepts presented, and some students challenge a few interpretations. We turn to the layout of *The Way to Rainy Mountain*. Students like the artwork, and they point out the use of different fonts to represent the three voices. Although I am only attempting to show them how they are to lay out their three-voices narrative, the students seem ready to begin discussing the content of their writing.

WRITING THE THREE-VOICES NARRATIVE: THE LAST THREE WEEKS

After hearing, reading, discussing, and analyzing a variety of cultural oral traditions, the students are ready for the writing assignment. Students are to write three stories, each in three parts, to cover a total of six pages. As in *The Way to Rainy Mountain,* the three different voices tell their stories in unison. That is, pages one and two are the first part of each story as told by the three voices. Sharing pages three and four are three different voices telling the middle portion of the three narratives. Pages five and six cover the end, or conclusion, of each story as told by each voice. I remind students that the stories should share a common aspect or element. A common symbol, theme, location, and the same story told from three different perspectives are all possible ways to connect the voices. Students are relieved when I assure them that one voice can be their own voice, a second voice a preferred folktale, and the third voice can, perhaps, be a relative, animal, or any other unique perspective. In other words, students can deviate from Momaday's order (mythical, followed by historical, followed by personal or reflective). At this point we also address the possible use of different registers (Joos, 1967) to distinguish the voices.

Even as we write during the remaining three weeks, I continue to begin each period with an oral reading of a folktale. I purposely choose from world cultures tradition stories that relate in one way or another. I place all the books I have on oral tradition, folklore, and folktales on the table in the middle of the room. We continue working on the three-voices narrative in a writers' workshop setting with peers helping with the revision and editing. For two weeks everything goes according to plan. Newspaper stories are mentioned and used as sources for a voice. Using Susan Lowell's *The Three Little Pigs/Three Little Javelinas,* we look at the use of fairy tales as a way of arriving at a voice and as a credible source for shaping pieces into a three-voices narrative. Even if some of the ideas never reach fruition, the suggestions foster openness and sharing among the students.

An exercise involving the folktale "How the Leopard Got Its Spots" introduces students to the idea of explaining how something came to be. This folktale becomes a favorite. Vacation stories are also used. The aspects of writing to learn become evident during this time as students do exploratory writing on many themes, elements, and voices. The learning that takes place is apparent when aspects of the activities from the contents of the anthology begin to appear as a voice in students' narratives.

The students are honestly and thoughtfully engaged in the activities and the experience of the three-voices narrative. By week six we begin to focus our efforts on completing the writing of the three-voices narrative. The remainder of the time is exclusively writing workshop time. I move around the classroom, spending the majority of the class period working with individual students, and I find myself becoming involved with my students on intellectual, creative, and personal levels—an involvement that I ordinarily do not experience during the first quarter of the school year.

Following are three examples of the students' creation of the three-voices narrative. The different fonts illustrate the different voices.

Brian's Narrative

Chapter 1

Voice One. He's asleep. What a lucky guy. I wish he could drive, so that I could sleep before we get to Mexico. Oh well, we're only another half an hour away. He needs to wake his tired self. He's fifteen; he can go without sleep.

"Come on, Brian! Wake up! Wake up!" He always does this. I might as well let him sleep. Ah! I can't wait until we get there so I can finally relax. I hope Joe's boat is running so I can dive at Bird Island.

Voice Two. Why won't he let me sleep in peace? Might as well get up. I wonder how Honcho is doing? Almost there. Soon I'll be able to have fun, walk on the beach, and get a tan. I hope Joe's boat is running so we can swim in the ocean.

Voice Three. *When are they going to get here? Man it's hot! Here comes someone. Time for me to protect my house. It gets really hot when your body is covered with fur. Look, they're here. "Joe, Joe they're here."*

Chapter 2

Voice One. Honcho quiet? I hate it when that dog barks. Time to get unpacked and ready to dive. "Brian, you put up the tents while I put up the ramada."

Finally, we got all the stuff up. It's time to get in Joe's boat and go. Ah! I love the smell of the ocean.

Voice Two. **Why do I always have to be the one to put up the tents? Well, now that the tents are put up, let's go diving. I love to ride in the boat. Look, seals! I wish I could be like them. So wild, so free.**

Voice Three. *Why couldn't I go diving? Just because I don't have hands doesn't mean I can't swim.*

Chapter 3

Voice One. Finally, we are in the water. Crap, the visibility is terrible. Oh well, it's so relaxing down here that I wish I could stay forever. Pity the fools that are afraid of the water. They don't know what they are missing.

Voice Two. **At last, we are in the water. It's so peaceful down here. It's funny, out of the chaos of getting down here, it's all worth it for this one moment. If only more people could see how beautiful it is down here, they would always want to come down here.**

Voice Three. *Alright, that's it! I don't care what Joe says, next time I'm going with them. I wish I were human.*

Cindy's Narrative

Chapter 1

Voice One. Science fiction came that much closer to science fact recently, when Honda Motors Company introduced a two-legged robot that could walk and even do a simple fix-it job. The six-foot, four hundred and sixty-two pound "P-2" has two arms, two legs, squarish head, small platform feet, and resembles a man in a boxy space suit.

Voice Two. **As a man sat waiting for public transport, he watched cars fly over head and thought back to a newscast he had seen the previous evening. There had been a frightening scare at the Honda Motors Company. Apparently some "P-2" robot experiments had gone terribly wrong and the huge human-like robots had begun to run amuck.**

Voice Three. *People think of us as just some kind of machine, but we are so much more than that. Aside from the everyday experiments and small petty jobs, we do very human things, and have very human feelings.*

Chapter 2

Voice One. The "P-2" is sophisticated enough to decide for itself when to try to step over an obstacle, and when to look for a way around it. That allows it to do uncannily and seemingly human things such as finding a work site, pushing a cart to it, and tightening a loose bolt there—all without continuous radio control. It needs only a simple initial command. "P-2" can walk up or down stairs, forward or backward, and keep its balance if given a shove, even on a slope it hasn't been on before. Susumu

Tachi, a robotics professor at Tokyo University, likened it to the androids of science fiction. "A truly humanoid robot was always considered to be just a dream or a product of fiction, but this proves that it is reality," he said.

Voice Two. **The "P-2s" had suddenly become very destructive and acted in somewhat of a violent manner toward the robotics professors. The professors' brilliance in building such advanced, almost truly living things, had suddenly become a nightmare. Many compared it to a science fiction horror movie. One of the professors commented, "It has been a dream of ours to build something so sophisticated, but now I think I may have some regret."**

Voice Three. *We weren't trying to harm anyone, we just wanted a little attention. For one day something besides poking and prodding, the experiments, and tests. An intellectual game would have been fun. We didn't mean to cause all this commotion.*

Chapter 3

Voice One. Unlike the most frightening robots of science fiction, the "P-2" only does what it is told to do. It can be switched to radio control at any time, or it can simply be turned off. Honda said it will continue to try to make "P-2" more sophisticated and Honda said it will try to find more practical use for it. One challenge that Honda realizes is the need for "P-2" to have more stamina. "P-2's" batteries can only keep it running for fifteen minutes.

Voice Two. **The "P-2" problem was solved right after it transpired. The robot's batteries did not have any stamina, they only lasted fifteen minutes. However, even fifteen minutes can be crucial. Normally the professors could have been able to control the "P-2" manually, but for some odd and incomprehensible reason the override program failed. The robots will be disassembled . . .**

Voice Three. *The idea of frightening or hurting people never crossed our minds. We usually are very good about listening to the professors. We could not stand to be shut off and put in that damp closet for one more night. I guess, however, it was a mistake because now they are going to disassemble us.*

Michael's Narrative

Chapter 1

Voice One. It was the nineteen ninety-six school year. Everyday we practiced. Our coaches pushed us so much. We ran until we couldn't run anymore and yet we still got up and ran again. We changed that game. It's quarters double to eight and the teams were now one against eleven. The game was all mental. Some of us understood. Our coaches understood. They knew what we had to do.

Voice Two. **She is my niece and I love her. She frustrates me and I cry. There are times when I couldn't take it anymore, yet I did. I wanted to, I still do. She is so very beautiful.**

Voice Three. *Humpty Dumpty sat on a wall,*

Chapter Two

Voice One. We went three and eight that season. We pretended like we were still winners and that we played our best. Yet, in our hearts we all knew we could have done better. That was all we would have needed, to go an inch farther. To be a second faster.

Voice Two. She isn't here anymore. She died awhile ago. Her funeral was sad. The mourning lasted for weeks. I wish that I could have done more. Her hair was always a mess. I miss her.

Voice Three. *Humpty Dumpty had a great fall;*

Chapter 3

Voice One. Next year our season will be even better. We'll practice harder and longer than we ever did, yet now it is different. The opportunity is there. The doors are open. No one is asking us to step inside. We have to have the will, the desire. I have it. I now know what I must do.

I can.
I will.
I must.

Voice Two. We still think of her all the time. It's easier now. I think that re-membering is the important part. I remember most her trying to stand up and her falling. I know she is happy. I bet she can stand now.

Voice Three. *All the King's horses and all the King's men couldn't put Humpty Dumpty together again.*

CONCLUSION: SEARCH FOR REASON

I wanted students to discover not only the place of literature and oral history in our cultural lives but also that place in their personal lives. Additionally, I wanted to get to know this class. Because I had learned so much about Momaday and his culture through this book, I knew that this unit would improve my knowledge of my students. Once during this unit a student remarked that she could now see things from her parents' perspective. After much reflection and rewriting, I have discovered that my real reason for this unit may be the opportunity to write to learn more about each of my students. Listening to three voices from each student tends to open communication and improves one's analytical, creative, and problem-solving potential.

Finally, students come to school with a casual language register (Joos, 1969). This voice is often marginalized and rejected in the English class. The potential for students to create in this casual voice, something they can do in this unit, empowers them to read, think, respond, and create in other voices.

EXTENSION ACTIVITIES

1. Anderson uses the reader response journal as a writing-to-learn activity to produce a piece of public writing. Have you ever used the reader response journal? If so, describe your experience. If not, plan a unit that has the reader response journal as an integral part.

2. Anderson uses one concept viewed three ways as a writing-to-learn activity. Consider describing a person, place, event, or object in three different ways.

3. Use detective stories that describe the same crime from multiple perspectives.

4. Provide and elicit extension examples from newspaper accounts, movies, and magazines that reflect the weaving of voices.

5. Take a historical event and view it from multiple cultural perspectives. Discuss cause and effect, compare and contrast, and create historical fiction.

REFERENCES

Banks, J. (1997). "Multicultural Education: Characteristics and Goals." In J. Banks & C. Banks (Eds.) *Multicultural education: Issues and perspectives*. Needham Heights, MA: Allyn & Bacon.

Hall, A. (February 15, 1994). *Oral tradition*. Paper presented at the annual spring conference of the Department of English, University of Arizona, Tucson.

Joos, M. (1967). *The five clocks*. New York: Harcourt Brace Jovanovich.

Kaplan, R. B. (1984). Cultural thought patterns in intercultural education. In S. Mckay (Ed.), *Composing in a second language*. Rowley, MA: Newbury House.

Momaday, N. S. (1969). *The way to rainy mountain* . Albuquerque: University of New Mexico Press.

Nye, R. (1996). *Classic folktales from around the world*. London: Leopard.

Rosenblatt, L. (1983). *Literature as exploration*. New York: Modern Language Association.

FOR FURTHER READING

Anderson, R. (Ed.). (1989). *Elements of literature: Fourth course*. Orlando, FL: Holt, Rinehart & Winston.

Andrews, W. (Ed.). (1992). *African American literature: Voices in a tradition*. Orlando, FL: Holt, Rinehart & Winston.

Erdoes, R., & Ortiz, A. (1984). *American Indian myths and legends*. New York: Pantheon Books.

King, T. (1994). *Green grass, running water*. New York: Bantam Books.

Kovacs, E. (1994). *Writing across cultures: A handbook on writing poetry and lyrical prose*. Hillsboro, OR: Blue Heron.

Sexton, J. D. (Ed.). (1994). *Mayan folktales: Folklore from Lake Atitlan, Guatemala*. New York: Anchor Books.

ORAL TRADITION

The oral tradition is that process by which the myths, legends, tales, and lore of a people are formulated, communicated, and preserved in language by word of mouth, as opposed to writing. Or, it is a *collection* of such things. . . . [T]he matter of oral tradition suggests certain particularities of art and reality. Art, for example . . . involves an oral dimension which is based markedly upon such considerations as memorization, intonation, inflection, precision of statement, brevity, rhythm, pace, and dramatic effect. Moreover, myth, legend, and lore, according to our definitions of these terms, imply a separate and distinct order of reality. We are concerned here not so much with an accurate representation of actuality, but with the realization of the imaginative experience.

(Excerpts reprinted with permission from Momaday, N. S. (1969). Man made of words. In G. Hobson (Ed.), *Remembered Earth: An Anthology of Contemporary American Literature*. Albuquerque: University of New Mexico Press. pp. 162-173.

Teaching N. Scott Momaday's *The Way to Rainy Mountain* (Albuquerque: University of New Mexico Press, 1969).

Goals
- To explore how myth and reality interact to create or define a culture
- To discover what the place of literature and history are in our cultural lives

I. **Critical Approaches**
    A. *Reader response* allows for positive and negative reader reports to be explored relative to non-Indian/Indian, "literary," and "social science"

attitudes about defining and communicating contemporary literature by and about Indians.

Ask students to read the text and respond to general questions such as the following:
What is the predominant effect the text had on you?
Why do you think the text had that effect?
- Examine nature of text
- Examine nature of reader
What does your response tell you about yourself?

B. *Structure:* Look at function of intensity of the one-paragraph voices and mixtures and juxtapositions of genres.

The tripartite structure of the book includes three voices, each with a different origin, format, and methodology. These voices are just three ways of approaching a single topic, of saying similar or related things.

The stories are organized chronologically under the headings "The Setting Out," "The Going On," and "The Closing In." There is also an introduction and an epilogue. As the book progresses, the three voices merge and each voice takes on characteristics of narrative, descriptive, and personal writing.

First Voice	Storyteller, mythic exploration of Kiowa narratives of tribal or family origins.
Second Voice	Objective, intellectual, historian: purpose is to recount historical, anthropological, factual information. Parallels first voice's chronological development by offering facts, definitions, and descriptions derived from written sources.
Third Voice	Subjective, poet, private, reflective: recalls significant personal memories often from childhood. Less chronological. Tries to capture aspects of subject, tone, or mood of the other voices that are meaningful to the writer. Links to other voices through acts of memory, association, and imagination.

C. *Genre:* Text has been called autobiography, epic, poem, nonfiction, tragedy, verse, drama, sonnet, prose, vision, and creation hymn. Momaday calls it "lyrical prose" and "quintessential novels." This approach asks students to understand the characteristics of different genres.

D. *Myth:* Joseph Campbell writes of the collapse of traditional mythology and its displacement by creative mythology. The personal voice in Momaday links to the traditional one. Some critics posit that Momaday goes a step further than Campbell in showing continuity between two kinds of mythology (both are acts of imagination and both are capable of generating some kind of belief).

E. *Identity formation:* The search for identity can be examined within a journey motif, relationship of identity to place, concepts of animal and human life in defining ourselves, and individual and society.

The journey motif can be linked to the tripartite structure as students explore a topic in three voices, taking three journeys as well: imaginative, intellectual, and real.

F. *Imagery:* Grandmother images, horse images, dog images, landscape imagery, and so forth all serve to connect the sections of the text.

G. *Language:* The theme of power of language shows how names of people, mountains, rivers, and plants in the text embody the ability to deal with the world on reciprocal terms, to encode and transmit culture.

II. Sample Essay Assignment

A. Retell a story or a few interrelated myths (from oral or written sources). You may be exploring the origin of an idea in myth or legend. You may use novels, short stories, journals, and interviews. Form must be in concise, summarized style. Cite sources.
Or recall a significant landscape, person, object, or experiences (spiritualize the ordinary).

B. Research the main topic. Bring in historical facts or documentation related to the subject matter. Paraphrase and document research. If you wrote on a myth or legend, give a reasoned explanation for it. Emphasize definition and factual illustration. This voice will link the first and third voices together.

C. Bring together the symbols and themes found in the other voices and apply personal memories and observations. Explore further patterns, analogies, and associations developed in the other sections. Your task is to make personal meaning from the mythical and historical perspectives, showing how the traditions live in you.

D. Final essay must be three chapters exploring the topic from the three perspectives Momaday uses. Create a three-voiced structure, arranged in some logical order (e.g., chronological, geographical, or thematic). Include an introduction and an epilogue.

12

BRIDGING THE GAPS AND SPACES AMONG LEARNERS IN A WRITING-TO-LEARN CLASSROOM

HARRIET ARZU SCARBOROUGH

TUCSON UNIFIED SCHOOL DISTRICT

ABSTRACT

Gaps and spaces among learners and between teachers and learners in classrooms are some of the consequences of the increasing diversity of the U.S. population and the great disparity between the relatively affluent and the very poor. These gaps and spaces must be eliminated if students are to achieve at their highest potential. Creating a community of learners in the classroom can help eliminate those gaps and spaces. Findings from brain research likewise show the need to create a nurturing environment in the classroom—an environment of low threat and high challenge. A few writing-to-learn activities that can be used to create community and build this kind of an environment are delineated.

Breaking through Barriers

One year I found myself teaching a social studies class in a middle school. Although it is fairly typical to find oneself teaching outside of one's area of expertise in my school district's middle schools, this was my first experience after six years at Pistor Junior High School (as it was known at the time). I was also going on my seventh year of working in an American junior high school, a challenge I had taken with trepidation because of the horror stories I had heard and read about American public schools. With a background in the insulated parochial school system of Belize, Central America, I found my nightmare coming close to reality at Pistor that first semester. After the initial vacillation, however, I adjusted, retooled, and was sold on junior high students. Six years later, I could not imagine teaching any other age group.

I was as different from my students as one could imagine. They were mostly European American, Latino American, Native American (just about all the students of junior high age from the nearby Yaqui Reservation came to Pistor), and African American. Of African Belizean descent, I surprised my students every year by speaking Spanish to them. Perhaps because of who I am, I readily saw the gaps and spaces between my students and me and the gaps and spaces among them. I recognized that somehow these gaps and spaces had to be bridged if we were to become a learning community. I never took for granted that that learning community would manifest itself magically. I did not have ready-made answers; I knew, however, that I had to work at establishing rapport with my students. So I used what I knew best—writing and literature. I scrounged around for writing activities that would help us get to know each other better. And every year it got a little easier.

Reputation has a way of either clearing the path or blocking it. After six years of teaching language arts at Pistor, six years of an unsullied reputation of being a "gentle" teacher, I was not only ready for a challenge but also prepared to be accommodating. Therefore when my principal approached me to ask if I would be willing to teach a class of seventh-grade social studies, I said yes. Little did I realize that my reputation would prove to be an obstacle this time around.

With the arrogance of an English teacher, I figured if one could teach students reading and writing, one could teach them social studies. And I was right, to an extent. The social studies class was a semester long, and during the first semester I taught a language arts–social studies block. I remember liking the social studies textbook because it provided reading and writing strategies and suggested some very innovative ideas for making the course relevant and authentic. My students participated in activity after activity, and I gloried in the fact that I was providing them the best learning experience they had ever had.

What I was not prepared for, however, was the reputation I was acquiring. Very quietly the word had been circulating that I was a hard taskmaster who "worked students to death" and that the new students I would have for the second semester were not looking forward to being in my class. And, indeed, when they came in, they were sullen and not very cooperative. This was a new experience for me. I have never been one of those teachers who relish being feared by students; I need to be able to have rapport with students if I am going to teach them. I needed to be able to connect with these seventh graders at the heart level before I could connect with them at the brain or mind level. Out of desperation, I turned to a tool I felt could help—writing.

I had the students acquire a notebook for the class, and before the end of every class I engaged them in a writing-to-learn activity.

> What are you having problems understanding in class so far?
> Write three things you learned today. How do you feel about what you learned?
> Having learned about _____ today, what else would you like to learn?
> What do you think of the Broncos' chances at the next Superbowl?

I collected the journals and wrote a response to each student every day. It was amazing to see the gradual transformation of the class. After three weeks, I did not find the need to respond every day. My students had become quite pleasant and very cooperative. I made sure that I gauged the amount of work I gave them, and that class became one that I remember quite fondly. What I remember most, though, is the power of nonthreatening, expressive, and informal writing—in other words, writing to learn, to break through barriers, and to foster that connection so pivotal to learning in a community.

What teachers instinctively have known educational theorists have given voice to. In his book *Actual Minds, Possible Worlds,* published in 1986, Jerome Bruner recounted his changing perspective regarding student learning:

> I have come increasingly to recognize that most learning in most settings is a communal activity, a sharing of culture. It is not just that the child must make his knowledge his own, but that he must make it his own in a community of those who share his sense of belonging to a culture. (p. 127)

The community defined by a shared culture that Bruner speaks of is the community I was in search of with my students at Pistor Junior High. In such a community students feel comfortable enough to risk learning. The shared culture here is not a particular ethnicity. Instead, it is an environment of equitable acceptance into which we bring our diversity. The varied experiences that we bring with us are shared and used as bridges to our new experiences.

THE NEED TO BUILD COMMUNITY: CHANGING DEMOGRAPHICS

The notion of a shared culture as a necessary setting for powerful learning and the notion that learning entails taking ownership of knowledge among others who have much in common are as imperative today as they were in 1986. The increasing ethnic, cultural, and linguistic diversity in the United States and the increasing poverty among children are demographic factors that make a shared culture as a setting for powerful learning an especially critical issue for schools and educators in the twenty-first century.

No one disputes that the children of the United States are becoming more diverse. The demographic predictions of yesteryear are today's realities. Estimates for the year 2000 is that 36% of students in American schools are children of color. (O'Hare 2000). This number is predicted to increase to 46 percent by 2020 (Banks, 1997). Together these students will represent diverse ethnic, cultural, and linguistic backgrounds. In some parts of the United States what used to be termed minority is now in reality majority.

These changing demographics have major implications for the way we create conditions in schools to allow for students to develop to their fullest potential. Cummins (1996) asserts that schools need to acknowledge the reality of cultural diversity in the United States and throughout the world. As a result there is an urgent need for school programs that promote sensitivity to, and understanding of, diverse cultural perspectives. He urges that cultural diversity be seen as a resource rather than an obstacle.

Freeman and Freeman (1994) likewise indicate that school is a place between two worlds for most students—the world of their homes and the world of the larger society. Particularly for culturally and linguistically diverse students, school may represent a very different world. Some students have difficulty navigating between these two worlds, depending on the instruction and attitudes they encounter. Moreover, too often the responsibility for navigating the chasm between these two worlds is left totally to the students. Overcrowded classrooms that prevent teachers from providing students with much-needed individual attention, the employment of just one method of instruction based on the assumption that "one size fits all," and the attitude of "I taught it; they didn't learn it" are factors that contribute to the gap that separates these worlds. The consequences of such a gap include a feeling of disenfranchisement and disillusionment with the system. Eventually, students may drop out.

Another demographic issue with major implications for educators is the increasing numbers of students living in poverty. Both Banks (1997) and Cummins (1996) attest to the continuing widening of the gap between the relatively affluent members of U.S. society and the very poor. Women and children make up a large percentage of the low-income population. Banks (1997) points out that in 1995 about 20.6 percent of the children in the United States lived in poverty. Bennett (1995) notes that an excessive number of ethnic minority and economically poor students are dropping out of schools, suspended, or expelled, and those who remain are achieving far below their potential.

Researchers (Association for Supervision and Curriculum Development Advisory Panel on Improving Student Achievement, 1995) caution that if America is to educate all its children to higher levels, there needs to be a major paradigm shift in our beliefs about the way students learn. Instead of requiring students to adapt to the prevalent teaching practices, instructional materials, and assessment instruments, schools must adapt to their clientele and see the entire community as a resource for learning. Central to this paradigm shift is the need to expend effort to create a community that fosters learning in classrooms.

The increasing diversity of the student population and the consequences of poverty make it more challenging to effect Bruner's (1986) shared culture in the classroom, an approach so necessary for developing students to their fullest potential. Complicating matters are confusing and conflicting views and attitudes that many people continue to cultivate. One attitude that still prevails is that all minority experiences are the same. Minority for our purposes here refers to African Americans, Asian Americans, Latino Americans, and Native Americans. Victor Villanueva, a professor of rhetoric at Washington State University, distinguished between the experience of the minority and the experience of the immigrant in an article he wrote in 1987. Immigrants come to the United States to look for a better life. Because they have a choice about whether to come (even if that choice may be between living freely or being persecuted), they more readily abandon their old cultural practices to assimilate into the mainstream culture. The minority, on the other hand, has had no choice in coming to the United States and struggles to slough off the effects of slavery, colonization, or conquest. The status of the minority is exacerbated by the visible differences of pigmentation and language.

Critics of multicultural education look at programs designed to raise the achievement of minority students (which lags considerably behind the achievement of European American students) and wonder why *those* people need special consideration when "my grandfather came here from Italy, Poland, Croatia, Germany (or wherever) not knowing English and look at what he was able to achieve without any special programs!" Bennett (1995) points out that the many nonnative speakers who do well in our schools provide evidence that students who put forth the effort can succeed. Ignored in this view, she notes, are the different histories that language minority students have experienced.

In a keynote address given at a National Council of Teachers of English (NCTE) convention, Walter Mosley discussed his book *Always Outnumbered, Always Outgunned* (1998), a very real story about the gaps and spaces that contribute to our conflicting ideas about each other. He spoke of the remoteness between lives that is reflective of the increasing polarization between those with homes, jobs, and money and those with none. Unfortunately, this increasing polarization characterizes our schools and our classrooms. So it becomes the schools' responsibility to devise ways to bridge that gap and eliminate those spaces that get in the way of student achievement. If learning is a communal activity, then deliberate steps need to be taken to create a learning community in which all our diverse students have a sense of belonging. Can teachers rise to the challenge?

THE NEED TO BUILD COMMUNITY IN THE CLASSROOM: BRAIN RESEARCH

Proponents of brain-based learning (Armstrong, 1998; Caine & Caine, 1997; Jensen, 1998; Olsen, 1995) also advocate creating a nurturing community for learning. This nurturing community is a brain-compatible environment at the heart of which is a strong relationship between the teacher and his or her students. Olsen (1995) cautions that if students do not feel that they have a relationship with their teacher, the classroom becomes for them just one more environment in which they feel disconnected, uninvolved, and uncaring about the welfare of the group. Gusmán (1994) states it succinctly with her motto: "Everything in the classroom is about relationships y nada mas (and nothing else)."

Gusmán's motto may appear simplistic; however, if one considers how much of our self-concept is developed in classrooms, one must agree with her. Gusmán goes on to say that a teacher cannot connect with students at the cerebral level unless there is first a connection at the heart level. This statement is rooted in the work of brain researchers who in their extensive study of the brain have provided educators with some insight into its functioning and the implications for teaching and learning.

Caine and Caine (1997) have identified twelve mind-brain principles. The following five are particularly germane to the need to create a nurturing community in the classroom for effective learning:

1. **The brain is a social brain.** Throughout our lives, our brains (or minds) change in response to our engagement with others. Learners need to be seen as integral parts of the larger social system.

2. **The search for meaning is innate.** We are constantly trying to make sense of our experiences, and this pursuit is lifelong. This search includes the need to develop relationships and a sense of identity. This principle points to the need to build community in the classroom.

3. **Emotions are critical to patterning.** What is learned is influenced and organized by emotions and the need for social interactions. This principle reinforces and supports the importance of connecting at both the heart and the brain level for meaningful learning to occur and the need to ensure a nurturing and collaborative environment in the classroom.

4. **Learning involves both focused attention and peripheral perception.** The brain absorbs both information of which it is directly aware and information beyond the immediate focus of attention. This principle points to the fact that teachers' inner attitudes and beliefs have a powerful impact on students. Students can perceive teachers' attitudes toward them whether or not they are stated.

5. **Complex learning is enhanced by challenge and inhibited by threat.** The brain (or mind) learns best when it is challenged and in an environment that encourages taking risks. When threat is perceived, the brain (or mind) "downshifts," becomes less flexible, and reverts to primitive attitudes and procedures. An environment of low threat and high challenge is essential for optimal learning.

These principles affirm the need to build community to foster strong relationships in the classroom and point to three major attributes of the setting that foster meaningful learning: (1) students learn best when they are important members of the classroom community, (2) students learn best when they have a positive relationship with a teacher, and (3) students learn best in a classroom in which they are challenged and feel safe and comfortable enough to take risks.

THE NEED TO BUILD COMMUNITY IN THE CLASSROOM: STUDENTS' PERSPECTIVE

Students also appear to reinforce the three attributes listed in the previous section. At a symposium on teaching and learning in secondary schools held at Catalina Foothills High School in Tucson, Arizona, a panel of students replaced the usual keynote speaker. The five student panelists were asked to respond to two questions: "Describe the most powerful experience you have had at this school" and "If you could change one thing in this school, what would it be?" Most of the educators attending this symposium were surprised to see that in addressing the questions, four out of five students focused not on academics but on relationships between teacher and student that made learning possible and enjoyable. One student described her experience in learning geometry. She said that she was able to do well in what she considered a very demanding subject because her teacher made her laugh. Later at lunch as we discussed the student panel, Ginny, a math teacher in attendance, recounted that when the student mentioned her math class as the one that had had the most impact on her, Ginny had expected to hear of a methodology that she could add to her repertoire. Although Ginny was a little disappointed not to walk away with that math strategy that might transform her classroom, her disappointment was tempered by the validation she felt when she heard that the magic had been the remarkable rapport between teacher and students.

THE NEED TO BUILD COMMUNITY IN THE CLASSROOM: EDUCATORS' PERSPECTIVE

The need for teachers to establish rapport in the classroom is not a new one. Even before educators could put a label on it, effective teachers have instinctively felt the need to connect with students at the heart level as a pathway to the cerebral cortex. In the context of the classroom, the relationship becomes broader to include student-student relationships and teacher-student relationships. Many educators (Kirby & Kuykendall, 1991; Kovalik, 1991; Zemelman & Daniels, 1988) advocate the use of community-building activities in the classroom. Because we now know the importance of positive relationships in the classroom, we no longer have to leave their evolution to chance. We can orchestrate experiences in our classrooms to foster the development of positive relationships.

WHY WRITING-TO-LEARN ACTIVITIES?

In responding to this need, many educators have developed activities for the purpose of community building in the classroom. These activities are sometimes set up in a progressive way designed to move students from becoming acquainted with each other to working collaboratively (Gibbs & Allen, 1987). However, one step missing from these activities has been a direct connection to other classroom activities. These community-building activities seem to stand apart from the writing lesson, the social studies lesson, the math lesson, the science lesson, and so forth. Because these activities seem separate from the subject matter being taught, high school teachers, especially, have been reluctant to spend precious classroom time on what they term "touchy-feely" activities.

So herein lies the dilemma. We do not want to leave community building to chance, yet we do not want to spend precious classroom time orchestrating activities that seem peripheral to instruction. So what can a secondary teacher do? Certainly, writing-to-learn activities can resolve this dilemma for teachers. Writing to learn has many attributes that make it especially useful as a community-building tool in the classroom. These attributes include the employment of expressive language, the way some of the activities are designed specifically to foster connections, and the ease with which writing-to-learn activities can be shared.

In most cases expressive language is the vehicle for writing-to-learn activities. Expressive language, according to Britton (1975), is language that is very close to the self. This informal language is the language that we use to talk or to write freely about experiences, feelings, beliefs, and understanding. The use of expressive language in writing-to-learn activities makes the activities nonthreatening and fairly easy for students to do, and the sharing of the writing is a natural extension.

Another reason for using writing-to-learn activities to build community in the classroom is that some writing-to-learn activities are designed to foster connections among learners. When we engage students in activities such as the fire drill or quickwrite, we are usually trying to direct instruction at Vygotsky's (1978) zone of proximal development. In other words, we are determining what individual students bring to the learning situation in order to find a common connection for the new learning among the class members. If we follow Vygotsky's postulation, then we want to ensure that instruction is not aimed at the "ripe function," where students may be bored, or at the "green function," where they might be frustrated, but at the "ripening function," where someone a bit more knowledgeable can help them on to the new knowledge. That "ripening function" is the zone of proximal development. Aiming instruction at the zone of proximal development is easier to do while working with students individually; in a classroom of thirty, it becomes more challenging. Writing-to-learn activities (such as the fire drills and quickwrites mentioned previously) that activate schemata (mental files) can help determine a common starting point for instruction that can benefit the whole class and in the process also build community.

A third reason for using writing to learn is the inherent quality of the strategies themselves that makes them easy to do and easy to share. Fire drills and quickwrites are strategies that celebrate students' contributions. These two strategies work well as an introduction to a lesson, although they could also be used quite effectively as a review at the end of a lesson or in the middle to check understanding. First, two or three concepts are identified from a lesson or a reading, and students are asked to write everything they know about each concept for about four to five minutes without stopping. If they get stuck, they can write the term over and over again until they find something to say. Students are encouraged to list, write phrases, write complete sentences, or write complete paragraphs. In sharing their writing students can read the whole piece or just a phrase or two. I am often pleasantly surprised during the times I have used the fire drill or quickwrite strategies with students at their willingness to share their writing, particularly when some of these students are in the process of developing proficiency in English.

BUILDING COMMUNITY IN THE CLASSROOM WITH WRITING-TO-LEARN ACTIVITIES

Until the summer that I attended the Southern Arizona Writing Project (SAWP) I had no idea what it was like to be a member of a community of learners. The Southern Arizona Writing Project is part of the National Writing Project, which has been instrumental in helping teachers kindergarten through college become better teachers of writing. During the six weeks of that summer, Margaret and Jim, the instructors, created for us an environment in which we felt comfortable taking risks. Our classmates took us through several writing experiences, and we cooperated willingly, always looking forward to hearing or reading what colleagues had written in response to a writing prompt. We solicited and offered feedback, and at the end of the six weeks we had become a very cohesive group.

A few years later I participated in the Summer Institute for Writing and Thinking across the Curriculum. This summer writing institute is a component of the University of Arizona Writing Improvement Program created by Dr. Roseann Gonzalez to improve the writing of minority students. Fifteen middle and high school teachers and forty-five high school students participated. This time my writing response group consisted of five high school students from all over Arizona. That first week of the three-week institute, John Rabuck, the instructor, led us through a number of writing activities designed to help us get to know each other. Because we were going to be sharing our writing with each other and learning from each other, John knew how important it was for us to become a community of learners. Allocating a few days to build community proved to be a wise investment. We wrote much that summer, learned quite a bit, had a wonderful time, and returned to our classrooms renewed.

My experience at the summer writing institute as well as my experience at the writing project may seem idealized. But I was convinced that such an environment— which contributed to my powerful learning experiences—could be actualized in a middle school or high school classroom. Those experiences helped me see the important function that writing can serve in the establishment of an environment that is conducive to learning. Therefore, during the first few weeks in my middle and high school language arts classes I immerse my students in writing-to-learn activities specifically for building community.

Sometime during the first week of the school year I introduce students to the *bio poem* (Gere, 1985).

Line 1	First name
Line 2	Four traits that describe character
Line 3	Relative ("brother," "sister," "daughter," etc.) of _____
Line 4	Lover of _____ (list three things or people)
Line 5	Who feels _____ (three items)
Line 6	Who needs _____ (three items)
Line 7	Who fears _____ (three items)
Line 8	Who gives _____ (three items)
Line 9	Who would like to see _____ (three items)
Line 10	Resident of _____
Line 11	Last name

(Reprinted, with permission, from Gere, A. R. [1985]. *Roots in the sawdust: Writing to learn in the disciplines*. Urbana, IL: National Council of Teachers of English.)

This pattern poem contains prompts that allow students to provide biographical information about their subject. I begin by introducing students to the pattern, and then we collaboratively write a bio poem on a public figure or a figure from fairy tales. We have written bio poems about movie stars, athletes, and fairy tale characters such as Jack and the Beanstalk and Cinderella. By the time we are finished with this collaboration, it is time to focus on the students themselves. I ask them to generate a list with the following information:

1. Favorite foods
2. Least favorite foods
3. Favorite movies or television shows
4. Favorite musical groups or persons
5. Favorite sports figures or teams
6. Favorite places
7. Favorite people
8. Favorite possessions
9. Favorite memories
10. Favorite pastimes
11. Best qualities
12. Worst qualities

13. Worst fears

14. Important goals

The brainstorming activity of *listing* is a writing-to-learn strategy that activates schemata and provides connections between students' background knowledge and what is to be taught. When students are involved in generating a list, clustering the list to make connections, and then sharing what they have composed, they learn from each other and they feel esteemed because every small contribution is accepted without criticism. Students next share this list with someone in the classroom. During this time the classroom, initially quiet, goes from a quiet hum to a more animated gathering, as the gaps and spaces among classroom members become smaller.

The next step is to have each student use the information that has been shared and the pattern that has been discussed to write a bio poem about his or her new friend. Introducing the new friend to the class by reading the bio poem out loud is a natural progression to this activity. Following is Reneé's example:

> Natalia
> Trusting, outgoing, nice and talkative
> Sister of Vivian
> Lover of food, animals, ocean
> Who feels lazy in the morning, hungry, and bored at home
> Who needs to study more, go out more, and a car
> Who fears drowning, going blind, and losing a body part
> Who gives attention to people, advice, and help
> Who would like to see the future, people getting along, and Hawaii
> Resident of Tucson, AZ
> Cardona

I have found Gere's (1985) bio poem pattern to be one that students find quite accessible. I also like the manner in which powerful ideas can be packed in the simple format of the bio poem. Other pattern poems that I introduce to my students during the first few weeks of the school year include the *"I Am"* poem and Hise's (1980) *"Mood"* and *"I Do Not Understand"* poems.

I Am

I am (two special characteristics you have)
I wonder (something you are actually curious about)
I hear (an imaginary sound)
I see (an imaginary sight)
I want (an actual desire)
I am (the first line of the poem repeated)

I pretend (something you actually pretend to do)
I feel (a feeling about something imaginary)
I touch (an imaginary touch)
I worry (something that makes you worry)

I cry (something that makes you very sad)
I am (the first line of the poem repeated)

I understand (something you know is true)
I say (something you believe in)
I dream (something you actually dream about)
I try (something you really make an effort about)
I hope (something you actually hope for)
I am (the first line of the poem repeated)

Mood Poem

a. State a mood.

b. Write three things the mood is not (two stated briefly, one stated as a comparison).

c. Switch to a statement of what the mood is.

d. State three more descriptions of the mood.

(Reprinted, with permission, from Hise, J. [1980]. Writing poetry: More than a frill. *English Journal, 69* [8], 19–21.)

I'm sad
Not crying sobbing sad
Not lose my best friend sad
Not break my leg can't play soccer sad
But just all over can't put my finger quite on it sad
Sad that summer vacation is over
Sad that I didn't do all that I wanted to
Sad that I'll have to wait another whole year for another summer

I Do Not Understand Poem

a. Begin the poem with "I do not understand."

b. List three things you do not understand about the world or people.

c. Name the thing you do not understand most of all.

d. End with an example of something you *do* understand.

(Reprinted, with permission, from Hise, J. [1980]. Writing poetry: More than a frill. *English Journal, 69* [8], 19–21.)

I do not understand
Why it is so hot
Why birds fly
Why airplanes fly
But most of all I do not understand
Why life can be so unfair
My cousin made the football team without much effort
And I have to wait a whole year to try out for cheerleading
What I do understand is
I'll have plenty of time to prepare

I introduce these patterns one at a time, with students writing these poems about themselves. Sharing the poems in small or large groups helps them get to know each other better and fosters a sense of community. Generally, every student is able to complete these writing activities because the patterns are fairly easy to follow, and the students are writing about a very familiar subject matter—themselves. Finally, this is a very low risk activity for them because there are no wrong answers. Sharing in pairs or in small groups also removes the threat of facing the whole class so early in the school year.

WRITING TO LEARN: A FOCUS ON PROCESS

I suffered a subtle putdown at the hands of a colleague one day when she saw my students' writing displayed in my classroom. She remarked, "I was thinking how creative Harriet's students were, writing all those poems about literary characters. I didn't realize that they were just following a formula." What was lost on my colleague is that whereas she was focusing on the product, I make the process important in my classroom. What I could have told her is that writing a formulaic or pattern poem is a means to an end, not the end itself.

Writing a bio poem, a Mood poem, an "I Do Not Understand" poem, or an "I Am" poem can be a step in a series of activities leading to a final piece of writing or it can be a community-building activity designed to help students get to know themselves better. Or writing any one of these pattern poems can be just that, an opportunity for students to interact with the subject matter as they try to make sense of the information they are encountering. At any rate, what brings me satisfaction is seeing my students later make that choice to write a pattern poem to help them process information from other subject areas. When I see this behavior, I feel that I am following Freire's (1989) recommendation that the goal of literacy instruction should be to help students become independent thinkers, not regurgitators of facts. Students will find it easier to remember information about Zora, Odysseus, or Última if they write a pattern poem about one of them than if they were asked to memorize some decontextualized facts. When used as writing-to-learn activities, pattern or formulaic poems are nonthreatening activities for students. The formulas remove for them the anxiety of looking at a blank piece of paper and agonizing about where to begin.

STUDENTS DEVELOPING PROFICIENCY IN ENGLISH

Educators always seem to be looking for a panacea, even though deep down we know no such thing exists. On the other hand, we know that even though using writing as a tool for learning may not be a panacea, it can serve as a powerful approach to instruction and learning. I am a proponent of writing as a tool for learning because of its many uses. The theories that undergird the use of writing to learn speak to the needs of all learners but particularly the needs of students developing proficiency in English. Writing-to-learn activities tap students' background knowledge, helping them make connections between new and old knowledge. Writing-to-learn activities can be used to develop a community of learners in the classroom. As the community develops, the gaps that occur among class members are bridged, establishing an environment in which students' emerging voices can be nurtured and celebrated.

CONCLUSION

The growing cultural, ethnic, and linguistic diversity in our schools and the widening of the gap between the very poor and the relatively wealthy populations in the United States contribute to the distances among students and distances between teachers and students. If we agree with Bruner that to take ownership of their learning students need to be among those who share their sense of belonging, then we will heed the findings of brain-based learning theorists that positive relationships help to create a sense of belonging. These positive relationships do not always evolve by chance. Therefore, it is incumbent on teachers to take deliberate steps to create a learning community in the classroom. Writing-to-learn activities can be used for this purpose. Writing to learn can be used to encourage open exploration and discovery in a community of inquiry and in the process foster communal learning.

EXTENSION ACTIVITIES

1. Write one of the pattern poems illustrated in this chapter. First write one about yourself and then write one about a character in a book you are reading. What are your observations about what worked and what did not? How did writing the poem affect what you remember about the character?

2. Make a list of other community-building activities that you have used in your classroom. How are they similar to or different from the ones discussed in this chapter?

3. Describe the demographics of your school. What are the implications for the kind of learning environment that you want to create in your classroom?

REFERENCES

Armstrong, T. (1998). *Awakening genius in the classroom.* Alexandria, VA: Association for Supervision and Curriculum Development.

Association for Supervision and Curriculum Development Advisory Panel on Improving Student Achievement. (1995). Barriers to good instruction. In Robert Cole (Ed.), *Everybody's children: Diverse teaching strategies for diverse learners.* Alexandria, VA: Association for Supervision and Curriculum Development.

Banks, J. (1997). Preface. In J. Banks & C. Banks (Eds.), *Multicultural education: Issues and perspectives* (3rd ed.). Needham Heights, MA: Allyn & Bacon.

Bennett, C. (1995). *Comprehensive multicultural education: Theory and practice* (3rd ed.). Needham Heights, MA: Allyn & Bacon.

Britton, J., Burgess, T., McLeod, A. & Rosen, H. (1975) *The development of writing abilities.* (pp. 11–18). London: Macmillan.

Bruner, J. (1986). *Actual minds, possible worlds.* Cambridge, MA: Harvard University Press.

Caine, R., & Caine, G. (1997). *Education on the edge of possibility.* Alexandria, VA: Association for Supervision and Curriculum Development.

Cummins, J. (1996). *Negotiating identities: Education for empowerment in a diverse society.* Ontario, CA: California Association for Bilingual Education.

Freire, P. (1989). *Pedagogy of the oppressed.* New York: Continuum.

Freeman, D., & Freeman, Y. (1994). *Between worlds: Access to second language acquisition.* Portsmouth, NH: Heinemann.

Gere, A. R. (1985). *Roots in the sawdust: Writing to learn in the disciplines.* Urbana, IL: National Council of Teachers of English.

Gibbs, J., & Allen, A. (1987). *Tribes.* Santa Rosa, CA: Center Source Publications.

Gusmán, J. (1994). "Inclusion Activities" Presentation at Integrated Thematic Instruction Institute, Granlibakken, NV.

Hise, J. (1980). Writing poetry: More than a frill. *English Journal, 69*(8), 19–21.

Jensen, E. (1998). *Teaching with the brain in mind.* Alexandria, VA: Association for Supervision and Curriculum Development.

Kirby, D., & Kuykendall, C. (1991). *Mind matters: Teaching for thinking.* Portsmouth, NH: Boynton/Cook.

Kovalik, S. (1991). *ITI: The model.* Kent, WA: Susan Kovalik & Associates.

Mosley, W. (1998). *Always outnumbered, always outgunned.* New York: W. W. Norton.

O'Hare, W. (2000). The overlooked undercount: Children missed in the decennial census. www.aecf.org/kidscount/census.pdf. Annie E. Casey Fdn.

Olsen, K. (1995). *Synergy: Transforming America's high schools through integrated thematic instruction.* Kent, WA: Susan Kovalik & Associates.

Villanueva, V. (1987). Whose voice is it anyway? Rodriguez' speech in retrospect. *English Journal 76*(8), 17–21.

Vygotsky, L. (1978). *Mind in society: The development of higher psychological processes.* Cambridge, MA: Harvard University Press.

Zemelman, S., & Daniels, H. (1988). *A community of writers: Teaching writing in the junior and senior high school.* Portsmouth, NH: Heinemann.

13

MAKING THE TRANSITION FROM HIGH SCHOOL TO UNIVERSITY WRITING ACROSS THE CURRICULUM

YVONNE MERRILL

UNIVERSITY OF ARIZONA

ABSTRACT

This chapter focuses on the common thread that links writing across the curriculum (WAC) between high school and university—writing as thinking in progress made visible. It provides heuristic questions for doing rhetorical analyses of context, text, and discourse communities for helping student writers appeal to different disciplinary audiences and demonstrate their academic knowledge and critical thinking effectively.

Having made the transition myself from high school WAC director to university WAC coordinator, I have discovered that, by and large, successful high school WAC programs have more faculty buy-in and coherence than do those at large universities. Of course, this difference is due to the greater size and complexity of the university structure, but it also has to do with the goals for WAC initiatives and the understanding about writing that the implementers hold. Important similarities, however, link WAC programs across these levels. They both emphasize writing as a mode of thinking.

The difference between them seems to be shaping up as an emphasis on writing to *understand* concepts at the secondary level and writing to *create* and *refine* concepts at the university level. This difference in emphasis reinforces our suspicions that thinking is a developmental skill influenced by and reflected in the language for concepts we are able to use. The effectiveness of our language is largely determined by the amount of verbal rehearsal we have in each new learning context: the more intellectually sophisticated and demanding the context, the more elaborated our language for the concepts becomes, provided we use and practice that particular language as much as possible.

The Importance of Writing as Thinking Made Visible

What both levels of WAC have in common is the centrality of writing to cognition and its role in conceptualizing. What we can articulate, we understand. What we cannot articulate, we have not grasped in a way we can use it. Language provides the abstract labels for ideas that we can then manipulate in our heads. Like mathematical symbols, words represent things and allow us to think about them, juxtapose them, relate them to each other, analyze them, interpret them, and even change their meanings. Without precision in language, we have only inchoate *feelings,* not clear *ideas*. What faculty and students at both levels come to WAC not understanding is that we do not think first and then merely transcribe those ideas onto paper. Unclear writing is unclear thinking. Writing is thinking made visible and always thinking *in progress,* subject to revision. There are no "final versions" of thinking.

The focus of high school WAC programs for the past fifteen years has been to raise student and faculty awareness of writing as a thinking tool, and the thrust of most programs is primarily to have students write—or write more—about course content and their personal relations to it. Classes that did not provide opportunities for students to write anything beyond short answers to study guide and test questions have added writing-to-learn activities to these traditional writing-to-demonstrate-learning activities. Ungraded, peer-reviewed, revised writing has become the new norm for classroom writing experiences. Faculty have shared and practiced activities such as those Anne Ruggles Gere described in *Roots in the Sawdust,* which has been a particularly helpful resource for teachers in departments other than English. The *process* has been valued almost as much as *product* because the learning it facilitates is the goal.

As my colleague Anne-Marie Hall has discussed in Chapter 2, we have to understand when enough writing to learn has taken place that students can then write effectively to demonstrate their learning for evaluation. At this point, both criteria for the text and the thinking it embodies must meet the standards for "public" texts of both the reviewer and the discipline, the conventions of the discourse community. In Chapter 2, Hall notes that, in the portfolios high school students submit for first-year composition placement, we see a noticeable disparity in the quality of thinking between the pieces from English classes and those from disciplines other than English. We have to attribute this phenomenon to the students not having enough opportunity to "rehearse" course concepts to have internalized them in their own language for abstractions in order to perform complex mental operations on them, such as synthesis, analysis, interpretation, or application.

At the university level, written products are highly valued and critically scrutinized, often for linguistic control and genre appropriateness, but writing remains largely an invisible activity. Though writing is the foremost activity of all academicians' professional lives, academicians rarely reflect on their process and never examine the theoretical commonalities that link writing across disciplines as an intellectual activity in its own right; they seem to prefer to think of their own discourse conventions as highly idiosyncratic ways to share their thinking and new information in their fields. They often believe their field's conventions for language, forms, and voice bear little similarity to the writing of other fields. They value written products for the thought they convey and are usually unconscious of the specific written conventions for conveying it—except for surface linguistic features. That is why both high school and college writing faculty need to raise these issues to students' awareness: what kind of thinking they must be able to articulate effectively and how the particular field expects it to be articulated. They need writing instruction that will give them necessary analytic skills to understand these rhetorical criteria and meet them.

DILEMMA: EXPANDING ROLE OF RHETORICAL CONTEXTS

What is even more problematic is that only now are academicians questioning the notion that the principal writing goal for their students is to help them write like other academicians. But practitioners in the professions and careers to which university graduates aspire are telling universities that the writing of their university-trained employees is ineffective and inappropriate in the workplace. As with students' exposure to the new writing contexts of university discourse communities, their introduction into the professional world of work also requires them to write in yet-unfamiliar contexts.

A useful analogy for understanding the real mission behind WAC programs at both levels is the foreign language analogy. In equipping students with the language for things and ideas and giving them opportunities to practice, we are helping them approximate the style and authority of "native speakers" in the discourses they are trying to participate in. We want them to know and use the ideas in the same way as the experts. Those who have taught second languages understand just how complex the act of imitation is in learning another language. We not only have to find precisely the right words for what we have to say but also attend to how native speakers say those words—their intonation, their use of politeness forms, the logic of their presentation, and so forth. In giving students tools to write in the languages of the various subjects they study, we have to be as deliberate and direct as a second-language teacher in teaching these other linguistic features. But, more importantly, until they speak like the natives, students do not understand the ideas as the natives do. We know that many complex concepts just do not "translate."

So what we at the university level are really trying to accomplish with our WAC initiatives is to give student writers the strategies that will help them move smoothly through, and write effectively to think, in the enormously expanded range of rhetorical contexts they now face. And these contexts are not the same contexts they will later face as they make the transition from university to workplace. Therefore, the job of writing across the disciplines at the university level is to identify both the thinking skills and the writing strategies that carry over from one writing situation and task to another. We need to know what cognitive abilities help students construct new knowledge in the disciplines they study and how they can adapt their writing strategies and practice them to meet the multiple constraints in every new context.

Our faculty development workshops at the university are attempting to identify the *specific thinking* that students have to demonstrate to succeed in all their classes and to help faculty understand that the complex thinking that goes into the writing process is very similar to the thinking required in the study of other fields. We accomplish these goals by showing them our critical thinking skills and how the faculty themselves actually apply them when writing texts to fit their own rhetorical contexts. In working with general education faculty, we have discovered the thinking skills valued in the large curricular areas of humanities and art, science and technology, and social and behavioral sciences. (Students must take course work in each of these domains of knowledge, as well as classes in the foundational subjects of mathematics, composition, and foreign language.)

The same thinking skills are sought by all these disciplines, but each tries to help students practice them in ways peculiar to the particular discourse community. For example, to study any phenomenon, students must be able to *observe* it, noticing its relevant features, and they must be able to *describe* it accurately. Of course these are activities students practice in high school English, math, science, and history (and more and more in their physical education and arts classes), but they become increasingly difficult as the phenomena being observed become more abstract and complex. Witness the difficulties presented and the specialized vocabulary required to describe concepts such as democracy in action, the processes involved in memory, or the quality of light in a painting.

Although they are fundamental thinking skills, observing and describing are not the main emphases of most university writing. Students have to do something with the phenomena under study to contribute to the understanding of those phenomena by a community of learners and scholars all studying the same things. Specifically, entry-level college courses expect students to:

- Analyze
- Synthesize
- Evaluate
- Apply
- Interpret
- Invent

They will be required to do more than simply recognize and characterize things, processes, or ideas, as may have been sufficient in the past. They must be able to take them apart and examine how the parts work, bring in information from other sources and experience to help them understand them, decide what aspects are important or relevant to examine, come to some decision about what they mean, use their new understanding in novel situations, and come up with original explanations and projects for inquiry.

Though we have found that we all value analysis, synthesis, application, evaluation, interpretation, invention, and the ability to observe and describe relevant data to do those operations, each discipline requires students to display those skills within quite different discourse conventions that may appear on the surface to have little in common.

And we often do not share a vocabulary for talking about the writing in which this thinking is inscribed because that is not the pedagogical goal of disciplinary faculty. For example, many professors tell us their students do not always have to have a thesis for things they write. They do not see the similarity between an interpretation of a literary work and an interpretation of a laboratory experiment or a historical event. But interpretation is what all of us want to see. The reader wants encapsulated versions of such interpretations succinctly stated in the introduction of these kinds of documents. Voilà! The thesis.

However, interpretation is a very sophisticated process of many steps. Before we can interpret any phenomenon, we have to observe it closely and describe it accurately. Before we can do that, we have to analyze the phenomenon and evaluate its salient features so we can focus on them and describe what is relevant. Thus, one of the most fundamental thinking skills we have to depend on and expect of our students is the ability to analyze. But without the categories for analysis, students have no idea where to begin. In high schools, we tell them what the categories are, but we rarely point out to them that these particular aspects of the phenomenon under study are the features that all members of our field consider the relevant ones and the ones they need to be able to find, observe, describe, evaluate, and interpret when they attempt to learn our subjects.

Being able to do this complex thinking is the most important learning students gain from their university experience because it gives them the flexibility to function creatively in diverse situations and adapt to their changing social and professional environments. Much of the concrete information and data they learn here will have been superseded by the time they need to use it, but their strategies for solving problems, overcoming obstacles, implementing ideas, and accomplishing goals rely on good critical and creative thinking and on writing as the activity in which this thinking is most effectively done.

The writing professors require primarily must show a mind at work, doing these complex operations on complicated concepts. What these professors often do not understand is that the concepts themselves do not become clear until students have had ample opportunities to "rehearse" them in their own language, preferably before a grade is attached to them.

So, how can students do these cognitive activities in ways that help them write effectively in their new academic "cultures"? In our pilot English 101 curriculum, we are trying to give students the tool, and that tool is *rhetorical analysis*. For thinkers to articulate their ideas effectively in writing whenever and wherever they have to, they need specific guidelines for sizing up exactly what the situation and readers require and for making effective choices in all aspects of their texts to meet those expectations. They need to choose the language and forms that their particular readers will understand and expect.

Using Rhetorical Analysis to Show Thinking in Multiple Contexts

When this rhetorical analysis becomes the WAC task, we have to examine carefully and provide concrete categories of descriptors for two phenomena: all the aspects of the writing situation and all the elements—physical, psychological, and substantive—of the written text that has to fit them. Because writing and cognition are so closely linked, we first have to identify the categories of concepts and thinking skills required in the discipline of writing itself, just as we have to do in any other field, and then give students the vocabulary for discussing and practicing the concepts and skills. Thus, writing is like other disciplines in that it is a phenomenon that first must be analyzed from observation and description. To do that, we have our own categories for analysis.

In our revised first-year composition course at the University of Arizona, we are thus building our curriculum around rhetorical analysis in the hope that the process and thinking that make effective writing will "translate" into the students' other rhetorical assignments. We are providing them with the categories for analyzing both the *context* and the *text* to help them make effective choices in the latter to satisfy the requirements of the former. Together, contextual analysis and textual analysis constitute rhetorical analysis. We are providing examples of our local faculty's work for them to analyze in both these respects and to use as models for their own texts.

Writing thus becomes for students a fully theorized discipline in its own right. It has its own categories for analysis, its own conventional ways of using and speaking about them, its own vocabulary, and its own principles, which to my mind are the defining features of any discipline. In this way, we can also model in our field ways for students to identify the relevant features of other disciplines that will help them participate in those discourses as well.

Teachers in any field have two subject matters to teach—theirs and writing. However, few disciplinary teachers want to shoulder this burden. It requires a training and a practice they do not have. If they do not have it but they all do it, it is difficult to imagine that some specialized expertise is required. Providing that expertise is the job of WAC specialists. We think providing both faculty and students with the tools for rhetorical analysis will lighten that burden and give us all a common language for discussing writing in our individual contexts.

The best way to undermine opposition from disciplinary faculty is to ask them to reflect on their own writing processes. Then we can show how, whenever we are in an unfamiliar writing context, our own writing is just as ineffective as any inexperienced writer's would be in our particular fields of specialization. Writing teachers need to be more honest in admitting that they would find writing in chemistry or anthropology difficult if these were not areas in which they regularly conversed. Disciplinary teachers need to be more honest in acknowledging how often their writing does not succeed and in accepting the responsibility to analyze why their original approach did not work. To *interpret* their failure, they first must examine the categories for analysis identified by writing specialists. These are the categories for analyzing their contexts for writing and for analyzing the texts they write in order to evaluate how well the features of their text address the constraints of their context.

Students come to the university with a fairly complete set of literary categories for analysis and sometimes an intuitive absorption of categories for historical, mathematical, and scientific phenomena. If they have been taught literary analysis, they have usually worked within the categories of plot, character, theme, meter, rhyme, figures of speech, and so forth. In history, they realize they have to know the who, the what, the why, the when, and the how of politicohistorical phenomena. In math, they learn what particular operations and formulas they need to apply to a given kind of problem. In science, they learn the classes of physical elements and biosystems and the principles under which they operate, as well as the conventional categories for presenting scientific data. The question high school teachers can equip students to ask is, "In this arena (whatever it may be), what are the categories for analysis? What exactly am I supposed to examine when I study these things?" And, more important for university studies, "Why these particular categories and not some other categories? Are these the only relevant features to analyze and interpret? What new categories do I see or can I create to study and interpret these phenomena?"

ANALYZING TEXTS AND CONTEXTS

Operationally it makes sense in our first-year composition course to have students analyze texts first. This activity appears familiar to them because they come with twelve years of experience in looking at texts. They already have specific categories and vocabulary for talking about essays and works of literature. But logically this approach does not give students any measure against which to evaluate reader effectiveness—either theirs or that of the authors they read. It is even difficult for them to describe features of texts accurately and explain them without understanding their contexts. To write effectively, we must first determine what we are writing to do. It is the standard assessment problem: How do we know if we have done a good job unless we have some standard by which to determine what good is? What behavioral objectives do we have to meet?

If we do a contextual analysis before and throughout the writing of a text, we have a much better chance of more quickly producing an effective document than if we wrote by trial and error. In a survey of both engineering faculty and practicing engineers, I discovered that practicing engineers who did extensive rhetorical analysis before writing their proposals, specifications, reports, design projects, and the like reported only four to six revisions before their documents were acceptable. On the other hand, engineering faculty who reported no rhetorical analysis claimed they required eighteen to twenty revisions before their reports and articles were accepted. These results indicate that analyzing the context is a necessary first step in producing an effective text with the fewest revisions. They also show that revision is the fundamental process in producing effective texts.

Once we thoroughly understand the context—and the best way to do so is by writing our analysis down—we can then apply analytic categories to the text we are trying to write and ask ourselves specifically how each feature of that text will work for the various aspects of its context. The discussions that follow provide the categories, vocabulary, and heuristic questions for analyzing both the writing context and the written text. If we analyze both, we can produce more effective texts faster than if we do not. We know that writing improves with practice on the same kind of task under similar circumstances, and we often can learn to do it effectively by osmosis, just through imitation and repetition. But at the university, students are faced with many unfamiliar writing situations and tasks, so each requires their deliberate and careful analysis before they can hope to participate effectively in those new rhetorical contexts.

Analyzing Contexts

The analytic categories for context bear some similarity to the categories for studying historic documents such as the Constitution or the Declaration of Independence, for instance. These texts, like the ones written in academic discourses, were composed to accomplish specific changes in the readers and their behavior. The readers were expected to use, believe, or act on their ideas in the particular situations that generated them. They had to be extremely clear and persuasive to be effective. Academic writing needs to do the same things. Writers have to persuade readers that what they have to say demonstrates important thinking in the fields they are studying and makes intellectual contributions in the areas they have staked out for their own research.

The potential effectiveness of writing for any academic context has to be measured against criteria created by the following aspects of that context:

- Audience (both primary and secondary readers)
- Purpose (desired goal of the text and audience response)
- Situation (the assignment objective or project goal)
- Stance (your position in relation to the subject and all of the preceding criteria)

These are the analytic categories for contextual analysis. When the writer examines each aspect and articulates a thorough description of each for himself or herself, the criteria will guide all the decisions about elements of the text.

To help student writers "look at the right things," you can provide them with the following heuristic questions (questions that elicit from them what they already know by requiring that they put that knowledge into words—preferably written). Their answers will start their thinking about what is relevant for each aspect of their text to accomplish. If they write out their answers as part of their prewriting activities, they will discover a focus and effective approach more quickly. Have them keep such preliminary writing in a journal or writer's log to show them how professional writers in all fields keep notes with ideas and directions to themselves for their various writing tasks.

Questions for Audience Analysis

1. Who will read this?
2. Who else will read this? (Most documents have peer and other passive readers who give necessary input to the writer on various aspects of the information and presentation.)
3. What is their background in this subject and document?
4. What is their interest in this subject and document?
5. How do they feel about me and my authority to write this text?

Questions for Purpose Analysis

1. What will the readers have to use this text to do?
2. How will this information and the way it is presented help them do it?
3. Why would they want to read it?
4. How are they supposed to feel after reading this text?

Questions for Situation Analysis

1. What made this text necessary?
2. How does it fulfill the course objectives?
3. How does it allow the readers to do what they have or want to do?
4. How does it help me do what I have or want to do?

5. How does this text meet the readers' information needs?

6. How does this text meet the readers' expectations?

Questions for Stance Analysis

1. What is my relationship to or interest in this topic? How do I feel about it?

2. What is my history and background in relation to this topic?

3. What is my relationship to the readers?

4. Is there a difference in power between the readers and me? Who has more power and why?

Let me give an illustration by telling you the answers I gave myself to the heuristic questions about audience and purpose for this chapter. In seeing them, you can judge for yourself whether I have an accurate picture of my context for this text. I hope it will model the "ungraded" writing that helped me articulate the things I wanted to say by focusing me on your interests and information needs.

Audience Constraints

1. My primary readers are secondary school teachers, both English teachers and teachers in other departments who participate in WAC programs.

2. My secondary readers are the editor of this collection, Harriet Scarborough, whom I know, and my colleagues who work in high school WAC outreach, composition theory, or disciplines other than composition.

3. Some of you, particularly English teachers, have a lot of WAC experience and are probably in the position of helping your non-English colleagues use writing effectively in their classes. Some of you have little WAC experience so far and have not incorporated extensive writing into your disciplinary courses.

4. You are mainly interested in knowing why writing can help students learn new and college-level concepts, including concepts about the writing process, and what strategies can help them write more effective assignments in your classes and later at the university level.

5. I presume that because you do not know me you hope I know what I am talking about from WAC experience and expect me to be able to share some ideas you may find useful in your WAC work.

Situational Constraints

1. Harriet Scarborough, Tucson Unified School District curriculum coordinator, proposed and edited this collection. She requested contributors who have expertise in different aspects of secondary WAC programs. She wanted a WAC text that secondary school teachers can use. My university colleague Anne-Marie Hall, who works more directly in high school outreach, approached me to contribute what I know about the bridge between high school and college WAC, because I have crossed it myself and worked on both sides for a number of years.

2. This writing fulfills the "course" or project objectives by providing a chapter that connects high school WAC to university WAC programs and sharing the tools we teach our students for addressing their much-expanded range of rhetorical contexts here.

3. I hope this chapter allows you to use our approach to strengthen your own WAC initiatives and our credibility to show your students that what you are doing with writing in all your courses will continue to be valued and built on at the university level.

4. This project allows me to do several things I have to do. I have to do considerable writing about these issues myself, primarily so that I can understand them well enough to work with faculty and students at the university. As an academic, I also have to publish regularly in my field. I also want to publicize what we are doing at the university to those who send us students. And I want to share what is becoming the focus of first-year composition courses in colleges and universities across the country—rhetorical analysis.

5. Hopefully, this new information meets your information needs as WAC practitioners in secondary schools by giving you some specific writing strategies for use in all your courses.

6. I also hope that the definitions and lists of heuristic questions provide the kind of specific ideas and strategies that you expected.

You can see that doing this sort of analysis involved considerable "ungraded" prewriting for me, but it is valuable writing because it helped me clarify exactly the contextual requirements for this chapter, which helped me decide what to focus on here to reach you. Now let us look at how to make the text itself "fit" these requirements or constraints.

Analyzing Texts

As I noted previously, your students already come with experience in looking at various aspects of written texts, so here I discuss the categories for analyzing texts specifically to determine their effectiveness for the contexts in which the texts have to do their work. These analytic categories will sound familiar:

- Content (what ideas need to be included or *not* included)
- Organization (what order of these ideas is psychologically most effective)
- Format (what *genre* is appropriate and what features of text design will help the readers read it and see its structure and content at a glance)
- Style (what degree of formality is appropriate)
- Tone (what writer attitude is appropriate to show)
- Language (what linguistic features, degree of accuracy, and diction choices will give this text authority with its readers)

As with the analytic categories for context, we can use heuristic questions to determine how to design and compose each feature to accomplish the goals of the text effectively with its readers. In writing each, we can use the results of our analyses to weigh our textual choices against our contextual constraints. Again, if we write out these analyses, they will focus our thinking more quickly and reduce our number of revisions because we are actively thinking about how and what to write by anticipating the readers' responses.

We only know how well our writing works by getting feedback from the readers. All university academics submit their writing to peers for feedback, but those in disciplines other than English usually fail to make that known to their students. Thus they are not modeling for students how effective collegiate writing is actually done. Once readers tell the writer what they understand, or do not, about the text, then the writer can revise the text to make it succeed. Without that feedback, it is a shot in the dark, and, as I said before, academics rarely do conscious rhetorical analysis beyond looking at the kinds of articles published by the specific journals and publishers they want to publish their work, so they spend a good deal of time and effort sending out their manuscripts and revising them—again and again. If we think deliberately about aspects of the text ahead of time, in light of who will read it and why, we put ourselves into the readers' shoes and can start closer to the most effective final version.

Following are heuristic questions to answer before and during the drafting and revising process:

Questions for Content Analysis

1. What information do the readers need or want?

2. What information do the readers not want (because they already know it, it would make us sound naive, or it is not relevant to the purpose of the text)?

3. What information will the readers be able or willing to entertain first?

Questions for Organization Analysis

1. What is the main point the text needs to make?

2. Where is the psychologically best place to state this point, and how often do I need to say it?

3. What order of reasons, examples, illustrations, and data helps make this point?

Questions for Format Analysis

1. What is the conventional genre for this kind of information in this context?

2. What physical features, such as headings, graphics, and font types, will give an overview of the content of the text and its parts?

3. How can these physical features show the reader how the text is organized?

4. Should there be headings?

5. How informative should the headings be, if headings are used?

Questions for Style and Tone Analysis

1. Is the appropriate style formal or informal and conversational?
2. Will this style be the most effective for this particular audience and purpose?
3. What writer attitude best suits the readers and purposes of this text? Personal or impersonal, friendly or distant, light or serious?

Questions for Language Analysis

1. What vocabulary is most appropriate to accomplish the text's purpose with these readers?
2. What grammatical and mechanical accuracy do these readers expect in order to respond positively to this text?
3. Do these readers expect the language to be both interesting and clear?

Following are the ways I answered some of these questions for features of this text:

Content Decisions

1. I thought you probably wanted to see my credentials for proposing these ideas first, in order to judge my credibility and not read further if you thought I had no experience from which you could benefit. You need specific information and writing strategies that you can actually use to help students write throughout the curriculum. You also probably want to know some current writing theory to stay abreast of the field—in this case, rhetorical theory.
2. You do not want any duplication of information from other chapters in this book and from other sources you have used. You do not want to deal with unfamiliar concepts that are not defined and illustrated. You do not want to be told what your experience is or have the general principles of WAC belabored.

Organization Decisions

1. The main points I wanted this text to make were that (a) the WAC emphasis changes from high school to college from writing to learn concepts to writing to produce concepts and (b) the way we approach it with students here is to teach them rhetorical analysis, so they can participate in the written conversations that will generate new knowledge for the vast range of discourse communities in which they will participate.
2. I thought the best place for the first point was in the thesis, but I delayed the second point because I thought it needed some background before you could see the logic of how I got there.
3. I approached the order of discussions to reveal that logic and to demonstrate the psychological order of most effective rhetorical analyses, following

each with a self-reflective description of my own thinking process to illustrate how the two analyses work.

Format Decisions

1. The conventional genre for this chapter is essay because this is a collection of nonfiction prose, each chapter defending particular points of view about Writing Across the Curriculum (WAC). Their defining features are theses and concrete supporting material.

2. Headings are appropriate for this essay because it includes several separate discussions, and you want to skim its contents to decide what parts of it you would like to read.

3. Italic type for emphasis is appropriate because it helps you focus on the important concepts and not get distracted by the definitions and illustrations.

Style and Tone Decisions

1. I thought that, because we are colleagues with a common interest in WAC, that a conversational tone would be the one you would respond to most readily and would convey to you that I see us participating in an ongoing conversation about our mutual writing concerns.

2. I tried to convey an attitude of helpfulness and friendliness by identifying with your needs and interests. Out of respect for your time, I wanted to treat this material seriously and give it value for you so you would feel it worth the effort to read.

Language Decisions

1. The only language I thought might be unfamiliar to you, or at least something you did not use every day, is the rhetorical terminology. So I decided that this vocabulary needed to be defined and illustrated clearly. I also wanted to choose collegial words in my choices of first and second person instead of third person. Much academic writing is done in third person in order to sound authoritative to its audience, but I imagined that you could guess very early whether I had any credibility in this subject and would prefer to be treated as the colleagues you are.

2. Naturally for fellow teachers, I wanted to use correct grammar, mechanics, and usage because not doing so would certainly hurt my credibility.

3. I know that if you have to read this chapter, you would prefer that it be interestingly written. Barring my ability to do that, it should at least have an interesting proposition for you to consider. I did not think you would appreciate having to struggle to understand what I was trying to say.

These were some of my assumptions that guided my textual choices. Accurate or not, they show you where a writer can go wrong if he or she is miscued and does not understand his or her rhetorical context very well. Hopefully, my secondary readers and editors will give me enough feedback to put this chapter on the right track before it gets to you. But I tried very hard to put myself in your shoes because I have been, in fact, in your shoes, so maybe I came close to the mark and have addressed your needs.

Now I would like to end by showing you the ways we help first-year students do these analyses more specifically for the particular disciplinary conversations they want to participate in.

Appealing to Different Disciplinary Audiences

To accomplish the university goal of producing new knowledge, most university scholars construct knowledge collaboratively. You already know the theoretical reasons for collaborative learning and are using it in most of your classes. Universities, which have used collaborative learning since their origins, have been surprisingly slow to acknowledge its importance, however, probably because university faculty have always taken it for granted. They have also been under the contradictory impression that, because knowledge is power, they need to hoard it because of competition for research dollars and professional advancement and to avoid giving their competition an edge. They guard their "intellectual property" assiduously and punish plagiarism severely. The social construction of knowledge is a somewhat underground activity here. Structurally, universities also put many obstacles in the way of collaborative efforts.

That said, though, the inquiry and intellectual work of universities gets done through the conversations scholars participate in—most of which are in writing. The only really useful knowledge we have is knowledge that we can express, share, refer to, and debate. We say, therefore, that disciplinary researchers join *discourse communities*. The writers in the different fields pose particular intellectual problems for themselves to solve in order to add to their field's store of knowledge. Their written work proposes their current solutions and illustrates their thinking as they found them. They share them to seek feedback that will help them refine their ideas and contribute to a better understanding by the whole community.

We know that we never stop learning, and the more we know about our fields the more we can learn. We attach new information to related existing knowledge, or *schemata,* in our brains, which helps us hang on to it, understand it, and find it when we need it. We synthesize it with what we already know to know more.

The most important schemata we have are the various *languages* we use to represent abstract concepts: English, mathematics, and other symbolic systems. We need such language, or symbols, so we can label and manipulate new concepts in our minds. To use these concepts, we have to practice the new language until we use it in the same way and with the same authority as the experts in our fields or discourse communities. Then we truly understand the concepts. That is why it is so important to give students ample opportunities to practice these specialized languages in appropriate disciplinary contexts.

For these "dress rehearsals," we recommend, as you do, that students do a lot of ungraded writing. Writing that accomplishes authentic objectives for students lets them practice using course concepts in real contexts. For example, we urge and encourage students to make lists of questions to seek answers from peers, instructors, and research. This ungraded writing gives them a supply of concepts they can articulate to perform effectively those assignments that are evaluated. Ultimately, students have to handle the language adroitly enough to participate in disciplinary discourse with the experts. Thus they have to apply rhetorical analysis to texts by these experts to discover how to use the language appropriately. We do that in our pilot 101 class with articles written by university faculty members so students have models they can use when writing about issues in their fields of research.

The overall question they must answer is, "How did these writers compose their texts to appeal to their particular audiences and get these readers to respond the way they wanted?" For students to answer the heuristic questions for context and text, they need to analyze some features of the discourse community itself as an aspect of their audience analysis because the individual writers' values are influenced by the values of their discourse communities. Then they can use two rhetorical strategies—identification and rhetorical appeals—in field-specific ways to get into the conversation and make readers willing to entertain their ideas.

Identification

Among the textual components to analyze closely is the *tone,* which plays a very important role in whether readers want to read a text. The tone has to welcome the readers into the text. Different readers expect to hear different tones in the various genres they read. They may want the tone to be friendly in some things, but in many academic texts readers want the tone to be serious and authoritative. Academicians want writers to sound as though they know what they are talking about because the readers want information that is reliable and interpretations that are credible.

But readers always have to want to read a text in order to do or think what the writer intends. Readers have to see some personal connection to the writer and his or her subject or they simply will not read the text. The writer has to establish immediately some kind of connection between them. We call this establishing *identification.* The writer is obliged to provide a way for the reader to identify with him or her and the topic.

Writers use all of the aspects of the text, not just tone, to create an identification with the audience. For instance, the *content* may refer to experience or interests shared with the readers, call attention to benefits for the readers of reading the text, or show how the readers can use the information. I tried to do all of these things early in this chapter. I called on our mutual WAC interests and experience, showed you the similarities between high school WAC and university WAC, and promised you information that would help your WAC initiatives.

The *organization* has to start with something important to the readers and make it easy for the readers to see the logic of the ideas—from the readers' perspective. That is why I started with what was familiar and important to us both, progressed to what is different and perhaps unfamiliar about university WAC, and used headings to announce and repeat the key terminology and concepts I was trying to get across.

The *format* should not make the text look impenetrable by creating long blocks of unbroken gray print with little white space and no headings to help readers identify the principal points and find specific information. The writing should be in the genre that readers expect to see in the particular context.

Most importantly, the writer has to use *language* the readers will respond to and understand. The language has the greatest influence on creating an appropriate *tone and style.* If the readers are alienated by too many unfamiliar terms, offended by being told the obvious, or insulted by being "talked down to" and made to feel that the writer thinks he or she is somehow superior to the readers because of his or her expertise, they will not identify with the writer or the subject. A writer may choose to use third person, for example, in favor of second because readers would prefer an authoritative tone to a tone personally including them in a "one-to-one" conversation as I have done here.

Following are some heuristic questions for analyzing the context of different discourse communities that will help student writers identify with their readers in those contexts:

1. What kinds of intellectual problems do the practitioners of this field like to work on? Will the one I am working on interest them?

2. What kinds of methods do these researchers use to find the answers they are interested in, and are my methods like theirs?

3. Am I using the same terminology they use in the ways they use it and not just trying to show them that I know the new vocabulary words?

4. Do I sound like I know what I am talking about with my tone and style?

5. Will the evidence or data I can give be the kind of evidence they find credible and persuasive?

6. Where do these people hold their written and oral conversations, and how can I get into those forums so they will listen to me?

7. What qualifications do I have that will inspire them to believe me?

8. Do I know and can I use the conventions scholars in this field expect in a written text? Some particular questions you can ask to discover the answer to this question are

   a. What genres are the usual formats for this kind of text in this kind of situation?

   b. Is there an abstract for most articles and reports in this field?

   c. Is the abstract informative, or is it just a list of topics covered?

   d. What methods of organization do these authors generally use?

      • Problem followed by solution?

      • Background then interpretation?

      • Survey of the literature on previous work followed by where the new information fits?

- A new way of interpreting particular phenomena after survey of earlier interpretations?

- A list of alternate interpretations or solutions followed by the one preferred?

e. What principles do these scholars take for granted, so I do not embarrass myself by stating the obvious?

f. What modes of thinking seem to be characteristic of the practitioners? Of those listed earlier, which do these scholars value the most and which do I see demonstrated in their work?

When writers know the answers to these questions about discipline-based texts, then they can "join the club." They will be accepted as writers who understand the particular discourse community and can participate in it as a member. As they discover these answers and practice the discourse, they lose their status as novices in the field. To be accepted into the club and to increase their status there, they can also employ rhetorical appeals to make their voices stronger with the other members.

Rhetorical Appeals

The theoretical discipline in which the study of effective verbal communication takes place is called *rhetoric,* which has a three-thousand-year history as a field. Most of the principles discussed in this chapter were articulated long ago by effective rhetoricians, such as Plato, Aristotle, Demosthenes, and Cicero, who participated in many disciplines— politics, art, history, natural science, and mathematics, to name a few. Aristotle catalogued these rhetorical principles in *The Rhetoric*. These thinkers saw speaking, and eventually writing, as being necessarily *persuasive* in that the listener or reader had to be persuaded that the ideas were important enough to consider, believe, or act on.

They found that all aspects of the text can be used to make specific appeals to the audience. The names they gave those appeals are logos, pathos, and ethos—the logical appeal, the emotional or pathetic appeal, and the ethical appeal. The logical appeal is what it sounds like. The writer wants the reader to think the ideas are logical and reasonable. The emotional appeal attempts primarily to make the reader willing to entertain, accept, or act on the ideas, but the writer may also want to create other emotional responses as well—pity, anger, sense of common cause, or feeling of urgency, for example. The ethical appeal attempts to make the writer credible through his or her qualifications, which include experience, expertise, and honesty. A strong logical appeal should be the foundation for effective emotional and ethical appeals. Without it, the ideas are often dismissed as "empty rhetoric."

As students analyze model discipline-based texts, they need to examine how each major element—content, organization, tone, and so forth—also creates a specific appeal to readers to accomplish the texts' purposes. They can ask heuristic questions such as the following:

- What information (content) makes this text sound logical?

- What content does the reader want to read, accept, or act on?

- What content is credible?
- How does the writer establish his or her credibility in the content, organization, tone, style, and language? What does he or she do in the text to sound authoritative?
- Is this order of points a logical way to go about making this argument?
- Will the readers understand and appreciate the psychology of the organization?
- Is this a believable organization, or does it omit or gloss over important ideas?
- Will the style and tone make the intended reader believe this piece of writing?
- Does the style and tone make the text interesting to the reader?
- What else about the text would make the reader sympathetic to this position and argument?
- Is the reader supposed to feel anything else?

Students' ability to answer these questions hinges on their having done an accurate analysis of the *rhetorical context* and will help them evaluate the effectiveness of the text. Sometimes the answers may surprise them. I always have my students evaluate the effectiveness of my textbooks in these ways, and often they are able to identify why they cannot understand them or do not want to read them. Their problems usually stem from lack of audience awareness and poor rhetorical appeals on the part of the writers, who often write as though writing to fellow academicians or make incorrect assumptions about student readers.

CONCLUSION

In this chapter, I have tried to contribute ideas for your WAC programs by showing you the university end of the writing development continuum, which is not the ultimate end of the continuum, but perhaps the last academic one. It focused on our common interest in helping students' cognitive development through acquisition of the language with which to conceptualize. The second-language acquisition analogy seemed an appropriate illustration.

At the university level, writing is valued primarily as the medium in which new knowledge is generated, whereas at the secondary level, writing is primarily valued as the medium in which students acquire existing knowledge.

In recommending rhetorical analysis, which we focus on in our first-year composition classes, I hoped to provide a tool that helps students identify important features of writing contexts in order to guide their choices for writing effective texts in multiple academic settings and disciplines.

The chapter provides heuristic questions for both contextual and textual analyses and for analysis of audience expectations in different discourse communities. It also discusses identification and rhetorical appeals as ways for writers to engage and keep their readers' interest and other ways to measure text effectiveness.

EXTENSION ACTIVITIES

1. Reflect on your writing process. What do you do when you compose?

2. How do you provide for students to receive peer feedback when they write in your classes? How effective are the strategies that you use?

3. What is the difference between writing to learn concepts and writing to create concepts? List some writing activities that could fit into each category.

4. Following Merrill's suggestions, provide an analysis of the context and the text for a particular piece of writing that you have to produce. Reflect on your answers to the heuristic questions.

5. Now, have your students use the questions to analyze the context and text of a particular writing assignment. Have them reflect on their process.

14

REARRANGING DESKS

ALYSON ISABEL WHYTE

FLORIDA STATE UNIVERSITY

ABSTRACT

This account describes how writing to learn during the initial year of teaching a large undergraduate introduction to education course catalyzed course revision and the instructor's professional growth. Private writing to learn, in this case, helped the instructor internalize the paradox that for learning to occur instruction must both respect students' experience and induct students into practices and habits of mind beyond their frames of reference. Through the private writing that the account describes, this paradox became not only the principle guiding the instructor's planning and assessment of lessons but also the conceptual keystone of this introductory course for preservice teachers.

I wish to thank the 500 preservice teachers who were enrolled in the sections of EDF1005, Introduction to Education, that I taught at Florida State University fall 1998 through spring 2000.

Writing during the First Year of Teaching a Large Lecture Course

Once each week August through December 1998, I walked to Milton Carothers Hall 201, several buildings away from my new office in the College of Education, to teach Florida State's introduction to education course. The course enrolls more than two hundred undergraduate students each semester, most of whom plan to teach school after they graduate. More than one hundred of these students attended my "01" weekly fall semester class.

The first class began with moving 126 desks out of long, long rows that faced a raised platform and into four concentric circles. As the class met for the second time and the third time, more students helped rearrange the desks as they arrived before class. I have gained new respect for the movable desk as one of the few reform efforts focused on student-centered teaching that has withstood powerful norms for teacher-centered practice that begin now even in kindergarten and that particularly impinge on the legitimacy and survival of high school teachers and administrators (Cuban, 1993). Carothers 201, the lecture hall in the building that initially housed Florida State's entire school of education and that now houses the large curriculum and instruction department, is the only large classroom at Florida State in which the chairs are not fastened to the floor, all facing a lectern or a stage. How the desks are arranged is important—important enough that I schedule introduction to education whenever Carothers 201 is available.

Fall 1998 introduction to education was the first college class I have taught. At the first two-hour session I announced the objectives of the course, which focused predominantly on the students. The syllabus announced

> Four objectives drive all aspects of this course: (1) that you complete the course with a clear sense of your working assumptions and values as a potential practicing teacher; (2) that you make connections between key pieces of theory and empirical research in education and your individual values to inform your working assumptions and your eventual classroom practice; (3) that you have a picture of what fine teaching looks and feels like, of how you can recognize when it is happening; and (4) that you leave the course with a small repertoire of high-quality teaching practices applicable across grades.

There had been nods, a smile here and there, nonverbal expressions of approval on some faces and of openness on most as I read the course objectives out loud. We had worked most of the first class on writing the stories of how each of us had come to be in the course and reading those accounts of our personal histories to one another. The students clearly felt comfortable and enthusiastic as they walked out of the hall on their way to other classes and to part-time jobs that day. Then I realized that I had forgotten to put the desks back. I pushed each desk, one at a time, back into the long, straight rows facing front. I learned in a hallway conversation later that day that if I had left the desks in circles, I would have been cited by the university for leaving the lecture hall where we met in disarray.

The way I remember feeling in that large, linoleum-floored hall, pushing and pulling the desks back into straight rows, parallels the way it has felt as I have written to learn how to teach this college lecture course. Through pages and pages of writing that no one but I will ever see, I learned that, as Dewey warned in the first chapters of *Experience and Education* (1938), good teaching means much more than abandoning traditional arrangements and that I have to occupy both a teacher-centered and a student-centered stance. Improving semester by semester, consciously pursuing both those stances, happened through a moment of awareness after dozens of pages of private expressive writing about my teaching, about the possibility, with twenty years invested in my identity as a teacher: "What if I'm not a good teacher? What if I won't ever be?" Without the practice I have maintained for years now of writing at least some mornings three pages in longhand that no one will ever see, that even I rarely reread, I would still be blindly wondering how in my classroom things could be going so wrong. Several months before the first semester of the course started, I had read what would give me the path to follow. But to know it I had to *re-cognize it*. The practice of writing to learn produced that *re-cognition*—and improvement in my practice as a teacher that, even the second semester I taught the course bore fruit: When we read the fall and spring final essays double-blind the most common score for the fall essays was a 2 in a range of 1 (worst) through 4 (best). The mean score among the fall final essays was 1.88. The most common score among the spring essays was a 4, and the spring mean score was 3.18. Interrater reliability was 95 percent. A list brainstormed by the scorers of characteristics of papers earning a 1 included the following descriptors:

1. Paper may demonstrate poor writing skills.
2. Paper does not relate to course.
3. There is minimal elaboration or development of ideas, content, or concept.
4. This is basically an incomplete paper.

The scorers reached consensus that the papers earning a 4 had the following characteristics:

1. Paper tells the story of the creation of the metaphor that is the topic of the paper, including key sources that were meaningful to the student.
2. Paper describes, in words, the metaphor in such a way that a person who has not seen what the student made can completely picture it.
3. The writer does not skimp on details. The writer uses descriptive words.
4. There is an explanation of the reason why what the student created is a good representation of the concept; there is also an effort to relate each element of the metaphor to the elements within the concept.
5. The writing draws from the student's experiences (these may include readings, observations, discussions, and so on).

My journal from fall 1998 looks dramatically different from the six or seven I had filled previously, three pages morning upon morning, month upon month, year upon year. Every previous journal is in neat, even cursive that follows exactly the horizontal lines printed on each page. The two years before I began the fall 1998 journal, when I was finishing my dissertation, I wrote in a small, white room in Palo Alto, listening to Gregorian chant—those same evenly written lines. No longer. October through November 1998 the neat script turned into wild, fast scribbling, slanted upward across the printed lines on the page, slanted downward, in boxes and circles, every which way. I heatedly mapped out version after version of the introduction to education course: a nearly frantic repetition of "How can I make this work? How can I get this to work?" After fall 1998 final exams and a week's writing, I turned to this chapter. Between Christmas and New Year's Day a draft that felt true began to appear, in red felt pen scribbles snaking across and up the margins and between the lines and paragraphs of a previous typed draft. In February, the week after the fourth session of the spring 1999 semester class, what I had learned about how to teach the introduction to education course had come clear.

When I began to turn those red felt pen notes into type on New Year's Day 1999, I had returned to the Tucson house where I lived when I taught high school for five years, 1991 through 1996. The desert light, the dry breeze moving gently through the garden I once lived in each day, reminded me of a day much the same three years before, in the company of the same trees, when I had written of difficulties teaching that would recur during fall 1998 in my first undergraduate course at Florida State. The same soft wind was blowing as had during the spring of 1996, at the beginning of what would become a three-year process of writing to learn to teach more effectively. On that day three years ago, I wrote,

> All day long today a hot, dry breeze has carried the precise beat of a tool assaulting wood through the garden and my house. As I slept late the second morning of spring vacation, past the cool hours, a woodpecker was carving a nest for itself through the trunk of my dying cottonwood tree. The tree got brief protection while I sat outside with morning coffee and a book, but now the pecking stops only at two loud shakes of the wind chimes—and there's a clean-edged cylinder stretching into the tree's heart.

"That cottonwood and I share a history," I wrote, describing how having left teaching after five years as a seventh- and eighth-grade English teacher (and then seven years of freelance textbook writing and editing, teaching college writing to newcomers to the United States, and graduate work), I had decided to teach high school. During my first year as a high school teacher one of my students had said to me, "You must really want to teach here."

"Why do you say that?"

"Because," she answered, "so many people are always coming in here to see if you're doing it right."

Early that year I had been talking on the telephone with a friend about how much I was struggling at school. In a loud splintering the cottonwood snapped in two, midway up its trunk, and fifteen feet of leafy tree crashed down an arm's length outside the window. Weeks before, the same thing had happened as I had sat in that friend's living room in northern California: A main branch of her plum tree, weighed down with ripe fruit, had splintered and fallen just outside the window beside us. "My professional identity would splinter into pieces during that same year," I wrote in 1996, "and like my cottonwood, it would not revive fully." During the quiet of the summer after that hard year, I watered the trees in my garden: "Day after day, and then week after week in the white June heat I watered the trees and listened to the locusts whirring," I remembered in 1996. By the time the *chubascos*—the warm, heavy midsummer rains—began, all the trees but the cottonwood, even the old fig, had come into full, strong leaf. But "two large branches of the cottonwood were dead. Its trunk . . . would soon open in a wide wound, to be bored by insects," and then ears of black fungus would begin to appear where the trunk gaped open, which I would chip off—and then watch reappear. Once the woodpecker had drilled through the only part of the tree's trunk that could still function, the tree could do nothing but die. Where it had once stood, shading the table where I wrote and rustling in the wind, there was now bare ground littered with a few scattered stones that had once encircled the base of the trunk.

It was the wrong kind of tree to plant right beside a house, especially in the desert; it required so much water that it could never have thrived where it was planted. But I loved it, continued to love it after I learned how wrong it was for that tree to be anywhere but alongside a river or in some other very wet place. It was intolerable to think about the bare ground that was going to be left where that tree had stood. As I looked ahead to the dissertation research coming up for me at the end of the 1996 school year, I wrote

> I've been noticing roses lately. Not vases of cut roses, but healthy rosebushes, rooted in the ground. When that battered cottonwood dies, I'll plant roses in its place. . . . I'll learn to cultivate roses. And when I return to teaching, I'll have the wisdom to . . . see my students as individuals rather than process them as institutional norms demand. . . . As the rhythm of nature replaces the rhythm of the assembly line in my classroom, as I learn to truly attend to each moment . . . each student . . . I'll feed the plants, prune their branches, and cut the roses each spring.

Three years later, I had returned to teaching. There were no roses planted where that tree had stood. After the second semester of the introduction to education course, when my teaching had begun to work, I would plant a good, drought-tolerant Mexican bird of paradise in that spot. Bare ground, not branches of roses, came next in my teaching. Writing spanning three years made me look straight at the aridity of my classroom, see that the anger among students and the lack of truly beautiful work in my high school classroom had recurred in my first college class. This chapter is the story of discovering what was fundamentally wrong with how I was teaching—and what has happened since I have begun to learn to teach differently. The mistake I made—in high school and in college, in Arizona and in Florida—was the same: focusing early during the term on pleasing students more than on teaching them and then toughening up the standards as the course proceeded. The students would slowly discover that there were standards for their work they had not participated in constructing and did not agree with, and disintegration and bitterness would result.

THE INSUFFICIENCY OF REARRANGING DESKS

It felt like cutting-edge, state-of-the-art college teaching those first weeks of the 1998 fall semester, rearranging those desks. But during the second session of class, the space in the center of the classroom began to lose vitality. I had prepared an outline of the week's assigned reading, by Elliot Eisner (1994), on educational ideologies that are currently in circulation. I could feel the students drifting away from the outline in their attentiveness. Switching to buzz groups working with the outline to compare the students' own school experience to the ideologies described salvaged that session. And the third session the students responded articulately and energetically to the assigned reading: an excerpt from the evocative trade book *South of Heaven,* by the *St. Petersburg Times* reporter Thomas French (1993), who spent a year in a central Florida high school. The classroom came alive somewhat when we discussed that reading. I had to cut the discussion short repeatedly that day when many hands were still raised, to turn the conversation to chapters that had not yet been brought in.

The assigned reading for the fourth class session was a chapter from Eugen Weber's (1976) *Peasants into Frenchmen,* a history of schools as an element of the establishment of France as a nation-state. At the center of those circles of desks that fourth week, I found myself standing in a dead zone, answering my own questions about the assigned chapter. A teacher I know once described a colleague saying in the school teachers' lounge: "I'd throw them a tidbit and—no fish swarming toward it. Just 'bluup.' I'd throw out another one. 'Bluup.' " Nothing but queries from me sinking of their own weight—and then me explaining what the answer could (implication should) have been. I called on some students to provide passages from the reading they thought were important. One of the first I called on I will call Erica, a small-framed senior who always emanated intensity. Erica had said hello on the footpath after class the first day, and we had talked about her determination to bring political science to life for high school students. That day, when I called on Erica to identify a passage in the Weber reading that she thought was important, she responded angrily:

> I would a lot rather read about students in Florida, where we are going to be teaching, than about schools a long time ago in France. I don't think we should have to read about things that have nothing to do with where we are going to be teaching.

Throughout the rest of the semester, Erica would interject complaints when I reviewed assignment requirements and deadlines and gave suggestions for how to do well on assignments during class. When I would respond that I was interested in talking further with her and with other students outside of class, the climate of the room would shift toward outrage that I had cut the student's outburst short. One evaluation of me as an instructor on a midsemester formative course evaluation describes the feeling that had arisen: "The class is so demanding that all I can do is worry about it. Everyone is stressed, and it seems to go unrecognized." Most students commented in their midsemester evaluations that they found me accessible and responsive. But most felt through the end of the semester that the demands of the course were unreasonable: The criticism of the course that characterized my end-of-semester evaluations was that there had been too much reading and that the reading had been much too difficult. I would fail to reconnect with Erica—she would alternate between obsequiousness and rage—throughout the remaining eight weeks of the course. I missed the optimism and direction that had been in her voice that first week when we talked, neither of which ever returned.

The fifth session I had provided a reading by David Tyack (1976) on the history of compulsory schooling, which was missing every other page. Only two students called my attention to the missing pages before class that day. When I led off by apologizing for the photocopy mistake, virtually all the students clearly had not looked at the assigned reading. I reran the botched photocopy job and set copies out in our department office for the students in introduction to education to pick up and read before the sixth session of class. Two days before that class meeting at the end of the afternoon hardly any of those handouts had been picked up. I had included in the syllabus and announced on the first day of class that students' responses during review of assigned readings would determine their final grade on assigned readings, in combination with a written test near the end of the course on Mike Rose's *Possible Lives*. I felt strongly—and still do—that without serious engagement with the ideas in the assigned readings, the hours of observing classrooms and the small-group research that constituted the course would not add up to a substantive experience for the students, that I would not be delivering on the course the college had hired me to develop and implement nor would I be responsibly preparing students to teach. So by e-mail I announced thirty-six hours in advance an oral exam to be administered during the sixth session of the course on the first five weeks' readings. I would draw names and call on students to respond to the question I had assigned the previous week: In four fictional portraits of teachers I had supplied, what features of the teacher portraits reflected big ideas about what schools should do that were in the Eisner, Weber, and Tyack readings? I knew, hesitating before I pushed the "send" button for the class listserv that evening, that I was forcing compliance with the syllabus—and there would be a high price to pay, emotionally, for having done that. I also knew there was no time remaining to persuade the students to do the assigned readings. Commitment to reading for ideas won out—a priority, I realize now, that is a bottom line for me as a teacher.

I made sure I got a full night's sleep before that sixth class. I gave the class two minutes after identifying which reading (Eisner, Weber, or Tyack) I wanted the students to connect to the fictional teacher portraits—and for the first time every student was closely attending to the assigned texts, just what I had wanted. The cost, however, was that the room felt tense and utterly mechanical. And most students called on had virtually no understanding of the readings that they could articulate. I invited those who had not been called on who had responses to the questions to e-mail those to me or to come in during office hours and discuss the assigned question with me. One to two dozen e-mails followed.

One e-mail documents the blatant exchange of remarks on the readings for grades that I had set up:

> Dr. Whyte,
>
> I am interested in speaking with you about the readings that we were tested on last week. I see and have documented the connections between the readings and would like to demonstrate that knowledge to you in order to get a good grade in class. Please let me know what times are good for you so that I can make an appointment to speak with you about the readings. I am making this appointment to help my grade. If not being called on in class last week has not hurt my grade and my grade in this area is good, then there is no need to speak with you. I want an appointment only if it will improve my grade in the area of participation. Please write me back and let me know if an appointment would be beneficial to me.
>
> Thanks for your time!

Student Voices on the Struggle to Manage the Course Requirements

Among the e-mailed responses to the assigned question I received, only one showed even satisfactory understanding of the ideas in the assigned readings. Florida State's students tend to be warm, cooperative, and respectful. Most of the e-mails thanked me for the opportunity to receive credit for the assigned readings instead of having to respond during class. Some students were also so upset, though, that they sent e-mails such as these:

> I have been reading and trying to participate in class and yet I have received [progress report] marks that are in the range of a "B" or a "C." I have, on different days, raised my hand and have not been called on. This class is proving to be a really stressful one for me. I would like to come away with something this class showed me or helped me understand better, but right now it leaves me not wanting to be in school—as a teacher or a student—at all.

and

> Dr. Whyte,
>
> I wanted to e-mail you about some serious concerns I have regarding our class. Up until this point I have felt that, although it has been a lot of work, it was still manageable. Now I feel otherwise. To be honest with you I feel like I fell into the deep end of a pool with weights tied to my ankles. Let me just tell you my concerns and then I'll explain.
>
> The work/reading for this class is extremely heavy. I know this is just a fact of life. However, this is a 1000 level course. The work doesn't seem to be consistent with the level this is supposed to be at . . . I really hope you don't take this as complaining. However, I truly feel that the e-mail assignment was unreasonable. It wasn't the nature of the assignment, but rather the method of getting it to us, and the time we had to

complete it. I'm sure you're aware of the problems many people had in getting the e-mail, or getting it very late. However, I felt that I didn't do a very thorough job, which is something that is just as important to me as getting the job done.

This class wouldn't be a concern for me if it was the only one I was taking. Yet with my other four class loads on top of this I feel completely overwhelmed. I don't want you to think I'm a slacker who is just complaining about our workload. I consider myself to be a very good student who is very organized and usually ready to go. My frustrations with this class are starting to affect my other classes and have quite literally made me hate school for the first time in my entire life. I really want to address these concerns so that I can feel like this class is possible and won't kill me. I'm willing to work!

Thanks for your time . . . .

A student in the department office signing up for hours at Florida State's laboratory school volunteered that week, "I know this is a weed-out course"—in an accepting, friendly tone of voice. Offering me forgiveness. She reminded me, disturbingly, that introduction to education is intended to be the opposite of a weed-out course: rigorous *and* a genuinely exciting, nurturing route toward the complexity and joys of teaching.

THE BEGINNING OF REACHING THE STUDENTS

My first response to students appearing not to have comprehended or perhaps even to have attempted the required reading had been to defend what I was doing and force the students through the next and then the next step in the syllabus. I am a seasoned classroom technician: I know how to engineer compliance. At the same time I began to hear an insistent inner voice, one that appeared on the pages of my journal between the frantic bursts of reconfiguration of the introduction to education course saying, "You've been here before. *Remember.*"

Before the same class when Erica's first outburst happened, another student, who has chosen the pseudonym "Michelle," had come to class early. Michelle, who is about twenty years old, with a direct gaze and an eager smile, wanted to tell me about a teacher she had observed who "was so *great*. She had such great control!" We had a good conversation—a real conversation about teaching—leading to the insight that one of Michelle's working assumptions was that moment-to-moment control by the teacher of what students are doing and thinking leads to student growth; it was not an assumption I agreed with (although I would live it out myself during the ensuing weeks), but I did not need to state my opinion. It interested Michelle to hear put into words the belief that led her to call this particular teacher "great." In that conversation I was my best self as a teacher, asking questions through which a student came to recognize a working assumption she had not seen before.

Michelle came to see me in my office as well. She was earnest, enthusiastic. Sitting facing me, those weeks when Weber and Tyack had been assigned, she said,

"The *readings,* Dr. Whyte. But we've talked to each other about it. We know it's your first year." As we stood in the doorway, saying goodbye, I recounted some experiences I had had as a teacher that had led me to choose the readings assigned. She responded, "You're so neat! There are a lot of things you could tell us in class that would really *help* us. . . ."

LACK OF ENGAGEMENT WITH THE ASSIGNED READING

I would like to be able to say that during the six sessions that followed my examining the students on the first weeks' readings, a gorgeous transformation of the class occurred. It did not. The students completed their group investigations of topics stemming from the following questions: "Who are the students in Florida's schools? What are the challenges? What actions are being taken in response to these challenges?" The students rated this experience highly in their course evaluations—and at the same time, many felt strongly that they should have earned higher grades than they did, usually "for the amount of work we put into this." The presentations I saw reflected little connection of the material presented to the questions posed—and little understanding of research as a search for information related to something one wants to understand rather than as cobbling together several published schemes or commentaries that reinforce one's existing opinion or impression of an issue.

I cut some readings from the syllabus. One of the five teaching assistants who worked with the students in small sections suggested that I allow the students to choose whether their names would be among those drawn to respond to questions about the readings, which eased the tension in class some. There was slight improvement in attentiveness to the readings and understanding of them on three occasions during the second half of the course. Once I provided an advance study question and a corresponding follow-up minilecture on a reading by Cohen, Lotan, and Holthuis (1997) on the robust relationship between students' talking and working together, under certain conditions, and gains in achievement test scores. A dozen or so students had prepared for this review, and most had understood the ideas central to this article. On a second occasion, interest among the students in a videotape that accompanied one reading helped the students comprehend that content. And during the final discussion of assigned readings, three weeks before the end of the course, the students animatedly discussed race in classrooms, appearing to have read an assigned excerpt from Grace Paley's (1979) *White Teacher.* Much of the enthusiasm in that final discussion of assigned readings, however, arose when I allowed the discussion to shift from response to the text to chains of comments recounting personal experience and beliefs regarding race. And the students had nothing of substance to say on the second and third selections assigned that week, by Lisa Delpit (1995) and Laurie Olsen (1997). The average score on a written test on Rose's (1995) *Possible Lives* at the end of the semester was 69 percent. The best of the final examinations, epistolary essays describing a nonverbal metaphor for something of lasting value learned during the course, included this writing, which reflects some under-standing of the ideas in the readings assigned and discussed:

> In my metaphor for ideas that I will take with me and use as a teacher, I decided to use numbers. I made this decision because numbers, like children, come in various shapes and sizes and can be manipulated. My numbers are all cut from different backgrounds representing the fact that I must be aware of each student's background. In order to get them where I want them I must first understand where they are coming from. I must look at them as individuals like a Progressivist. Just as numbers are manipulated, chil-dren can be added to and changed (positively or negatively) through a class.
>
> Once I know each of the students, or numbers, I am dealt, I must decide on the goal, or solution, I will set for them. I, then, must figure out which ideology, or for-mula, to use in order to help them reach the goal, or solution. The formulas, which represent different ideologies, can be used singly or jointly with other formulas. This will depend on what I am trying to achieve in my classroom, my pedagogy.
>
> The variables on my collage represent things that enter my class that I will have no control over—things I cannot change. These are things such as standards, policies, and politics. These things become a part of the equation and must be dealt with.
>
> The infinity symbol represents that education is an ongoing and everchanging en-tity. As one teacher in *Possible Lives* said, it is an ongoing experiment. As a teacher, I must also be willing and ready to grow and change with it.
>
> The set of factors of nine represents the group work that will take place in my classroom. I must express that, like this set, each member plays an important part and the group is not complete without each member.
>
> The theory of relativity ($E = mc^2$) represents the important role that relativity plays in the classroom. Whatever I am teaching, I must ensure that it is something I make rel-evant to the students. It must also be relative to their lives. They must be able to relate to it and see the importance for it in their lives and future. If I do not succeed at this, they will not be interested in learning it at all. We saw an example of this in studying the history of public education in France. It was not until they saw the usefulness of education that it became something they wanted for their children.
>
> Just as in mathematics, I am sure I will make a lot of mistakes with my students I only hope that, like in mathematics, I will learn from these mistakes and become better at manipulating the numbers and variables into an equitable solution.

I would like to see more explicit logic, including quotation of material from the readings, in this essay. The student appears to understand, however, the ideas in the readings that as an educational ideology Progressivism includes attentiveness to growth of the student as an individual, and she states that multiple ideologies, often overlapping, shape classroom practice. She mentions that regulation of schools through standards for students' academic performance is currently an element of the environment within which teachers work. All these points parallel points in the read-ings. This essay refers to specific skills for collaboration that foster discussion within student work groups and that the students in introduction to education experienced through skill builders during class. Finally, this student refers to some extent to the point in the Weber reading that school attendance during the early years of nation-hood in France followed from families' recognition that school attendance had eco-nomic value.

More typical final essays were these, neither of which approaches what I have in mind for even minimal demonstration of learning at the culmination of the course:

> I am writing in regards to my final project. In my metaphor I was able to relate it to what we have learned in this course throughout the semester. I took a few colors of candle wax that represent the different areas of education and melted them together to create one candle. The completion of my candle represents a classroom and by melting together the different colors of wax I feel I was able to show how the many different areas of education must work together as one. My first impression of education before taking this class was from the students' point of view. After learning the experiences that teachers have, this greatly changed my opinion. I learned that education has a great deal to do with how people interact and work for a common goal. For education to work teachers, students, and parents must work together to create a lasting experience.

and

> The object that I have created that can compare and contrast to this course is a wooden doll. This doll represents how children are already cut out and framed into who they will become when they enter the classroom. However, as an educator it is my responsibility to cultivate and enhance the skills that the child already possess[es]. Wood is a fine and delicate material. And it is necessary for an individual to polish and protect wood to keep it looking its best.
>
> It is also necessary to polish and protect children. Children need to be polished into successful adults in society. Children also need to be protected from scares [scars?] and scratches that will hinder their development. As an educator I must be constantly aware of the hindrances that prohibit children in their development. And I must protect them by not allowing these hindrances to be near them until they are strong enough to handle the temptations.
>
> This course has taught me many lessons that I can apply in the classroom as well as in my daily life. Therefore I will be more equipped to deal with societal problems.

These final essays include no mention of the ideas central to the readings assigned throughout the fall semester.

INSIGHT THROUGH WRITING TO LEARN

I had made a promise in writing—and published it three years before the fall of 1998—not to force compliance at the expense of learning. My journal pages of revised course plans had accumulated through September and into October 1998, most of those plans jettisoning the goal of close reading for ideas and the goal of precise oral and written analysis, because those goals seemed to have cost the students and me mutual affection and respect. I told myself—scolded myself, really—that I had to stop trying to make the students read what they did not want to read.

My heart would sink as I said it. It felt like "folding the tents and slinking away in the night," as I remember my father saying. Like capitulating. Then, as I sat at the keyboard one October day attempting to turn what I was learning into the chapter you are reading now, suddenly, ringing with clarity, one clause came through: "the center does not hold." I then saw the image of those circles of desks and felt the cellular memory of how the center of those circles was not holding, at the midpoint of the semester.

The Internet instantly supplied the title and full text of Yeats's "The Second Coming," including the image of the falcon spiraling out so far from the falconer that the ability of one to hear the other is lost:

> Turning and turning in the widening gyre
> The falcon cannot hear the falconer;
> Things fall apart; the center cannot hold . . . .[1]

Exchanges of electronic chat discussing the poem included someone describing a vision Yeats had of two spirals, the point of origin of each at the center of the widest expansion of the other. The image, as I understood it from the discussion on the Internet, resonated. Here is how I picture it. Each of the cones drawn here represents a spiral:

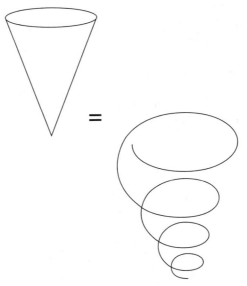

[1] Reprinted with the permission of Simon & Schuster, Inc. from THE POEMS OF W. B. YEATS: A NEW EDITION edited by Richard J. Finneran. Copyright© 1924 by Macmillan Publishing Company, renewed 1952 by Bertha Georgie Yeats.

The interacting spirals fit together like this:

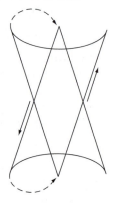

When only didactic teaching occurs, expanding and expanding without accompanying movement to student-directed teaching (and corresponding expansion of that), as in Yeats's words, "the best lack all conviction." The most beautiful ideas fail to connect with students' capacity to learn. The same is true of student-driven teaching attempted without the guidance and grounding of didactic instruction. The insight I needed was that neither can expand indefinitely, except into meaningless noise, without the aid of the other.

When I had first taught in 1979, I had hung words from Yeats's "The Celtic Twilight" on my classroom wall, not knowing why. I had brought those same words, on paper faded since its framing two decades before, in a carry-on bag on the plane to Florida, where they now hung on my office wall:

> We can make our minds so like still water that beings gather about us that they may see, it may be, their own images, and so live for a moment with a clearer, perhaps even with a fiercer life, because of our quiet.[2]

Those lines, as I understand them, match the conclusion in my writing three years before I arrived at Florida State: what is integral to students has to be central to my teaching. I had found the language three years before to say that didacticism must not exclude what is inherent in the student, but what I had missed is that attentiveness to students' interests and desires is insufficient. What Yeats's image of double spirals represented was that either purely teacher-centered or purely student-driven teaching is untenable. If teaching that attends to the student's agenda for himself or herself or didactic teaching is exalted to the exclusion of the other, the center of my classroom will not hold.

Who I am as a teacher includes that preservice teachers will learn—and demonstrate that they have learned—to read for ideas and to reason precisely. I had to find a way to put into practice what I now knew: a way to move out wide in a didactic

---

[2]Reprinted with the permission of Scribner, a Division of Simon & Schuster, Inc. from THE YEATS READER by Richard J. Finneran (New York: Scribner, 1997).

stance and then straight from that widest didactic expansion to students' experiential theories, values, and interests. But how?

WRITING TO FIND MY WAY

Peter Elbow's (1986) *Embracing Contraries* had come into my hands just before I arrived at Florida State. Elbow writes,

> good teaching seems a struggle because it calls on skills or mentalities that are actually contrary to each other and thus tend to interfere with each other . . . . [W]e have an obligation to students but we also have an obligation to knowledge and society. Surely we are incomplete as teachers if we are committed only to what we are teaching but not to our students, or only to our students but not to what we are teaching, or half-hearted in our commitment to both. (p. 142)
>
> (From EMBRACING CONTRARIES by Peter Elbow. Copyright © 1986 by Peter Elbow. Used by permission of Oxford University Press, Inc.)

The teacher in Arizona who had given me this text has been an exemplar for me because she begins where students are—and takes them to levels of quality and power as writers that few adults ever experience. Her classroom feels alive—questing, truthful, fertile—and exact. I loved the piece but soon forgot about it. After the first months of fall 1998, though, I knew "through the skin" (Fenwick & Parsons, 1997) the futility of failing to teach with an active recognition of the paradox Elbow names, of acting only on

> the "paternal" version of the paradox, which is to stick up for standards and firmness by insisting that to do so is good for students in the long run, forgetting the "maternal" version which is to stick up for students by insisting that to do so is good for knowledge and society in the long run. (Elbow, 1986, p. 146)

I had executed a "bait and switch" "soft" the first session of class, exhibiting loyalty to the students, then switching to "hard" teaching, with loyalty to knowledge and society winning out—the same error that had undermined the high school classroom where I had begun writing about my teaching three years before.

Elbow gave me the path to follow to begin to achieve the marriage of the "in the head" and "through the skin" learning I want for my students. Elbow cautions that his suggestion is one "rough picture" among widely different possible means of putting this paradox into practice. He describes how open emphasis on requirements and criteria for an A, B, or C at the outset of a course—even exaggeration of this gatekeeper function at the beginning—can serve to make it clear to the instructor and to the students that the instructor has a loyalty to knowledge and to schools and the university as institutions. This open emphasis lays the groundwork for subsequent work as "an extreme ally to students." Elbow writes that having been "wholehearted and enthusiastic in making tough standards," he then can say:

> Those are the specific criteria I will use in grading; that's what you are up against, that's really me. But now we have most of the semester for me to help you attain those standards, do well on those tests and papers. They are high standards but I suspect all of you can attain them if you work hard. I will function as your ally. I'll be a kind of lawyer for the defense, helping you bring out your best in your battles with the other me, the prosecuting attorney me when he emerges at the end. And if you really think you are too poorly prepared to do well in one semester, I can help you decide whether to trust that negative judgment and decide now whether to drop the course or stay and learn what you can. (Elbow, 1986, p. 155)

Elbow suggests that once genuinely high standards have been set, there is no longer any such thing as being " 'too soft,' supportive, helpful, or sympathetic." There is no longer any reason to curtail seeing things entirely from students' points of view, to curtail worrying about students' problems. Accompanied by forthright loyalty to knowledge and standards for students that reflect that loyalty, respect for students' experience no longer carries with it the danger that by focusing on students' experience, the teacher will be taken advantage of and learning undercut. Elbow concludes

> If we are teaching less well than we should, we might be suffering from the natural tendency for these two loyalties to conflict with each other. In such a case we can usually improve matters by making what might seem an artificial separation of focus so as to give each loyalty and its attendant skills and mentality more room in which to flourish. (Elbow, 1986, p. 158)

At the beginning of spring semester 1999, we circled the desks again for the first session of the spring introduction to education course, but instead of bamboozling (Elbow, 1986) the students by implying through the structure of the first lesson that their feelings and experiences were the nucleus of the course (and leaving the students on their own to contrast that with the details of the syllabus), I started out by emphasizing that the students would be required to read for ideas and to write logically and exactly about how the ideas in the readings connect to what they are seeing in classrooms and how they will teach. Students for whom this was more than they could do in combination with their other classes or with their part-time jobs had the chance to drop the course until another time when they could take on the work involved—or to switch instructors. Several did. The course objectives on the spring 1999 syllabus read

> The course has four objectives, all aimed at helping you arrive at an accurate understanding of a number of big ideas about what schools should do that are in circulation, overlapping, and sometimes competing with one another. You will be responsible for identifying these ideas in the course readings and for connecting concepts in the readings with the classes you observe and with how you will teach or do the other adult work you plan as an occupation.

1. You will read selections from the history, philosophy, sociology, politics, economics, and anthropology of education, with close attention to the ideas central to these readings and demonstration that you understand these ideas.

2. You will connect the ideas in the course readings with your observations of K–12 classrooms during the course and with specific plans for your own teaching or other adult work.

3. You will collaborate in a small group of four to five students to investigate a question such as "Who are the students in Florida's schools?" "What are the challenges?" "What actions are being taken in response to these challenges?" You will prepare a multimedia lesson plan, which you will use to teach others in the course what you have found through this research, and by assigning and assessing homework you will assess your classmates' understanding of what you taught. You will revise the assignment you made based on your classmates' performance.

4. You will explain, argue, analyze, and synthesize ideas, using language precisely, orally and in writing.

I talked the first day of class about how I felt an obligation to the young people the students in introduction to education would soon be teaching and to the society to make sure these preservice teachers could read for ideas and synthesize ideas from their reading with ideas based on direct observation and with their plans to teach—or to manage a baseball team or practice law or whatever occupation each individual in the class was planning. The mood in the room was sober, even anxious, as I broadcast the initial signal: "To succeed in this course you must read for ideas and find precise, logical language to link what you are seeing in classrooms and what you value to the assigned readings."

The biggest change in the course between the fall and the spring was that an eight- to ten-page paper was the most heavily weighted assignment during the course. Two other professors and I annotated and graded these "connections" papers, which were due in late April. This paper, the greatest single contributor to students' final course grades, held each student responsible for understanding the ideas in the assigned readings and for synthesizing those ideas with his or her observations of classrooms and plans for work after graduation. The instructions for this assignment were as follows:

> This paper is an opportunity to reflect on the intersection of readings, class discussion, and your field experience during the semester. The paper will have three major sections evaluated on the following criteria:
>
> 1. (Four pages) Summary of major concepts in the readings (Except *Possible Lives*) that captured your interest. Give specific examples. Include at least five authors and ideas.
> 2. (Four pages) Summarize your practical experience in a coherent, chronological manner, including how your ideas and your attitudes toward the students and teachers changed during the semester as you read (Especially *Possible Lives*) and learned about concepts of education. Give specific examples.

3. (Two pages) From what you read, observed, and so forth this semester, what are your thoughts on entering the field of education as a teacher—or on entering your chosen occupation? Be specific. Explain why.

How Class Discussion of Assigned Reading Improved

The second session of the class during spring 1999, I assigned three readings: a *U.S. News and World Report* commentary called "Dumbing Down Teachers," accusing teacher education programs of being silly and anti-achievement; three pages of Linda Darling-Hammond's *The Right to Learn,* arguing that in sociological terms teaching does not presently qualify as a profession; and the excerpts from Thomas French's *South of Heaven* that the fall semester class had enjoyed so much. In addition to the new course requirement of the culminating "connections" paper, other new features of the course to help the students understand the ideas in the readings included a study question[3] that I assigned for each reading, due with supporting evidence from the text on an index card at the beginning of class, and the requirement that an honor code pledge that students had done their own work be written out as *pledge* on every assignment and signed.

The second session of class during the spring semester of 1999, one student, whom I will call Will, asked, "What's this term 'knowledge base' mean?" A good discussion that involved a number of students followed; we defined the term and contrasted what one can expect a medical doctor to know ("Where my appendix is!" one student called out. "What drugs to prescribe," offered another) with what one can expect every teacher to know (the only suggestion with which the class tentatively agreed was one by a teaching assistant that all teachers probably know some ethical points such as that one should not charge one's own students for tutoring after school).

By the third session, the groundwork for the small-group research projects that took place from early February through mid-March was well enough laid that we could devote more than half of the plenary hour to discussion of that week's assigned readings, classified as "Voices from the Past." I was able to start the discussion by reminding the class of Will's excellent question the preceding week. And because this semester we took time the first day for me to give some personal information to demonstrate to the students how to complete a "culture wheel" about themselves, I could refer to Will, who is preparing to teach math, by his complete name and as a preservice mathematics teacher.

About forty students had been assigned "Plato's Allegory of the Cave" (Lee 1961); about forty Jefferson's "A Bill for the More General Diffusion of Knowledge " (Reed 1996); about forty "Of the Training of Black Men," by W. E. B. DuBois (1902); and about forty the first two chapters of Dewey's (1938) *Experience and Education.* When

---

[3] I am indebted to Victoria-Maria MacDonald, Florida State University, for the format and wording of this assignment.

I asked, "OK, what don't you understand about these readings?" the pause was a long one, as had been the case at the outset of discussion the week before. There were a number of very long pauses that day when I asked for the students to shift to what they did not understand about the reading by Plato, by Jefferson, and by DuBois. I faltered near the end of the hour and did too much telling the class about the DuBois reading. But as the conversation that hour unfolded, haltingly, I could see most of the students had read the assigned selections. And the discussion was starting where students were and helping them better understand what they had read.

The first question was from a young man who follows the band Phish in the summers and plans to practice law. He wears his hair back in a neat ponytail. Michael, we will call him, said that what he did not understand in the Dewey reading was how an experience could be miseducative. One or two students concurred: Could one not make something constructive out of any experience? Another student then contributed a rapid summary of points from Dewey, clarifying that it is the outcome of the experience that defines it as miseducative, and another student located the passage where Dewey discusses this concept. We reread it, and I recapitulated, as accurately as I could, what the student who had summarized Dewey's points had said. (Another time, ideally, I would ask a student to help by doing that.)

The next question was from another young man, tall, with an athletic build and close-cropped hair, whom we will call Steve. The Jefferson reading, he said, had been hard going; was there anything more to it than the idea that we should have public schools? Another student answered that yes, right here on the first page was the idea that even a government with a strong constitution, with strong protections in its laws, would tend toward tyranny if the citizenry was not widely educated. She mispronounced *tyranny*. We talked about what the word *tyranny* means. It was a new word for many of the students. I was proud of this student for pointing out the passage her classmate needed to see at the risk of mispronouncing a word in front of 125 other people, for caring more about helping her classmate understand than about possibly making a small mistake. The conversation was a very different kind of conversation about assigned readings than we had ever had in the fall.

PRESSURES TOWARD PREDOMINANTLY STUDENT-CENTERED PRACTICE

Elbow warns that the approach he describes is likely to confuse students at first "because they are accustomed to teachers being either 'hard' or 'soft' or in the middle—not both" (Elbow, 1986, p. 159). Once I had set my heart on taking the path Elbow has laid out, I wrote in one of the abandoned drafts of this chapter, before the spring semester began:

> The atmosphere in my classroom may not be happy and comfortable at times—perhaps for sustained periods of time—and I may not be able to embrace the contraries of teacher as gentle, soft, and flexible and teacher as "hawk-eyed, critical-minded bouncer at the bar of civilization" (Elbow, 1986, p. 159). I may have to stretch as far as I can,

grab one pole of this paradox with each hand, and hang on hard, reaching back out as far as it takes when my grip slips—for semesters, for years.

The first response from a student spring semester was indeed that I was being too "hard." This e-mail came after the very first session of class, from a young woman whom I will call Lisa. Lisa was quick, mentally and verbally; emotionally intense; ambitious and focused—qualities that reminded me of Erica from the previous semester. My responses to this first e-mail from Lisa interweave with her words to me:

> Dear Dr. Whyte,
>   This class seems very overwhelming!!
>   ****When have you felt overwhelmed in the past and then succeeded? Think back to what you did then that helped you succeed.
>   The first project [a case history of oneself as a reader] and the observation hours don't bother me. I am very excited to do those. It's the group project and all the reading that we have to do. I like to read, but you made it seem like that 75% of the reading we will be doing will be such a bore! The group project seems murderous!
>   ****As I said on the first day of class, I will be interested in your opinion of the readings and the group projects mainly after you have learned to read this kind of material for ideas and to synthesize those ideas, including connecting the ideas with your classroom observations and with how you plan to teach. I will be interested in your opinion of the group project mainly after you have successfully completed it.
>   ***I meant what I said the first day. I feel a strong obligation to the young people you will teach, to the college, and to the society to teach you to read fluently for information (a different kind of reading than reading articles as literature). I feel that same strong obligation to teach you to work with others to carry out high-quality inquiry into educational issues. You will need to work hard to earn good grades on your work on the assigned readings and on the group investigation: That's really me—the person who will be grading your work. Provided you are willing to work hard, I believe you can do well in the course. If you feel you are so unprepared for the course requirements that you may not be able to succeed, I can talk with you during office hours (which begin January 27) and help you make the decision whether to take the course.

I made mistakes during the spring 1999 semester, forgot often—as I did toward the end of the preceding e-mail—that I did not need to be stringent moment to moment, that the way I started the course and the structures to help students complete it genuinely well really do allow me to attend unstintingly to what experience the students are having. But even when my grip slipped, as I was fighting to correct missteps, extend myself more to help, the character of the course improved. One Saturday, before the fourth session of the spring course, I spent hours answering student e-mails, most having to do with the need for logistical help. Here's one exchange with a student I will call Scott:

> To Alyson Whyte:
>   I am in your EDF-1005 class that meets at 4:30. I have been having a real problem lately with work and classes. At work the other cook for the catering business I work for is out of town and I have to go in to work and make sure everything is ready for

two parties next week. I also have two tests Tuesday in Latin American politics and economics and a group presentation in Latin American politics on Thursday. I would like to apologize for not being able to meet with my entire group but I will be meeting with individuals from the group this weekend to discuss what we did and what my ideas are. This is a very stressful week for me and it is hard to find a time when everyone in the group can meet but things will hopefully work out and I hope me just meeting with one person from the group will help the group as a whole. If any members of my group complain I will be able to start meeting with them after Thursday when everything blows over and my life is back to normal.

Thank you.

Dear Scott,

It's good that you let me know what the circumstances are that surrounded your not meeting with your group this past week. I'll forward a copy of this to your TA, too.

I've made allowances for groups to have problems this first week of the project. The final group decisions on the Stage 2 questions are due February 10, though: the day after your tests and the day before your group presentation on Latin American politics and economics. You are going to need to find an hour between now and the end of the day on Wednesday when your whole group can meet. It's the only way that groups can come to good decisions on what the group is going to study, who is going to do what, and what the purpose of the research is going to be.

Something I can do to help is extend the due date for you of the readings due Monday, February 8, through February 15. That way this weekend you can put in more time on your Latin American politics projects and your job and free up an hour to meet with your group between class on Monday and the Wednesday deadline for the decisions by your group on the Stage 2 questions.

I'll try to reach you now at the phone number on your phone to suggest this.
Dr. Whyte

To Alyson Whyte:

Thank you very much for the extension. It really will help me a great deal. I will try and arrange a meeting with my group Sunday night. I will be in touch with them today when I have free time. I am very sorry to have to ask for more time but a lot of unusual circumstances have come up with work and it created a lot of stress for everyone there and the people like me are just caught in the middle. I really appreciate your favor and I know you talked [on the first day of class, showing the students how to complete the culture wheel] about how you like to read about cooking so if you ever want some recipes for anything just let me know.

Thank you.

Dear Scott,

I am glad I could help.

Something I've had in restaurants here and liked but don't know how to cook is grouper. Any suggestions? Not right now, though!! When you have time. . . .
Dr. Whyte

To Alyson Whyte:

A good way to cook grouper that I learned is to take about a 1/3 lb. piece and put a little olive oil or butter (olive oil is healthier) on both sides of the piece. Throw a little salt and pepper on both sides of the grouper. Then put the piece in a pan and put a few ounces of white cooking wine in the pan (there should be about 1/4 inch of wine in the pan). Cut a whole lemon in half and squeeze the juice onto the piece of fish. Then throw both pieces of lemon in the pan with the wine and the fish. Bake it for about ten minutes at 350 (remember the oven has to be preheated too). After ten minutes throw some uncooked peeled and deveined shrimp into the wine in the pan. Let it cook for another ten or so minutes or until the shrimp and the fish is done.

I am not sure on the exact times on how long it takes to cook because the ovens we use work differently than the ones people have at home. The times should not be that off, just throw the shrimp in after 10 minutes and then wait until the piece of fish is cooked, it should be flaky and white on the inside. . . .

Scott came up to the lectern, where I was organizing transparencies to use during class, to say hello before the next class. His entire group had met Sunday night and was on track.

Michael was in the foyer of our department office one day, signing up for classroom observations. The day before, I had been thinking about an expression I saw cross his face during class when I was talking about the first writing assignment, which I had begun reading. "You looked like a big piece of granite was suddenly right on top of your head," was the only way I could think of to describe how he had looked to me at that moment. Yes, Michael had been wondering: Did I want more of—well, not writing from feeling? I had read Michael's paper the night before, I wanted him to know. There were sentences in his reading case history that had truly enticed me to want to keep reading. We talked about the fact that he likes to write from feeling, and, yes, that was what I wanted together with the control of prose that was in those compelling sentences. And what exactly was the connections paper, Michael wanted to know. We talked about some strategies for Michael to connect the readings and his classroom observations with his plans to practice law.

Awkwardly, usually two steps forward and one step back, I was finding a way for my students to learn through the large EDF 1005 course. With only a handful of exceptions, during the fall my students accomplished nothing beyond playing the role of student. The students and I began the spring semester to talk to one another mostly about ideas: a shift from *doing school* to *doing learning* (G. Papagiannis, personal communication, August 1999). The essay I wrote in 1996, when I was beginning to search out what was wrong in my classroom, is archived now, under plastic in the teaching portfolio I keep shelved in my office. Romantically, I forecast there would be roses when I returned to the classroom, but in the end, something brighter, tougher, and faster-growing took root and, although still small, is thriving.

Extension Activities

1. Whyte describes her dilemma in teaching a rigorous and relevant curriculum (Daggett & Houston, 1998). Her dilemma stems from requiring her students to ground their feelings and observations about education in theory and research. It is a conflict between teaching a student-centered versus a teacher-centered curriculum. It can also be perceived as a conflict between allowing students to remain at one end of Britton's (1975) writing continuum instead of requiring them to navigate the entire continuum. In your teaching, have you ever experienced such a dilemma? Write a description of your experience. Any insights?

2. What do you do to provide that balance in your teaching between student demands and course requirements?

3. If you have access to e-mail, see if you can correspond with your students electronically to try out Whyte's idea of writing to learn about class matters. If you do not have access to e-mail, do this interactive activity through journals.

REFERENCES

Britton, J., Burgess, T., McLeod, A., & Rosen, H. (1975). *The development of writing abilities* (pp. 11–18). London: Macmillan.

Cohen, E. G. (1994). *Designing groupwork: Strategies for the heterogeneous classroom* (2nd ed.). New York: Teachers College Press.

Cohen, E. G., Lotan, R. A., & Holthuis, N. C. (1997). Organizing the classroom for learning. In E. G. Cohen & R. A. Lotan (Eds.), *Working for equity in heterogeneous classrooms: Sociological theory in practice.* New York: Teachers College Press.

Cuban, L. (1993). *How teachers taught: Constancy and change in American classrooms (1890–1990)* (2nd ed.). New York: Teachers College Press.

Daggett, W., & Houston, S. (1998). *Facilitating learning.* New York: Leadership Press.

Delpit, L. (1995). *Other people's children: Cultural conflict in the classroom.* New York: New Press.

Dewey, J. (1938). *Experience and education.* Boston: Collier.

DuBois, W. E. B. (1902). Of the training of black men. *Atlantic Monthly, 90,* 289–297.

Eisner, E. (1994). *The educational imagination: On the design and evaluation of school programs* (2nd ed.). Columbus, OH: Merrill/Prentice Hall.

Elbow, P. (1986). *Embracing contraries: Explorations in learning and teaching.* New York: Oxford University Press.

Fenwick, T., & Parsons, J. (1997). *A critical investigation of the problems with problem-based learning.* East Lansing, MI: National Center for Research on Teacher Learning. (ERIC Document Reproduction Service No. ED 409 272).

French, T. (1993). *South of heaven: A year in the life of an American high school.* New York: Bantam/Doubleday/Dell.

Lee, G. (Ed.). (1961). *Crusade against ignorance: Thomas Jefferson on education*. New York: Teachers College Press.

Leo, J. (1998). "Dumbing Down Teachers." *U.S. News and World Report*, p. 15.

Olsen, L. (1997). *Made in America: Immigrant students in our public schools*. New York: New Press.

Paley, V. G. (1979). *White teacher*. Cambridge, MA: Harvard University Press.

Reed, R. F. (1966). *Philosophical documents in education*. New York: Longman.

Rose, M. (1995). *Possible lives: The promise of public education in America*. New York: Penguin.

Tyack, D. B. (1976). Ways of seeing: An essay on the history of compulsory schooling. *Harvard Educational Review, 46,* 355–389.

Weber, E. (1976). *Peasants into Frenchmen: The modernization of rural France, 1870–1914*. Palo Alto, CA: Stanford University Press.

INDEX